TECHTV'S STARTING AN ONLINE BUSINESS

Frank Fiore

CONTENTS AT A GLANCE

A Division of Pearson Technology Group, USA
201 W. 103rd Street
Indianapolis, Indiana 46290

TECHTV'S STARTING AN ONLINE BUSINESS

International Standard Book Number: 0-7897-2564-9

Library of Congress Catalog Card Number: 20-01090366

Printed in the United States of America

First Printing: August 2001

04   03   02   01   4   3   2   1

Trademarks

Warning and Disclaimer

ASSOCIATE PUBLISHER
Dean Miller

EXECUTIVE EDITOR
Jill Hayden

ACQUISITIONS EDITOR
Angelina Ward

DEVELOPMENT EDITOR
Howard Jones

MANAGING EDITOR
Thomas Hayes

PROJECT EDITOR
Tricia S. Liebig

COPY EDITOR
Sossity Smith

INDEXER
Sharon Shock

TECHNICAL EDITORS
Bill Bruns
Harrison Neal

TEAM COORDINATOR
Sharry Lee Gregory

INTERIOR DESIGNER
Anne Jones

COVER DESIGNER
Anne Jones

PAGE LAYOUT
Stacey Richwine-DeRome

TECHTV VICE PRESIDENT/ EDITORIAL DIRECTOR
Jim Louderback

TECHTV MANAGING EDITOR
Andy Guest

TECHTV MANAGING EDITOR- HELP
Phil Allingham

TECHTV LAB DIRECTOR
Andrew Hawn

CONTENTS

To Sell on line business

ABOUT THE AUTHOR

Frank Fiore is an e-business expert and consultant, and author of e-business books entitled *The Complete Idiot's Guide to Starting an Online Business*, *e-Marketing Strategies*, and *Successful Affiliate Marketing for Merchants*, all published by Macmillan/Que, and *Dr. Livingston's Online Shopping Safari Guidebook*, published by Maximum Press. He has been involved with e-business from its inception on the Net and with his experience as an e-business expert and direct marketer of products, he knows e-business from both sides of the transaction. He is currently the Official Online Shopping Guide for About and has been interviewed for numerous TV and radio talk shows and print media on the subject of e-Business and online shopping.

ABOUT TECHTV

TechTV, the only cable television channel covering technology news, information, and entertainment from a consumer, industry, and market perspective 24 hours a day. Offering everything from industry news to product reviews, updates on tech stocks to tech support, TechTV's original programming keeps the wired world informed and entertained. TechTV is one of the fastest growing cable networks, currently available in more than 23.5 million households and distributing content to 70 countries around the world. With nearly one million unique visitors per month, techtv.com is a community destination that encourages viewer interaction through e-mail, live chat, and video mail. TechTV, formerly ZDTV, is owned by Vulcan Ventures, Inc. Check local television listings for TechTV.

DEDICATIONS

To Mario—my tutor, business partner, and friend. I miss his guidance and laughter.

To all the TechTV fans and future fans.

TELL US WHAT YOU THINK!

As the reader of this book, *you* are our most important critic and commentator. We value your opinion and want to know what we're doing right, what we could do better, what areas you'd like to see us publish in, and any other words of wisdom you're willing to pass our way.

As an Associate Publisher for Que, I welcome your comments. You can fax, e-mail, or write me directly to let me know what you did or didn't like about this book—as well as what we can do to make our books stronger.

Please note that I cannot help you with technical problems related to the topic of this book, and that due to the high volume of mail I receive, I might not be able to reply to every message.

When you write, please be sure to include this book's title and author as well as your name and phone or fax number. I will carefully review your comments and share them with the author and editors who worked on the book.

Fax: 317-581-4666

E-mail: feedback@quepublishing.com

Mail: Dean Miller
Que
201 West 103rd Street
Indianapolis, IN 46290 USA

INTRODUCTION

Back in 1999, dot-coms were going DOT-CRAZY—*complete with the attendant media hype*. And unless you've been living in a cave somewhere in the Himalayas, you know that today the dot-coms have DOT-BOMBED—*complete, of course with the attendant media hype*.

So, should you still consider starting your own online business? Most definitely. Here's why.

Most of those high flying dot-coms that have come down to earth with a loud DOT-THUD were examples of business ideas that looked great on the back of a napkin but had little resemblance to a business plan. Adding to the problem were the venture capitalists. Those wonder kids who were more interested in building wealth than building a business poured billions of dollars into high flying start-ups that had more technical ability than marketing smarts, hoping to unload their investment and recoup their venture capital by selling these poorly run companies to the general public.

e-Commerce is not going away, but the insane assumptions of the media hype are. So where is e-business today? IBM Chairman Lou Gerstner knows and we quote: "Today, e-business is just business—real business. And real business is serious work."

And if you're serious about starting an online business you DON'T start with those offers of "build a free Web site and never have to work again." You know the ones we mean. You see them on late night TV or they show up in your mailbox. Like those weight loss ads that claim you can lose weight while you sleep, these new snake oil cyber-salesmen offer testimonials and promises of making money selling stuff on the Net while you snooze away your bedtime hours. All you have to do is buy their Internet moneymaking package. It's yours for the asking.

THEY'RE asking $79.95 plus shipping and handling—paid out in three equal installments.

Too many people believe the hype thinking they're going to sleep until they're 65, wake up thin, and have lots of money to enjoy it with! Unfortunately, making money on the Net is NOT easy. To paraphrase an old investment quote that applied to many of the well-funded DOT-COMS—"If you want to make a small fortune in e-commerce—start with a large one."

So where are the dot-com opportunities today?

According to recent research from IDC, a market research firm, the next wave of online growth are not dot-coms financed by greedy venture capitalists, but from small and home-based businesses.

Uh huh—that's right. You!

We're living in an historic period of time. A time when anyone with an idea, some guidance, and a lot of hard work can start their own business and share in the fruits of one of the biggest opportunities of this century. The things you know, the products you make, or the services you can provide are all ingredients for cooking up a successful online business. And because of the nature of the Net, you don't have to be Jeff Bezos or Wal-Mart to compete.

We'll give you a good example.

Alvin Toffler—the guy who wrote *Future Shock* years back—talks about a small Colombian village where the villagers are connected online and selling products to Denver. Years ago he was having dinner with friends in Denver and they served him fruit for dessert. The fruit was absolutely delicious. Toffler asked what they called it and where he could buy it. They told him the name of the fruit but said he couldn't buy it anywhere in the United States. The fruit was grown only in a tiny little area just outside Bogota because of climate conditions, soil, and so forth.

The Internet allowed this small village and its villagers to sell their fruit into Denver—a market that they could never reach offline because Denver would never know the fruit existed. There are many niche and specialty products and services like that—products and services that you can provide with an online business here and abroad that you could never reach before.

That's the power of the Internet and the promise of an online business.

But what about the Wal-Marts, Macys, and IBMs of the world, you ask? Aren't they going to dominate cyberspace as they dominated "meatspace?" And what about the current crop of e-tailers like Amazon, eToys, and CDNow? Would you dare compete with the likes of them?

Well, ponder this.

The turn of the next century will look more like the turn of the last. The end of the last century saw the last of the cottage industries. These home-based businesses went the way of the carrier pigeon as the population marched lockstep into the factories and offices of the Industrial Age. Working for oneself was replaced by working for the firm and individuality was consumed by the faceless corporation. But the Internet is changing all that and bringing back the cottage industry.

The Internet levels the playing field and gives any business of any size—home-based or not—the image of a larger company that creates the perception in the potential customer that your online business is credible and able to perform. The Internet gives you the power to compete with established brands, providing you not only the opportunity of branding your business—but branding *you*!

Sure. It's a long journey from idea to cyber-mogul but as the old sage said, "A journey of a 1,000 miles starts with but a single step." So, let's shift our eyes away from the future for now and focus on the task at hand—where to begin.

HOW TO USE THIS BOOK

TechTV's Starting an Online Business begins with an explanation of e-commerce, what to sell, how to sell it, how to plan it, and where to find the money to fund it. Then it gives you the basics of setting up shop on the Web, where to host it, some e-commerce Do's and Don'ts, and how to take orders and ship them. Finally, it covers the essentials of marketing and promoting your new business. For the latest coverage of industry market, and consumer forces that may impact the success of your venture, tune in to TechTV or visit us at www.techtv.com.

The book is organized so that you can quickly find a topic and get the information you need to set up your own online business.

Part 1, "Staking Your Claim," includes Chapters 1 through 6 and leads you through a process of identifying a need to fill with your new business, positioning yourself in the customer buying cycle, exploring the different ways of selling on the Internet, and creating your Unique Selling Position. It also walks you through building a business plan and the ways to fund your new business.

Part 2, "Setting Up Shop," includes Chapters 7 through 11 and shows you how to plan, deign, and set up your online business. It describes e-commerce and Web site essentials and helps you decide whether to build your own or use one of the many store builders available on the Web. It then goes on to explain where and how to host your Web site.

Part 3, "e-Commerce Basics," includes Chapters 12 through 14 and covers the basics of e-commerce—the Do's and Don'ts, meeting the customer's expectations, making money hosting affiliate content programs, staying up to date in e-commerce, selling to the world, keeping customer information private, and the importance of informational content and a sense of community on your e-commerce site.

Part 4, "Delivering the Goods," includes Chapters 15 through 17 and explains how to take an order from your site, how to take credit cards, debit cards, and personal checks, and how to take advantage of new payment solutions on your Web site. It then describes how to fulfill an order, ship it, and track it. Finally, it covers the essentials of good customer service and managing returns.

Part 5, "Promoting Your Online Business," includes Chapters 18 through 24 and shows you how to get your customer's attention, market and promote your new business through paid advertising, free marketing, give-aways, contests, and promotions, the ins and outs of permission marketing, and protecting your brand and company reputation. It also gives you the tools of how to market on the Web, the importance of PR and how to use it, and how to start your own affiliate program to leverage the power of the Net.

Finally, you'll find a list of valuable e-commerce Internet resources and an eBusiness To Do List in the Appendices and a Glossary of technical terms so you not only can walk-the-walk of e-commerce but talk-the-talk, too.

So before you charge out into cyberspace with your great new e-business idea, stop, pick up this book, take a deep breath, and study the step by step guide we've created that will help build a solid foundation for the success of your business.

CONVENTIONS USED IN THIS BOOK

All through the book, you'll be presented with tips and advice to help you understand the technical language used in the text to help make your online business more successful.

Important text will be called out with a special typeface. For example, if you are instructed to press **Ctrl+C** or select a particular **menu item**, it will appear in **bold**. Web addresses and other text that you must type will appear in monospaced type.

In addition you will find special tips and advice in these sidebars:

JARGON

e-Talk

Hey. The Internet is about technology. But that doesn't mean we have to settle for the techno-babble. So look for these sidebars to bring you quickly up to speed on technical terminology.

TIP

TechTV Tip

Check these out for quick tips and tidbits from TechTV's editorial team on how to promote your online business, find much needed resources, and keep your site customer friendly.

Book Reference

From time to time there are some other references you just can't afford to miss, and all such items are handily found under this icon.

Web Reference

The Net has a surprising way of quickly making tomorrow today. So, when creating your online business strategy, keep these e-commerce trends in mind.

Dot-Bomb

Watch out for these common and not so common e-commerce mistakes. They can quickly stop a customer—and a sale—in its tracks.

GET IN THE GAME

Still here? Hey, time's a-wasting. You're on Internet time now! So turn the page and let's get started!

PREFACE

Dear Online Entrepreneur,

So, you're thinking about starting an online business.

You've come to the right place.

In this book, we'll show you the Hows, Whats, Wheres, and Whys of starting a business online—and without all the hype. You'll find no high-tech jargon, and the text won't be in a tone that is difficult to understand. You'll see practical, real-world advice for establishing your online business and an easy-to-follow set of instructions to get you there.

We'll show you how to take your business idea to a working business plan—and then we'll show you how to fund it. You'll learn where and how to set up shop online (how does FREE sound?), take orders, service your customers, drive shoppers to your Web store—and keep them coming back for more.

We'll give you dozens of tips and tidbits on how to establish and promote your online business and keep your site customer-friendly—and profitable. Just as importantly, we'll alert you to common and not-so-common e-commerce mistakes that can quickly stop a customer—and a sale—in his or her tracks.

When you're finished reading our book, you'll not only talk-the-talk of e-commerce, but walk-the-walk, too.

Good Luck. See you in Cyberspace!

Frank Fiore and TechTV

P A R T I

STAKING YOUR CLAIM

CHAPTER 1

PUTTING THE "E" IN COMMERCE

In This Chapter

- Discover what e-commerce is and who's doing it
- See the opportunity and what it means to you
- The numbers tell the tale—find out who's buying online

Just a few short years ago there were no Web sites—now there are more than 10 million of them. According to NEC Research which is a wholly owned subsidiary of NEC Corporation—an international organization active in computers, communications, electronics, and advanced technologies—by 2002 the number of Web pages will exceed the number of people on the Net.

And it's not just the number of Web sites that are growing. The population of the Internet is growing, too. According to the Strategis Group, which publishes in-depth market research reports and provides customized consulting services and continuous information solutions to cable TV, half the people in the United States are connected to the Internet while the worldwide number of people with Internet access is rapidly growing towards one billion people. Thousands of new people are coming online each and every week. And that's not all. The Internet is going mobile. Millions of cell phones around the world can now access the

Internet, and purchase products from almost anywhere. In fact, some researchers say that in five years, more people will access the Internet from their cell phones than from computers! Those in business have noticed the numbers and they've seen the handwriting on the wall. Their response? They're opening new Web sites at a furious pace, selling products and services to online consumers.

And so can you.

If you have the right kind of business, the Internet can open up a vast market of customers at a price unheard of even a year or two ago.

THE E-COMMERCE EXPLOSION

e-commerce seems to be everywhere these days. On the radio and TV, in magazines and newspapers—it seems you can't escape the dot-com craze. Your neighbor's kid down the street has dumped his newspaper route and became a cyber-merchant on the Web. Your mother in Florida is cleaning out her garage and her neighbor's by selling the contents on eBay. And your husband is spamming your e-mail list enticing your friends, family, and co-workers to buy his Amway products.

So, what's happening here? And can you still get a piece of the e-commerce pie?

At first look, e-commerce (or its more formal name—electronic commerce) seems to be a well-established entity. In reality, e-commerce has been in existence for only a few years. In fact, commerce on the Internet wasn't even allowed until the early 1990s. That's when Former Vice President Al Gore declared the Internet the Information Superhighway and sought to make the Internet—then a private enclave of the government, researchers, and university professors—open to the general public. And he did.

> **JARGON**
>
> **e-Commerce Is Short for Electronic Commerce**
> Electronic commerce is quite simply selling online over the Internet. An e-commerce site will display, offer, and sell its product or service electronically through personal computers connected to the Net or through Internet-enabled information devices.

After the doors to the Internet's World Wide Web were flung open to the public, millions flocked to newly formed ISPs, fired up their PCs, and boarded the Information Superhighway. The invention of the Web browser made it easy to surf the Net. Text and images appeared on our monitors enticing us to join in the new global block party. Millions did. And where there are millions of people, there's a potential market; and where there's a potential market, business soon follows.

Just a few years ago, there were only a scattering of e-commerce sites—a bookseller here, a T-shirt seller there—but soon they were sprouting up everywhere on the Web. One of the first online merchants to put e-commerce on the map was Amazon.com. It proved that people would buy books off the Net if you gave them a convenient way to save and to buy. Soon thousands of imitators followed, selling everything from flowers, chocolates, and greeting cards to CDs, videos, gifts—even automobiles. Nothing was sacred. Today, you can even buy your funeral arrangements over the Net at WebCaskets.com at `www.webcaskets.com`.

JARGON →

What's an ISP?

If you want to get on the Net, you'll need an ISP. ISP stands for Internet service provider and provides Internet access to its subscribers. Like a phone company, your ISP connects you to the Internet. A good place to look for ISPs is at `www.isp.com`.

There's nothing mysterious about e-commerce. If you ever bought an item from a catalog or from an advertisement in a magazine, the purchase process is pretty much the same. The only difference is that instead of purchasing from a person over the telephone or sending a check through the mail, you're conducting the transaction with a mouse through your PC. For the business, the fulfillment process that takes place is no different from taking and fulfilling an order over the phone.

What puts the "e" in e-commerce is that the transaction is completed electronically and without human intervention. After the order is accepted, the e-tailer, or online retailer, fills and ships the order the same way any brick-and-mortar store would. The fact is, a dot-com company faces the same challenges of building a presence, marketing and promoting the business, taking orders, fulfilling and shipping them, and has all the same customer service issues to solve that a "no-dot" company has.

JARGON →

To "Dot" or Not to "Dot"

The "dot" referred to here is the little dot in .com (`www.i-am-in-business-online.com`) that identifies a business as doing business on the Net. Just a few short years ago a no-dot company was the traditional brick-and-mortar business we see in the real world. No longer. Now many brick-and-mortar companies have opened e-commerce sites and now call themselves "clicks-and-mortar" or "bricks-and-clicks" companies.

What Makes e-Commerce Special?

What's so special about e-commerce? Why does it offer a unique opportunity to those who go searching for business online?

It's very simple. What e-commerce does is level the playing field.

If you design your business right, your Web site can make your business look just as large as those that are many times your size. The Internet also can build in a potential customer's mind the perception that your business is as credible as any other that's just a mouse click away.

Three simple words can make or break your business: It's not location, location, and location as in real estate, but execution, execution, and execution. The dirty little secret of e-commerce is that ideas are easy. It's their execution that determines whether an online business is a success or failure. And in that area—the ability to execute properly—your new business idea has the same chance of succeeding as any other business on the Net—large, medium, or small!

The truth is, the Internet is still an open marketplace for small startups, home businesses, and one-person operations that can *and* do build profitable online businesses.

One Man's Testimonial

To see how a one-person operation can flourish, meet entrepreneur Jim Daniels. He started his publishing business with $300. Six months later he was earning enough to quit his day job. Check it out at `www.bizweb2000.com/howiquit.htm`.

In fact, you don't even need a site to conduct a successful business on the Internet. At person-to-person auction sites such as eBay (`www.ebay.com`), individuals have established their own home-based business buying products and auctioning them off to the highest bidder. Other Net entrepreneurs don't bother to carry inventory at all! Their business model is to set up small content and community sites, join an online merchant's affiliate or associate program, and sell the merchant's merchandise off their site. The merchant takes the order, ships it, and performs all the customer service.

You're probably thinking that heavy hitters with state-of-the-art technology have the e-commerce edge. Or setting up a commerce-ready Web site costs tens of thousands of dollars. Well, think again. You can launch a respectable online store for what you spend on video rentals each month. Net companies such as Yahoo! Store (`store.yahoo.com`), which we'll discuss in Chapter 9, "Hosting with an ISP," can set up and maintain your online store for as little as $100 a month—and there are some companies that will do it free!

e-Commerce Success Stories

Do you have to be a well-known merchant to be a success? Not at all! Read how small startups like Just Balls, Flying Noodle, and 1-800 Birthday used the Net to build a successful international business on the Web. Check it out at `www.ecommercetimes.com/success_stories/`.

How Many Products Do You Need?

You might be wondering if you need to offer shoppers hundreds of products for sale at your online store to be successful. The answer to that question is *no*. Research done by ViaWeb (now Yahoo! Store), a host for online merchants, showed that adding more items to an online store doesn't guarantee more sales. Stores that sold fewer than 10 products had almost as many orders as stores selling 50 products.

In fact, you don't even need to sell products at all! Many online businesses sell services or expertise. Others use the Web as a way to sell a physical item, like vacation home rentals, travel packages, and so on.

Finally, just because the new business model is e-commerce, old business models are not obsolete. Customer service, customer care, a good product or service at a fair price, integrity, and above all proper execution of your business plan are principles that still hold true in business whether its online or not.

THE "DOT-COM" CRAZE

Do you recognize these e-commerce companies?

Amazon and CDNow? They're responsible for what we now call the dot-com craze. When they first hit the Net and opened for business, they were generally ignored by their counterparts in the brick-and-mortar world. The brick-and-mortar crowd saw the Internet as another fad equal to the civilian band radio craze of a couple of decades before. They dismissed it.

That proved to be a mistake. A *big* mistake.

Original no-dot companies like Barnes & Noble, Toys-R-Us, and Compaq were "Amazoned" and soon in a race for their customers who were buying more and more from these electronic upstarts. They in turn created their own dot-coms and were soon competing with the upstarts.

Putting the "e" in Retail

An online retail store, or Web site, is commonly referred to in this book as an *e-tailer*—an electronic retailer.

Getting Amazoned

Amazon and its aggressive merchandising first-to-the Net strategy blindsided many no-dot companies who thought that the Net was a fad and not a serious competitor to their real-world business. They discovered otherwise. A perfect example is Barnes & Noble, which now has to play catch-up to Amazon on the Net.

You can't escape the dot-coms. You see and hear them almost everywhere. On TV and the radio, on billboards, in magazines and newspapers. Go to a sports event and right beside the real estate ad on the scoreboard is one for an e-commerce company. There have even been dot-com ads on the Super Bowl.

Today, there's a frenzied rush to get companies online, but success will not necessarily go to the biggest or well known—or even the well funded. Take Toys-R-Us as an example. First, being "Amazoned" by eToys, they have had a difficult time creating a viable business strategy for selling online. Toys-R-Us is a company with years of experience in its industry, sufficient funds, and good product sources, yet was unable to create a competitive presence on the Internet.

Their solution? They partnered with Amazon and sell their toys on Amazon's Web site!

On the Net, size does *not* matter. You can still build a small- or medium-sized profitable business if you can identify a need, move quickly to meet it, and execute your business plan properly. The Internet can add tremendous marketing power to a small business. As a dot-com company you can conduct business with both national and international customers with costs far below those of brick-and-mortar stores.

Think of it. Because the Internet is global, the cost to reach someone in your local community is the same as it is to contact someone on the other side of the world. Using the technology of the Net, you can take orders and easily and inexpensively build a company's image, provide customer support, make available technical and troubleshooting information, develop prospect lists, and conduct customer surveys with a click of a mouse.

All well and good. But what's the opportunity here? What kind of money are we talking about?

THE E-COMMERCE POTENTIAL

Although e-commerce represents a small part of retail sales today, the potential for e-commerce is immense. Retail consumer shopping revenues hit over $26 billion in 2000. As for 2001, the U.S. Department of Commerce reported that e-commerce sales hit $7 billion in the first quarter, up 33% from the first quarter in 2000. Forrester Research (www.forrester.com) expects U.S. online retail sales to hit $184 billion by 2004.

The demographics of the Internet cover the gamut from children, to teenagers, to young and old adults. Ages 18–54 are well represented on the Internet and make up a profitable target market for e-tailers on the Net. And who's buying now? Boomers in their peak earning years and seniors with deepening pockets. Close on their heels is Generation X—and the offspring of the   Boomers—Generation Y.

Today's eShopper

People who shop online are older than you think. The average age is   years old. Online shoppers have a lot of disposable income. The medium annual income is approximately $40,000 a year. But a significant number of people make $100,000 or $200,000 or more a year. People who shop online are much more likely than average to be married and those who shop online are *twice* as likely to be college graduates.

The gender demographics are shifting as well. More women have come on to the Internet and are making an impact on e-commerce. Media Metrix and Jupiter Communications reported in May of 2000 that for the first time more U.S. women than men used the Internet. Women made up 50.4% of all unique visitors to the Web compared to men at 49.6%. And the proportion of women online in Europe is also growing steadily.

e-Marketer at www.emarketer.com reported in February 2001 that nearly 49% of Internet users are female, and they comprise 41% of all Internet purchasers.

Internet Economy Indicators

Check out these indicators. They can give you a quick study of the economics driving the Internet. The indicators are derived from analysis of four layers of the Internet Economy: Internet Infrastructure, Internet Applications, Internet Intermediary, and Internet Commerce. Find them at www.internetindicators.com/facts.html.

Keep Your Eye on the e-Commerce Puck

As Wayne Gretzky said, "The real key to success is knowing where the puck is going, not where it is."

To keep track of the e-commerce puck, you need to stay on top of the Internet statistics. There are several good sites on the Net that can keep you up to date on what is happening in e-commerce: the latest online research, demographic information, and newsletters, reports, and surveys on all facets of the online world.

CyberAtlas

www.cyberatlas.com

CyberAtlas can provide you with valuable statistics and Web marketing information, enabling you to understand the online business environment and make more informed business decisions. CyberAtlas gathers online research from the best data resources to provide a complete review of the latest surveys and technologies available.

InternetStats

www.internetstats.com

InternetStats is an excellent source pointing to Web sites that have the business and market information, statistics, and trends you need (see Figure 1.1). Although InternetStats doesn't offer numbers directly, it does point you to the proper sites to find the statistic you need. One useful feature is its search engine, which you can use to find statistics or market data on a specific industry.

Easidemographics

www.easidemographics.com

Get up-to-date demographic data to target your market from the Right Site. Use their search interface to narrow your search by geography (ZIP Codes, regions, and so on) and type of data (quality of life, income, and so on) for detailed market-specific statistics and reports.

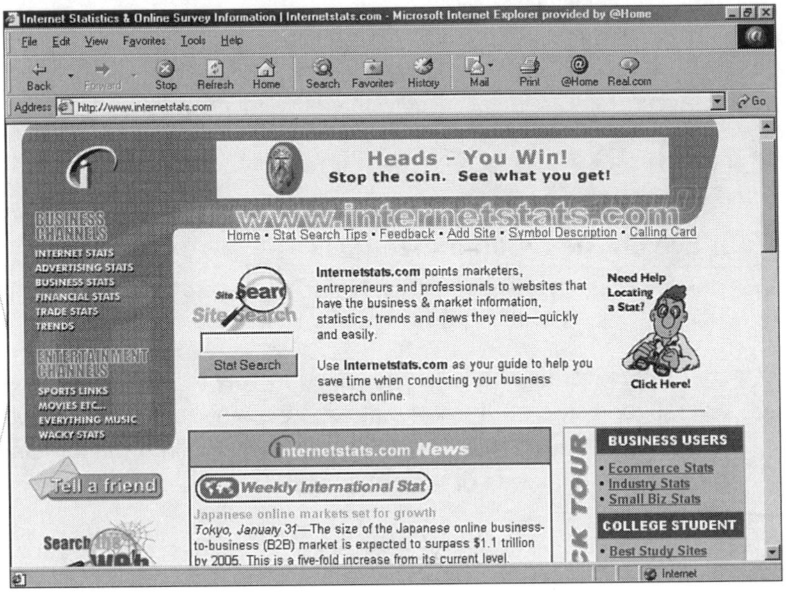

Figure 1.1

InternetStats will keep you up-to-date on what's happening in the online world with links that point to
Web resources offering market information, statistics, and trends.

Nua
www.nua.ie

Nua offers a compendium of news articles, reports, and surveys on all facets of the online
world. The Nua Knowledge Base is a central, authoritative resource for news, opinion,
trends, and the latest thinking about the Internet and the World Wide Web.

IDENTIFYING A NEED

In This Chapter

- Learn what types of businesses you can run online
- Discover how to choose an idea for your online business
- Learn how to identify your customer's specific wants and needs
- Determine whether you should sell your own products or those of others

The first step in starting an online business is to find a need and fill it. The Net can make that easy because it offers you the opportunity to reach and sell to a very targeted market. It's the perfect place for niche marketing.

> **Niche Marketing**
>
> A *niche market* is one where you meet the needs of a particular consumer audience. For example, selling fitness equipment to health buffs, or hip clothing to teenagers, or foreign films to movie experts.

Let's say you have a product or service that would make someone's life easier—a new way to sew buttons on a garment without a needle and thread. A single product like that could never support a retail storefront. However, on the Net you could reach thousands, even millions, of people who could use such a timesaving device.

So what do you do once you've found and filled a need? You need to know what motivates a shopper to buy. Keep in mind that different things motivate different shoppers—even at different times. When trying to choose a product or service to sell, keep the following human motivators in mind:

- Information
- Economic
- Entertainment
- Social

A great human motivator is the need for information, and that's where the Internet shines. The Internet is like the Library of Congress multiplied millions of times. But it's also a vast information storehouse that is hard to navigate. If you provide a ready source of information that meets a shopper's need, you can sell that information and turn a shopper into a customer.

A second very strong motivator is economic. It goes without saying that commerce is a fast growing segment on the Net. After all, if you didn't believe that you wouldn't be reading this book! And what motivates a shopper to buy? A quality product, a nice selection, a secure and convenient way to buy—even a great deal! All these motivations and more would entice a shopper to open his wallet and buy from your online store.

Entertainment is another motivator. We all love to be entertained. We'll even pay for it if we feel the value is there. So think about ways of selling entertainment products and services to the online shopper.

Finally, human interaction is a strong motivational force. The opportunity to hobnob with those of similar interests can be turned into a profitable business. Think about community sites that provide live chat or ways for people to meet one another. Fill the need to interact and you can build an effective business on it.

Business Opportunity Scams

If you've been on the Net for any length of time, "they" have pitched you. What I'm talking about are the get-rich-quick schemes that you get via e-mail. These scams masquerading as business opportunities should be avoided like the plague. These are *not* business opportunities! If the business opportunity seems too good to be true—then it is! If you think you've been a victim of a business opportunity scam or just want to learn how to avoid them then go to www.ftc.gov/bizop.

SHOULD I SELL A PRODUCT OR SERVICE?

That's a good question. Luckily you can easily do either one on the Net. It makes no difference whether you sell a product or a service from your Web site. Both have their advantages and disadvantages.

Selling products online has certain advantages. When selling products, you're not constrained by a limited amount of inventory. When selling products, you can grow your business more quickly because the more products you sell, the more income you make.

The disadvantage of selling products is that they normally require you to stock and ship them. Unless you have a very high profit margin on a product, you have to fulfill a large number of orders to make a reasonable amount of sales.

The advantage of an online services company is that making a profit is quicker and easier because the entire price of the service is paid to you. Also, there is the opportunity to generate repeat business if your clients are pleased with your service. The main disadvantage is that there is only so much *time*. We're only human and a person can perform only a certain number of services in a 24-hour period.

Selling services can provide you with immediate revenue but will never give you the biggest bang for your buck in the long run. In short, you can sell only so much of your time, whereas you can sell an unlimited amount of products. The trick is to turn a successful online service into a product. An example is to have a service that helps people market their online business—such as search engine placement—and then sell them a book on how to do it.

THE MAIN TYPES OF ONLINE BUSINESSES

An online business is not limited to selling just products and services. In fact there are five primary ways of doing business on the Net:

- Become an Online Retailer
- Become an Online Information Seller
- Start an Online Consultation Service
- Become an Online Services Seller
- Become an Online Subscription Seller

Let's check each one out.

Online Retailers (e-Tailers,) as they are called, are the popular and well-known dot-com companies. They started out selling the basic commodity products—books, videos, and CDs—then branched out to almost every conceivable product that you could buy in the real world. If you become an e-tailer, you can sell your own products or market those of another merchant.

Should You Buy an Existing Business?

One online business strategy you might consider is buying an existing e-commerce company. This has several benefits, such as a current product to sell, a Web site already established, and a customer base to sell to. A good place to start looking for an e-commerce business to buy is at www.bizbuysell.com.

Online Information Sellers   Information sellers offer information products for sale. Unlike buying a product, the customer pays for the information and immediately downloads it to his or her computer. A good example of this kind of merchandise is a piece of software. Another is an online newsletter or publication or perhaps a how-to manual that you pay to receive electronically.

Online Consultation Services   Consultants are different from Online Information Sellers. They're an online business with a human touch. If you're a consultant, you sell advice. Your customer contacts you directly with a question and you respond personally. This is usually done via e-mail but the business also might offer a live chat room where customers can speak with the consultant or advisor directly.

Service Sellers   There are online businesses that just sell services. They perform an actual service on behalf of the customer, such as lawyers giving legal advice, CPAs doing taxes, doctors giving medical advice—even Web-site designing and computer programming.

Subscription Sellers   Some online businesses sell subscriptions. A good example of this type of business is the *Wall Street Journal*. Other online businesses might charge membership fees to view the content of their site or participate in one-on-one chat communities.

You can get creative with different types of online businesses and combine one or more of them into a unique online shopping offering.

Should You Sell on Price or Value-Add?

There are two main ways to distinguish your products from your competitors. The first is by price and the second is by adding value. Selling on price is simple—and the least expensive. But you can charge higher prices and still get the sale by adding value to your product offering such as good customer service, guarantees, easy exchange policies, or overnight delivery.

MEETING BASIC HUMAN NEEDS

One of the easiest ways to decide on a product to sell is to find a problem, then offer a product or service to solve it. The first step is to decide who your target customer is.

Are your customers consumers or other businesses? What are your customers looking for? If your customers are consumers, what are their ages? What are they interested in?

What are their needs? If they are businesses, what products and services will help them solve their day-to-day business problems?

Then you have to decide what to sell them. There are products that sell well online and are easy to fulfill and ship, such as books, software, CDs, housewares, and apparel. Services such as travel packages, information, and professional services work well also. If you're selling products, stick with nonperishable items that are easy to store and ship.

Get Product Ideas by Observing Consumer Behavior

Ask yourself these questions. What do people buy and why? What do they want to buy but can't? What do they buy and don't like? What are people buying a lot of? What's trendy and in vogue?

The first step is to analyze your potential customers' needs and organize them into the basic human needs. For this, we will need to call on the services of Dr. Abraham Maslow.

Dr. Maslow was a twentieth-century psychologist who spent a lot of time categorizing human needs. If he were alive today and on the Internet, I bet he would have made a pretty effective e-tailer. He could easily define a list of human needs and be good at choosing the products to satisfy them. So can you.

They are

- Physical needs
- Safety needs
- Belonging needs
- Esteem needs

Meeting Physical Needs

The basic physical human needs are food, shelter, and clothing. If you were going to sell products that solve the problem of finding these physical needs, you would consider these types of products and services.

Physical Needs—Product Ideas

We all need to eat and drink, so selling non-perishable food products online is a natural. It's something that we all need and is consumable—meaning we can buy the same product over and over. That's good for business. In addition, the food products you sell can be gourmet in nature or ethnic or regional food types that certain customer segments would be want buy.

The need for shelter from the elements is right up there with sustenance. Outdoor products such as camping and hunting gear and goods for the patio and garden make very good merchandise to sell on the Net as long as they are not so big as to incur high shipping and handling costs.

Finally, though we might not buy clothing as often as we do food, covering our bodies is a social necessity. Apparel meets both the needs of the fashion conscious and protect us from the elements.

Physical Needs—Service Ideas

Our physical needs can be serviced as well. Many who eat also cook. Providing consumer information on how to cook, what to cook, and where to cook is an information product that makes a very good service to sell online. Perhaps you can start an "Ask Mr. Chef" site where consumers can ask cooking questions of expert chefs. Here's another idea. We all eat out. Many of us eat out frequently. An online business that lists and categorizes restaurants and their reviews is another service that can be provided online.

As for clothing and shelter, a site could provide the best places to camp in an area or a directory of places to fish and hunt. One might even include the ways to catch, clean, and cook the fish and game that you get. You then have a site that does double duty: where to hunt and fish and how to cook what you catch.

Stumped for Ideas? Try These Techniques

Talk to family and friends. Have a brainstorming session over dinner or drinks. Try to think outside the box. Ask others what they would like to buy and what could be improved. Read the trade magazines and don't just focus on what's happening in your country. Remember, the Net is global: What's a good idea in one country, might not apply to another.

Meeting Safety Needs

Feeling safe and secure is one of our strongest basic needs. The safety needs of protecting self, family, and home offer an online business the opportunity to sell a variety of merchandise and a nice selection of services to the online consumer. An additional safety concern is our health. Think about these product and services ideas if this is the type of customer that you are targeting.

Safety Needs—Product Ideas

Security products like self-defense items and security devices to use when traveling would make very good products to sell on a Web site. Books and tapes on self-defense are other product ideas. Child safety products like baby seats and identification systems would sell well, along with home safes and surveillance equipment.

As for health, diet books, exercise tapes, and health and nutrition products are very big sellers on the Net. First-aid equipment and home medical supplies also are good products to sell, as well as products for people with disabilities.

Safety Needs—Service Ideas

Many types of safety services can be delivered online and would make a low-overhead, profitable business. They would include private investigative services, directories of alarm services and their reviews, and emergency alert services for the infirm and elderly.

Another service idea would be to provide nutrition and health information. The Nutrition Guide at About.com is an example of a site that provides a wide variety of information on living a healthy life through nutritious eating (see Figure 2.1).

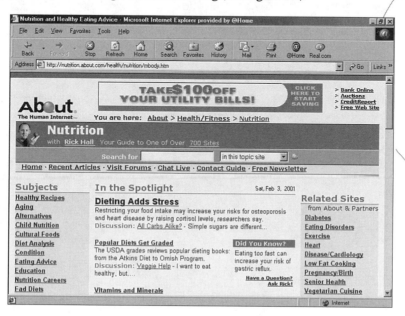

Figure 2.1

The Nutrition Guide at About offers a vast array of information on Nutrition and health.

Weight-loss information; nutrition services and guides; and even life, auto, and health insurance can be delivered over the Net.

Belonging Needs

To be loved, to have friends, and to be part of a family fills us with the need to be a part of something greater than ourselves. This need to belong and to express our appreciation for being part of something offers a variety of online business opportunities.

Belonging—Product Ideas

One of the best ways to express our affection for lovers, friends, and family is by giving gifts. Online gift shops are a natural for the Net. When people want to express their affections in a more tangible manner, gifts are one of the best ways to do it. Other products that do just as well are the traditional flowers, cards, and candy. Any of these should be considered as merchandise ideas for your online business.

Belonging—Service Ideas

If you would rather not sell gifts online, then perhaps setting up a gift registry service like the one at www.wishclick.com is the next best thing (see Figure 2.2). This type of service enables visitors to your site to list the actual gifts they want and then inform the potential gift givers. You can then send orders to a gift house that would fulfill and ship them to your customers.

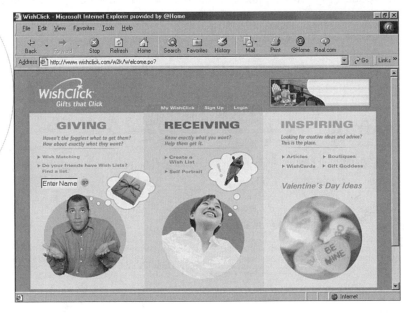

Figure 2.2

Here's a good example of a gift registry service. WishClick matches gift givers to gift recipients.

Another service idea is a genealogy service. Tracing one's roots has become very popular over the last several years—especially with the baby-boom generation. Another popular service that meets the belonging need is an online dating service.

Esteem Needs

We all like to be recognized and feel good about ourselves. Products and services that cater to our esteem needs offer a great opportunity for an online business. How we feel about ourselves and how others perceive us is important. Recognition and vanity are strong personal needs that we seek to fulfill.

Esteem Needs—Product Ideas

Beauty and grooming items and other personal care merchandise are the most popular products to sell if your online business is targeting the esteem needs of the consumer. For women, perfume, bath and body lotions, cosmetics, and even fashion products are key items to sell. For men, cologne, razors, and electric shavers would fill the bill.

Next to consider are jewelry items for the ladies—rings, diamonds, bracelets, precious stones—and for men, watches, cufflinks, and rings. Then there are books and videos on personal care, dieting, and products to reverse the aging process.

Esteem Needs—Service Ideas

If meeting the recognition and esteem needs of consumers is your target, then think about these types of services to offer.

Many types of training and educational courses can be offered over the Net, like computer certification classes or real estate courses. You can sell beauty tips to your customers or offer a jewelry appraisal service. Finally, you can offer advice on how to succeed in business or even—after reading this book—offer a course on how to set up your own online business!

SELLING YOUR CREATIVE WORK

You don't have to limit yourself to selling other people's products or even services. Consider selling your own creative work.

Can't Think of a Product to Sell? Try This...

You've tried and tried, but still can't come up with a product to sell. Then why not find a merchant who already is selling products—but *not* online—and offer to sell them on the Net. You create the site, the merchant supplies the product, and you both make money.

Ask yourself this. What one thing do you do better than everyone else? Maybe you're a good photographer. Or perhaps you enjoy writing. Maybe you enjoy working with your hands creating works of art or unique items that can be sold as gifts.

Here's a Way to See Whether Your Idea Is Original

The US Patent and Trademark Office holds the mother of all patent databases. If it has been patented, it's here. Check out patent descriptions at www.delphion.com/.

Sit down some evening after work with a pad and pencil or drop by your local coffeehouse and make a list of what you enjoy doing. You might be surprised that what you like to do can be turned into a product or service you can sell online. The key thought here is to do what you enjoy!

CHAPTER **3**

WWW—SELLING ON THE WILD AND WOOLY WEB

In This Chapter

- Find out the different ways you can sell off the Net
- Learn what affiliate selling is and what to look out for
- Should you sell products without a Web site? Are person-to-person auctions the way to go?
- Learn how to use e-mail to sell your product or service
- Should you consider setting up shop in an online mall?

You've decided what need your e-business will meet and you've chosen a product or service to meet it. Your next task is to figure out where to sell your deal. Luckily, the Internet offers you a virtual universe in which to get your product offer in front of potential customers.

When most people want to set up shop on the Net, the first thing they do is build a Web site. That may or may not be the right approach, depending on your customers and their habits. You might be able to take advantage of an alternative way of selling on the Net that doesn't require a Web site.

Although this point might be obvious, the first thing to consider when selling your product or service is to find out where your customers congregate. Depending upon whether customers hang out at your Web site, at auction sites, at classified sites, or at online malls, you can use any of a number of methods to reach them:

- Selling from your own Web site with your own product or service
- Selling someone else's product or service from your Web site
- Selling your product at person-to-person auctions
- Selling your product or service through e-mail
- Selling your product or service through online classified ads
- Selling through an online mall

Any one of these sales models can produce profitable results and help you launch your online business. And each offers its own unique opportunities and challenges.

SELLING FROM A WEB SITE

Although later chapters focus on the mechanics of setting up your e-commerce Web site, you need to take a few moments to consider a few of the basic principles of selling from a Web store.

Where you host your Web store and the type of store you need to build depends a lot on what you plan to sell. If you have only a few products to sell, you can list them on a few simple pages with HTML forms to accept orders.

JARGON

What's HTML?

Web pages are built using Hypertext Markup Language, or HTML. The HTML code is a set of commands embedded in a Web page that tells the page what text to display, how to format the text, and how and where to display the graphics on a Web page.

If you have a very large range of products, you'll need to build a Web store using a database and an electronic shopping cart.

What do I mean by using a database to manage your product offering? If you have a simple site with a small number of products, you would place those products on individual Web pages. If you had to edit or delete those products on your site, you would just go to that product page and make your changes. But, If you have a very large number of products to sell and have to make changes frequently—like product availability or price changes—then placing your product information in a database that automatically populates, edits, or updates your product Web pages is the best way to go. That way you make changes to your database and NOT individual Web pages.

Another issue to consider when selling from a Web site is security. Providing an online payment method like accepting credit or debit cards will greatly increase your chances of making a sale. But with these sales opportunities come security problems. Later on in the book I explain what these security problems are and how you can protect against them.

> ### What's an Electronic Shopping Cart?
>
> Just like in a grocery store, shoppers use an electronic shopping cart to collect items they want to purchase at a Web store. By placing items in their electronic shopping cart, shoppers can go from product offer to product offer without having to buy each one separately. When they're ready to check out of the Web store, shoppers complete just one order form, pay once, and are on their way.

Keep in mind that the more features you add to your store, the more sophisticated your software and hardware need to be. Features such as databases and shopping carts require a lot of customization and support.

SELLING THROUGH AN AFFILIATE PROGRAM

If you don't want the hassle of listing, warehousing, fulfilling, and shipping your own orders, then you should consider Network Selling. *Affiliate programs* allows you to sell other merchants' products and services through your site. The advantage: You don't have to source, warehouse, or ship products. The disadvantage: You only get paid a small commission on each sale.

Putting Someone Else's Product in Front of Your Customers

Currently, there are over one million Web sites participating in some kind of affiliate program. The products and services sold through affiliate programs run the gamut from hard goods such as books, CDs, toys, and movies, to credit card applications and marketing programs.

Web sites in a merchant's affiliate program normally display a merchant's banner on their Web site, and receive a commission based on each successful sale. The merchants advertise through these programs and use them primarily to draw traffic to their site. They figure if Mohammed (the shopper) won't come to 'the mountain (the merchandise), they should take the mountain to Mohammed.

Keep in mind that when you participate in an affiliate program, you do make a commission if your visitor clicks a merchant's banner and buys something from the merchant's site. Chances are though, that you've lost that visitor from your site; the visitor's unlikely to return to *your* site after moving to the merchant's site, and the visitor may use the merchant's site in the future, too, (rather than yours). So, in a way, you act as a salesman for the merchant and earn a commission when your visitor buys, but you may not be courting your *own* visitors.

The key to making an affiliate program a success for your site is to target your customers. If you have a sports-related site, sell sporting goods or personal electronic equipment—not housewares. If your site caters to women, avoid products that primarily target men.

Catch the Next e-Commerce Wave—Syndicated Selling

Syndicated selling or *distributed commerce* is another term for affiliate selling. Forrester Research states that "Syndicated selling will take over…[and] rapidly outpace both Internet shopping malls and destination-only stores." Jupiter Communications reports that affiliate programs account for 11% of the $5.8 billion of consumer transactions online. They project that figure to grow to 24% or $37.5 billion in total sales by 2002.

Then, be sure the products you sell either have a high retail price or that you're paid a high commission on lower-priced products. Remember, you're being paid on commission. Be sure the payment is worth your effort. Associate Programs Directory, www.associateprograms.com, lists a wide variety of affiliate programs and also ranks them (see Figure 3.1). Click the "Affiliate programs: Our Top 10 Best Sellers" link at the top of the page to view them.

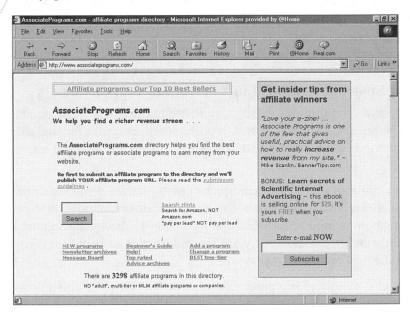

Figure 3.1

Check out the Associate Programs Directory's Top 10 affiliate programs.

Choosing the right product or service to sell will go a long way toward generating a meaningful revenue stream. And don't make the mistake of selecting too many merchant partners. Concentrate on only one—or just a few—programs and then target them to your Web site visitors.

Finally, what kind of help does the merchant offer its affiliates? Many merchants may fade from the scene after the affiliate signs up. But if you're going to sell their product or service, merchants should offer you sales ideas, promotions, and guidance to help you sell their product or service. Don't hesitate to ask for that help, and consider finding another program if you don't get the answers you need.

Some Words of Warning

Affiliate programs are one of the hottest e-commerce plays on the Net. They're easy to join and they don't involve up-front costs or costly overhead. But working successfully with an affiliate program isn't a no-brainer, either.

Get the Real Scoop on Affiliate Programs

Declan Dunn is a well-known affiliate program consultant who understands the pros and cons of affiliate selling. His book *The Complete, Insider's Guide to Associate & Affiliate Programs* is a must-read if you're considering joining an affiliate program. Order it at www.marketingassistance. com/affiliates/dunn1.htm.

Some programs are either outright scams or structured so that you'll have to sell tens of thousands of dollars of product a month to earn even a meager income. Read the fine print in the Affiliate Agreement that should be posted on a merchant's site. See what you are agreeing to do and what the merchant is agreeing to pay you—and when. Some programs are worded so that they will *never* pay you!

Investigate the programs you want to join. Don't pay to join *any* affiliate program and be careful to read the fine print about charging you any fees *after* the sale. Some merchants actually charge back against the commissions you earn and some merchants will not pay you at all if you don't meet a minimum amount of sales in a period.

Finally make sure that your sales and commissions are being tracked correctly. Many merchants track their own programs and unless you are completely comfortable with their tracking system, you should consider affiliate programs that use an outside third-party tracking company such as BeFree at www.befree.com or Linkshare at www.linkshare.com.

TIP

Affiliate Tracking Companies—A Good Place to Find Reputable Programs

Third-party affiliate tracking companies like BeFree and Linkshare manage and track merchant affiliate programs.

Where to Find and Join Affiliate Programs

If you want to go the affiliate selling route, start with these affiliate program directories. Those listed here are some of the best because they offer advice on choosing a program and—in some cases—even review and rank programs.

Get to Know These Gentlemen

There are three affiliate program advisors that you should visit. These three men offer unbiased reviews of many of the most popular affiliate programs on the Net. Check them out. Glenn Sobel's Affiliate Advisor.com at www.AffiliateAdvisor.com, Mark J. Welch's list of Commission-Based Affiliate Programs at www.adbility.com/wpag/bc_main.htm, and Allan Gardyne's AssociatesPrograms.com at www.associateprograms.com.

Start with the review sites:

- AssociatePrograms.com at www.associateprograms.com
- CashPile at www.cashpile.com
- ClickQuick at www.clickquick.com
- Revenews at www.revenews.com
- Clickslink at www.clickslink.com
- AffiliateGuide at www.affiliateguide.com
- i-revenue.net at www.i-revenue.net
- Refer-it at www.referit.com
- Associate-it at www.associate-it.com
- 2-Tier at www.2-tier.com
- Associate Search at associatesearch.com

These sites are your best sources for separating the affiliate wheat from the chaff.

TIP

The Mother of All Affiliate Directories

AffiliateManager.net has a very comprehensive list of affiliate program directories at AffiliateManager.net/directories.htm.

SELLING THROUGH AUCTIONS

Selling from your own Web site is not the only way to do business on the Net. Over the last couple of years person-to-person auctions have opened up a whole new way of selling products online.

eBay at www.ebay.com pioneered the concept, which was soon followed by a host of imitators including Amazon at www.amazon.com and Yahoo! at auctions.yahoo.com/. The advantage to selling off person-to-person auction sites is that you don't need your own web site to market your product. Many home-based businesses have been started and flourish on these auction sites.

One of the reasons the person-to-person auction sites are so successful is that they're so easy to use. To offer your product up for bid on eBay, for example, you simply fill out a form (available at the eBay home page), enter a short, descriptive title of the product you have for sale, then provide a complete description of the item (see Figure 3.2). Following eBay's instructions, you can even include a picture of your product.

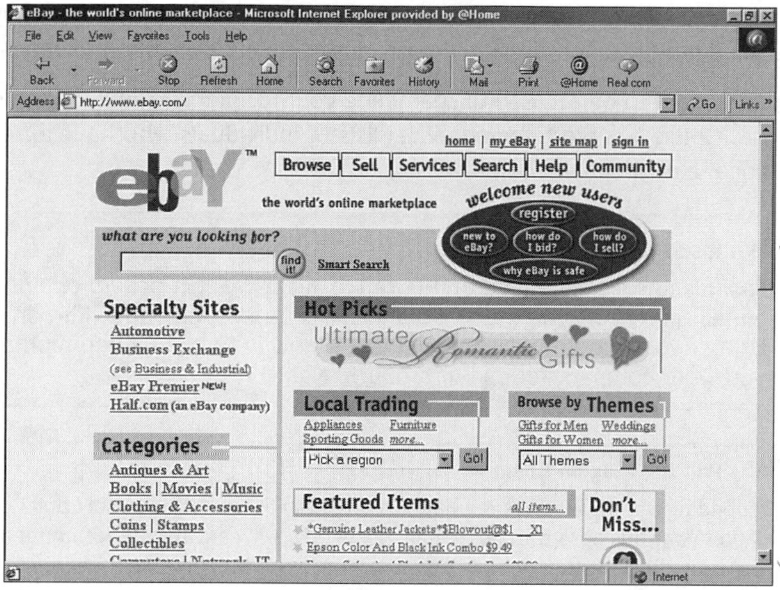

Figure 3.2

The granddaddy of all person-to-person auctions is eBay. You'll find individuals and merchants selling just about any product you can think of—along with some you'd *never* imagine.

From there, eBay takes over. You set a minimum price that you would sell at—called the minimum bid—and their software automatically assigns a bidding increment. The increments are kept small to encourage more bidding. You can even advertise the existence of your auction to all of eBay.

Other Large Person-to-Person Auction Sites

Besides eBay, there are several other large person-to-person auction sites for you to use to sell your wares:

- Yahoo! Auctions at `auctions.yahoo.com`
- Excite Auctions at `outletauctions.excite.com/`
- Amazon Auctions at `www.amazon.com`.
- ZDNet Auctions at `auctions.zdnet.com`.

SELLING THROUGH E-MAIL LISTS

E-mail direct marketing is a hot area for e-commerce. Using this technique, you craft a sales message for your product or service, then send it out in an e-mail message to a list of recipients (and potential customers). Typically, you buy a list of e-mail addresses from one of many companies that make them available for merchants. E-mail selling can be very effective, but you have to be careful about the e-mail lists you choose to buy. The fastest way to kill a product-offer through e-mail is to *spam* your potential customers.

If you don't want to be accused of spamming your recipients, you need to use only *opt-in e-mail lists*. Opt-in lists are targeted e-mail lists of individuals who have agreed to receive promotional e-mail.

What's SPAM?

Spam is unsolicited e-mail that's used to sell a product or service. Spam clogs e-mail servers around the world and sucks up needed bandwidth on the Net. Using it to promote your business is a sure way to build a bad reputation for you, your company, and your product.

ISPs Pull the Plug on Spam

Depending upon your ISP's regulations, an opt-in list may be the only practical way to market your business through e-mail. Many ISPs will cancel your account if they think you're sending spam.

Buying an opt-in e-mail list is more expensive than using unsolicited bulk e-mail, but it's also far more effective. Opt-in e-mail marketing is quickly becoming a popular way to sell on the Internet. Some surveys show that the response rate from marketing to the proper opt-in e-mail list can be five to ten times higher than the response rate from a banner ad.

What's Opt-In E-mail?

Opt-in e-mail is a marketing technique that, unlike spam, gets your message out to people who have *asked* to get it. People who opt-in to an e-mail list have said in advance that they are willing to receive unsolicited e-mail from companies on the Net that meet the list's criteria. For example, someone who would like to be kept informed of newly released software might opt-in to an e-mail list that announces new software products.

Here are some rules to keep in mind when selling through e-mail.

- **Identify yourself**   Let your prospective customer know who you are right up front. If you've rented an opt-in list, remind them that they opted in. Include a sentence reminding them why they're receiving your e-mail.

- **Keep it short—real short—less than one page**   E-mail is most effective when it's short and simple. After you introduce yourself, give a brief description of your offer. Within the offer, give them a link to click or refer them to the URL of the buying page.

- **Provide value for their time**   Make it a compelling or a limited-time offer. Offer something that they couldn't already buy from your site. Perhaps an exclusive offer only made through your e-mail.

- **Be ready to apologize**   People can have a short memory and they can forget they opted into the list, or their tastes or needs might have changed. So, if they complain or ask to be removed from your list, respond quickly and politely.

- **Make it easy to unsubscribe**   Place your unsubscribe instructions both at the beginning and at the end of your e-mail message. Don't make them call a phone number to unsubscribe. The unsubscribe process should be fast and simple.

Finding Companies That Offer Opt-In E-MAIL Lists

If you want to e-mail responsibly, then first turn to these sites to purchase targeted opt-in lists.

NetCreations—The first company to collect, categorize, and offer for sale non-spam opt-in e-mail lists is PostmasterDirect (now called NetCreations) at w3.netcreations.com. If you're looking for numbers, this is the place. You can choose from more than three million e-mail addresses in 3,000+ categories.

Bulletmail—Bulletmail at www.bulletmail.com gives you a choice of more than 100 targeted, opt-in e-mail lists not available elsewhere. Bulletmail offers advice on building an e-mail campaign, and it lets you use an unlimited number of hotlinks in your e-mail to your site offer and even your own e-mail box.

Targ-It—If you want to e-mail using demographic information, then check out Targ-It at www.targ-it.com/. Their lists are all 100% opt-in and have more than 350 lists available for purchase.

Get the Scoop on E-mail Marketing

E-mail Marketing News is a monthly e-mail newsletter covering subscription e-mail lists, opt-in, corporate e-mail marketing, advertising in e-mail, e-mail ad techniques, metrics, countering spam, and evolving standards. Check it out at www.emailmarketingnews.com/.

Htmail at www.htmail.com/customer.html gives an interesting twist to their list offer. First they claim that their list will generate as much as a 27% response. Second, they guarantee at least a 10% response from your e-mail message or they'll give you your money back.

Finally The Direct E-Mail List Source at www.copywriter.com/lists/index.htm is a directory of voluntary e-mail marketing lists. The site also offers a resource for opt-in lists, newsletters, e-mail discussion lists, advertiser supported e-mail services, and e-mail list brokers where you can advertise without spamming (see Figure 3.3).

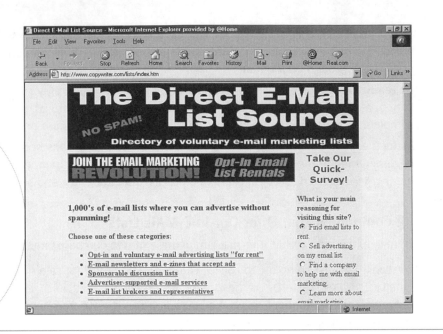

Figure 3.3

The Direct E-mail List Source is a great place to start for both opt-in e-mail lists and ideas for selling your product via e-mail.

SELLING THROUGH CLASSIFIEDS

"SWM looking for devout vegetarian into camping, Barry Manilow records, and Jell-O wrestling. No freaks."

This may be the first type of ad that comes to mind when you think of classifieds. But there's another type of classified ad—one that can be used to sell products. The trick is to find the right sites on the Net; sites that cater to businesses and attract customers who will be looking to buy your product or service.

Though selling through classifieds is one of the least expensive ways to sell online—there is no need to build a Web site, for example—it does have its downside. Potential customers could be leery about buying a product from some company without a Web site presence. A well-designed Web site lends credibility to an eTailer. In addition, offering a secure way for customers to purchase with a credit card is difficult without a Web site. The trade off of a little expense in exchange for credibility, is an important factor if you plan to build a large business on the Net.

To see an example of a site that's designed specifically for selling products online, take a look at Buy & Sell (www.buysell.com). One of the most popular classified ad sites is Yahoo! Classifieds, at classifieds.yahoo.com. Because of the visitor traffic Yahoo! generates to its site, their classified ads are viewed by millions of people each month. Individuals who are selling one or two products place most of the ads; still, you can't ignore the traffic numbers, so it would be worthwhile placing your product for sale there.

Another classifieds site for businesses is i752.com at `www.i752.com`. They offer a wide variety of items that are essential to today's businesses.

Finally Promote Plus at `promoteplus.hypermart.net/classifieds.html` offers a source of low cost advertising through their classified ads. Categories include both business services and products.

SELLING THROUGH ONLINE MALLS

When e-commerce on the World Wide Web was just starting, online malls were the place to be. They provided a convenient way for shoppers to find a variety of stores in one place. But as stores on the Net developed, the destination sites were the stores themselves and online malls fell from favor.

One of the reasons for this fall from favor was that most of these online malls were nothing more than a directory of stores. The malls didn't add any value to the shopping experience and as the search engines became more mature and efficient, eTailers could be found more easily. Nobody needed a shopping mall that acted as only a directory.

Some online malls did offer additional value, such as a built-in central purchasing system in the form of a shopping cart. That meant e-tailers didn't have to pay for shopping-cart software up-front, but instead paid for it in higher fees over a period of time. But the main problem with selling from the old online malls was traffic; the malls really didn't advertise and the stores in the malls saw few sales. Although these old-style online malls are in decline, some bigger players in the market are replacing them.

The major search engines like Yahoo! realized a few years back that they could convert their site visitors into customers. Yahoo! was the first to offer an online mall in the form of its Yahoo! Store. When you join the Yahoo! Store mall as an eTailer, you have the benefit of a major search engine offering its visitors sites to buy products associated with their searches.

Major search engines—such as Yahoo!—realized some time back that they could convert their site visitors into customers. Yahoo! offered one of the first online malls in Yahoo! Store. Yahoo! Store was the first to offer eTailers what other online malls didn't—one shopping cart and one interface. Then just last year, Amazon created zShops to compete with Yahoo! and upped the ante. Now anyone selling products can open a store on the Net. The result for eTailers is that they can share an online shopping space that uses one return policy, one privacy policy, one shopping cart, one interface, and one customer-support center.

I'll talk more about these do-it-yourself online stores in Chapter 8, "Hosting Your Store for Free." They offer a quick and easy way to get into e-commerce without the large expense.

CHAPTER 4

CREATING A UNIQUE SELLING POSITION

In This Chapter

- Learn how to sell on the Net now that the customer is more in control of the transaction
- Decide on a pricing model for your business that will attract this new type of buyer
- Learn how to differentiate yourself from your competition

Ask a random sample of business owners to tell you what makes them different from their competition and you'd get a blank stare or perhaps a response like "My prices are the lowest." "I guarantee satisfaction." "My products are high quality." "I give great customer service."

The problem is that none of these responses is a *Unique Selling Position* (USP). Many businesses can claim the same things. After you find a need to fill, you must fill it in a unique fashion. A business must know what they offer a customer besides general statements and why they think a shopper should buy from them. That is, what makes them *unique* in the market and in the eyes of a potential customer.

So what is a Unique Selling Position? Let's put it this way. A USP

- Gives your company a unique *advantage* over your competition.
- Gives consumers a distinct *reason* to buy from your company.
- Portrays in the consumer's mind a compelling image of what your business will do for them that others cannot.

Advantage, reason, and image are what your goal should be in creating a Unique Selling Position. Creating a USP is the first thing you need to do before you even consider building your online business. Your USP creates the framework and lays the foundation for your compelling offer. And here's another reason. A good USP also keeps your business pointed in the right direction.

Finally a good Unique Selling Position helps you deal successfully with the new type of consumer that the Net has created and the different ways of selling that they are demanding.

COMMERCE TURNED ON ITS HEAD—THE SHOPPER IN CONTROL

A long long time ago in a Mall far, far away retailers set the price and consumers had little choice but to pay it. Today—because of the Internet—fixed prices are a thing of the past.

The pricing of products and services as we know it has been turned upside down by the Net. The consumer, more and more, is in control of the transaction. Fixed pricing is giving way to all kinds of dynamic pricing schemes ushered in by the technology of the Net. Auctions, reverse auctions, Dutch auctions, comparison shopping, group buying—even bartering—and a host of other buying schemes has put the consumer in control of how much they will pay for an item.

Not that any of this is really new. Auctions, group buying, and bartering have been around in the real world for many years but the Net has made them more efficient. In the real world, it's very difficult for retail stores to change prices after the price tag is applied. But on the Net, prices can be changed in a second.

The technology of the Net offers another advantage to the online consumer—quick and easy comparison shopping. Although most of the Net-based shopping *robots*—or *personal shopping agents* as they are sometimes called—of today are primitive, they are maturing fast. A good example of a comparison-shopping bot is mySimon (see Figure 4.1). They cover the field in the number of merchants and the products shopped. Some day, you and I can simply tell a shopping bot what we want to buy, give it some basic parameters to follow—such as size, color, shipping costs, warrantees, and return privileges—and it will scamper across the Net searching and negotiating on our behalf for the best deal.

Figure 4.1

mySimon is a good example of a comparison-shopping bot.

What's a Bot?

Bot is short for robot. A Shopping bot is a piece of software or service that you can personalize and send onto the Net to search for specific products, services, or information that you request. These intelligent software agents, as they are sometimes called, are becoming more and more popular and will change the face of e-commerce. For a list of shopping bots currently available, check out the BotSpot at www.botspot.com/search/s-shop.htm.

And what about the consumer? How will their newly won control of pricing impact the design of your new online business? Will they be buying strictly on price alone and will the low price leader win every sale?

That's not likely. Consumers buy for different reasons and price is not the only determining factor, although it is an important one. That's why it's important to have a strong Unique Selling Position that explains the *full* selling position of your company. Your full selling position could include one or more of the following:

- **Pricing policies and discounts**—How much will you charge and how can the customer buy it?

- **Product and service selection**—Do you offer a narrow line of specialized products and services or a broader category of them?

- **Site convenience factors**—Do you offer a site, product, or service search capability?

- **Customer service and purchase guarantee information**—What kind of purchase guarantee will you provide? 100% satisfaction guarantee or something less?
- **Order security**—Is your online credit card transaction process secure?
- **Shopper communities**—Will you offer discussion boards and chat rooms for customers to exchange opinions and ask questions about your products, services, and company?
- **Product and service reviews**—Will you offer detailed product reviews of the items you sell?
- **Rebates**—Will you offer rebates, coupons, or points to entice shoppers to buy?
- **Personalized services**—Will you take special requests from customers for products or services not offered in your online catalog?

Still, flexible pricing models are going to be very common in the years ahead. When creating your Unique Selling Position it would be wise to understand and incorporate these new models if you want to stay atop the e-commerce wave and not be swamped by it.

THERE'S MORE THAN ONE WAY TO SKIN A PRICE TAG

Let's face it. Your online business will succeed or fail based on what you charge a customer. Set prices too high and customers won't buy. Set them too low and you're not profitable. At either extreme you go out of business.

Fixed pricing has been the norm in U.S. commerce. With fixed pricing, the seller sets the price and the buyer can take it or leave it. But today the fixed pricing model is only one of many on the Net—and one by the way, that doesn't seem to have a very good future.

Tomorrow's pricing models will surpass the fixed-pricing model and include a variety of auction types: online haggling, and aggregate or group buying. The following sections take a look at each of them.

Online Haggling

Haggling, although not new in the real world, has come to the Net. This type of pricing model is a one-to-one exchange. You either personally haggle—or negotiate—a price with a seller or you can use an intelligent software agent. You're beginning to see sites use this pricing model because the technology of the Net makes it possible.

eWanted.com at www.ewanted.com and MyGeek at www.mygeek.com (see Figure 4.2) are two examples of haggling services.

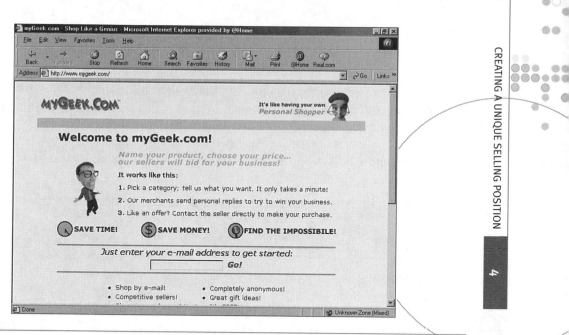

Figure 4.2

The geeks at myGeek will present your product or service needs to their merchant members and they will bid for your business.

Online Auctions

The next flexible selling model is the online auction. As in the real world, online auctions come in three different flavors:

- Standard online auctions
- Dutch auctions
- Reverse auctions

> ### (TIP) Place an Auction on Your Site
>
> Want to add an auction to your site? Instant Auction lets you auction-enable your Web site with their easy-to-use software. You can run an online auction right from your own Web site. Check it out at www.instantauction2000.com/.

The *standard online auction* has grown exponentially on the Net over the last few years. It was the first alternative to fixed pricing and the number of sites offering this pricing model has grown steadily. The standard online auction is a seller-dominated market that pits buyers against each other to determine the highest price of an item. The highest bidder gets to buy the item. A good and venerable example of a standard auction is eBay.

Next is the *Dutch auction*. Whereas the standard auction sees prices steadily climb, the Dutch auction works backward. Dutch auctions such as Klik Klok Productions (www.klik-klok.com)

are used when there are many of the same items for sale (see Figure 4.3). In this case many buyers can win a bid and buy as many of the items for sale as they want. The seller who bids the lowest amount for the most items is the winner.

Reverse auctions turn the standard and Dutch auctions on their head. When buyers dominate an auction, the reverse auction is used. In the case of reverse auctions, buyers name the desired quantity and price of an item or service and sellers bid down to get the sale. Here the seller is competing against other businesses instead of the buyer competing against other buyers. To see an example of a reverse auction, head to Respond.com at www.respond.com.

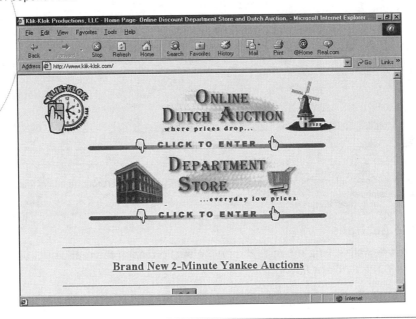

Figure 4.3

At Klik Klok Productions, products in their department store move off the shelves fast. Prices decrease over a period of two minutes.

Group Buying

Demand aggregation or group buying, is different from the other pricing models. In the other models buyers commit to a price they name and sellers decide whether to accept their offer. In the group-buying model, buyers accept an offer at a maximum price that falls as more buyers decide to buy the product.

It's sort of like an electronic coop. Buyers band together to negotiate a better price from the seller. Examples of the group-buying model can be found at MobShop (www.accompany.com).

You should seriously consider these different pricing models when creating your Unique Selling Position.

USP—YOUR UNIQUE SELLING POSITION

Having the right USP doesn't matter if you can't explain it to your customers. Consider the situation Federal Express found themselves in. They had a new concept of delivering packages overnight and wanted to say that their package delivery service was better than using the services of the buses and airlines. And they needed to say it in one simple phrase.

Up until then if you wanted to ship a small package across the country, you had to ship it on the bus and airlines schedules. It might take up to several days to have your package delivered—and then *you* had to pick it up!

FedEx saw an opportunity here. All they had to do was convince the public that they could deliver their package in a speedier fashion. After much thought, they decided that what differentiated them from their competitors was that they owned their own planes. This meant that customers could ship products on *their* schedule and not the schedule of the airlines and buses.

So what was the USP of FedEx? It was this. "We have our own planes."

It didn't fly with the public. They didn't understand it.

"So what?" they said. "What does that mean to me?" So FedEx went back to the drawing board and came up with this. "When you absolutely, positively have to have it overnight!" That worked. The pubic responded and the rest is commerce history. Consumers didn't care if FedEx had their own planes. They could care less. They didn't care if their packages were delivered by Pony Express. The benefit to the consumer was that their package was delivered overnight right to their door.

> **JARGON**
>
> **Spree.com—A Good Example of Differentiating**
>
> Over one million Web sites participate in affiliate programs on Net. So how do you differentiate yourself from those? Spree.com did. Spree.com sells the same products that any other affiliate program does. But they've learned to package the programs in such a way to create a Unique Selling Position. What entices a customer to buy from their Web site? Rebates. Customers who buy get back, as a cash refund, a percentage of the affiliate commission paid to Spree. Check it out at www.spree.com.

There's a lesson here—one that you can use when creating your own Unique Selling Position. Keep in mind WIIFM—What's In It For Me? This is what a customer is looking for when he or she buys. Phrase your USP in those terms and you will go a long way toward creating an effective and successful Unique Selling Position.

Another good example is Domino's Pizza. How do you differentiate one pizza service from another? Domino's did by promising to deliver your pizza in "30 minutes or less—or the pizza is free!" One unexpected side effect unfortunately, was that Domino's employees were getting speeding tickets and having car wrecks trying to meet that 30-minute deadline. So be careful how you plan to execute your USP!

Both FedEx and Domino have had a measurable and beneficial USP. They're measurable—"Overnight" and "In 30 Minutes"—and have a unique benefit—"Delivered to Your Door" and "Free If Not Delivered in Time."

Remember that a good USP is specific, measurable, and conveys a customer benefit.

Creating Your USP

Put this book down, take out a pad and pencil, and ask yourself these questions. Answer them as *simply* as you can. You're not creating a corporate mission statement here.

- Why is my business special?
- Why would someone buy from me instead of my competition?
- What can my business provide a consumer that no one else can? What's the benefit to the consumer that I can deliver?

Keep your answers specific, measurable, and show a benefit to the buyer. Here's the hard part—answer these questions in just one sentence and make it so anyone can understand it. Test it on your spouse, family, friends, and neighbors and ask them what they think it means.

Before you can build your online business, you must have a clear understanding of what your USP means and how to deliver it through your online business.

Don't Put the e-Commerce Cart Before the Horse

Planning your Web site before deciding your Unique Selling Position is bad enough, but even worse is diving into your site design using a lot of pretty graphics and whiz-bang technical tricks. Your job is to sell the customer—not entertain the visitor.

Here are some additional aspects to consider when fleshing out a Unique Selling Position. They're called the four Ps: pricing, positioning, packaging, and promotion.

- **Pricing**—If you're going to compete on price, don't just say you're the lowest—say why. For instance, perhaps you can sell at such a low price because of your ability to source product from the closeout industry, buying products at pennies on the dollar. Play up this uniqueness in your USP. But be cautious here. Many consumers do not buy on price alone. They are looking for not just a good price but a good value.

The Price Is Right!

Like many sites on the Web, US Wings sells leather jackets. What sets them apart from the others? Quality. They sell only US made leather jackets—not cheap imports. Customers don't mind paying more because the jackets will last more than 30 years.

- **Positioning**—The Marines are looking for just a few good men—not all men, just a few. This is a great positioning statement and makes their business unique and differentiates them among the armed forces. Look for a similar positioning with your business. Perhaps your focus is gender based. Perhaps it's age based. Or perhaps it's interest based like L.L. Bean at www.llbean.com (see Figure 4.4). Sell to a unique segment of the population—not to all of it.

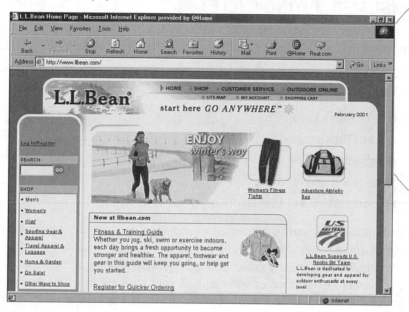

Figure 4.4

L.L. Bean offers a lot of information on outdoor sports and living. Their clothing designers actually test the products in the field. This reinforces their Unique Selling Position by branding them as *the* place to buy outdoor clothing.

- **Packaging**—Take a common product that others sell and re-package it in a new way. For instance, take the iMac. It's just a computer, but look at the packaging. Not only did it sell, but it also had a positioning statement with it—get on the Internet in 20 minutes and "Think Different."

- **Promotion**—Finally, look at the promotional possibilities of your product or service. Can you tie your product or service to a season or holiday where you can benefit from the promotional activities and mind set that already exist at that time of year? Or perhaps there are other time-based connections like the birth of a child, birthdays, or anniversaries. The key here is to tie your product or service to activities or life events that are normally promoted by others. You then can identify your USP with those.

Above all else remember that your USP is not about you, it's not about your business—it's about your customer. Speak to the needs of the customer—the needs you identified in Chapter 2, "Identifying a Need."

Don't Forget the Call to Action!

The hard work you put into a Unique Selling Position is all for naught if you don't have this in your offer: *Ask for the sale!* So many times a business with a great USP and the ability to deliver it forgets to end it with a call to action by asking for the sale.

THE CONSUMER BUYING CYCLE

A lot goes into a consumer's decision to buy. In fact, it can be looked at as a process. And where you position your online business within that cycle will help you create your USP.

According to MIT Media laboratories, the Consumer Buying Process consists of five elements:

- Need Identification
- Product Brokering
- Merchant Brokering
- Negotiation and Purchase
- Product Service and Evaluation

Need Identification   Any purchase of a product or service starts with a consumer's perception of a need. This can give your business its first opportunity to build a relationship with a potential customer by either anticipating or stimulating a consumer need. By helping a consumer fill a product or service need, your business can collect—voluntarily—information on a potential customer. A reminder service is a good example. There are several dozen reminder services on the Net today where consumers can list their important dates and be reminded via e-mail about an upcoming event. Candor's Birthday and Anniversary Reminder Service (www.candor.com/reminder/) is an example of a service that reminds you about upcoming birthdays via e-mail.

The value to the consumer is the timely reminder—the value to your business is the collection of specific information on the consumer and a potential sale.

Product Brokering   After a consumer has realized a need for a product, he or she needs to locate information on what to buy. The consumer needs to not only locate the product or service but also evaluate the different product or service options available to create a consideration set. In this case, the primary function of your business would be to provide the information that the consumer needs and, in the process, build a stronger relationship with the potential customer. Web sites such as Epinions (www.epinions.com) helps people make informed buying decisions. It offers consumers unbiased advice, personalized recommendations, and comparative shopping. In this way, Epinions collects consumer information to further personalize the consumer's shopping experience. Another way to create stickiness is to create a sense of community among consumers. Discussion boards, chat rooms, discussion lists, and electronic newsletters are great ways to create shopping communities at your e-business. Monitoring these community-building activities gives a company the opportunity to collect information on its users to build a better shopping experience.

Merchant Brokering   After finding the right product or service, the consideration set moves from what to buy to where to buy it. At this stage, the consumer starts the process of evaluating the merchant itself. Price, convenience, availability, service, warranty, delivery time, reputation, security and other factors all enter the merchant choice equation.

Negotiation and Purchase   Every customer wants a good deal. But what's considered a good deal is different from buyer to buyer. Most everyone would admit that they got a good deal when they purchased their last car. Yet the chances of any two buyers paying the same price for the same car are slight. Another example is an airline ticket. The odds that two travelers sitting next to each other paid the same price for their airline tickets is not good. Still, both probably felt they got a good deal on their tickets at the time. The car and airline game of different pricing for different people will pale in comparison to the dynamic pricing schemes that are hatching on the Net. Over the last few years, companies such as Priceline (`priceline.com`), uBid (`ubid.com`), MobShop (`mobshop.com`), and Respond.com (`respond.com`) have given consumers the power to negotiate the price they pay for products and services. Perhaps you can offer a similar service or better with your new online business.

Product Service and Evaluation   After the product or service is delivered, a buyer then evaluates the entire purchasing experience. This experience can be communicated to the merchant in the form of a compliment or complaint—or no comment at all. The buyer can relate his or her experience to consumer-oriented organizations such as BizRate, other shoppers on community bulletin boards.

Customers also can file complaints with one of the complaint services on the Net. On these services, consumers not only can air their grievance, but the service will actually take up their cause and seek to resolve the customer complaint with the merchant. Companies such as eComplaints.com provide complaint resolution services. The procedure is simple. The consumer with a complaint registers their complaint with eComplaints.com. The complaint is passed directly to the company, which is then invited to respond to the consumer directly or through the site. By having a public forum for publishing these complaints, consumers gain leverage in their dispute. Furthermore, by reading the published complaints, other consumers who visit the site gain insight on a company's product and service problems before they buy from them. The question is where can your online business fit in the Customer Buying Cycle? Do you need to become one or all these information companies to succeed? The answer is *no*. By understanding that valuable information can be collected on customers and potential customers, and seeing the importance of this collected information in developing an online business, you can consider one of these as a focus of your USP.

One final thought: Whatever you promise in your Unique Selling Position—be sure you deliver on it. Don't make the mistake of adopting a USP that you can't fulfill. Remember the old adage "A good experience is told to one person, but a bad experience is told to 10 people."

CHAPTER 5

PLANNING YOUR ONLINE BUSINESS

In This Chapter

- Learn what a business plan is and why it's important in creating your online business
- Discover where to find sample business plans
- Learn the elements of a good business plan

A business doesn't plan to fail—it fails to plan. So if you want your new online business to be a success you'll need to plan for that success. To do that, you need a business plan. A business plan acts as a roadmap for your company. It clearly states who you are, what you do, and how you do it. It's also essential if you ever want to raise money from established capital sources such as investment banks and venture capitalists.

GET A PLAN, MAN!

It's not enough to plan to be in business. A good business plan helps you focus on your business concept, provides a framework to develop your business idea, serves as a basis for discussion with investors, and gives you a way to measure your business assumptions and performance that can be reviewed over time. A good business plan also should give a clear understanding of your business objectives, strategies, and financial viability.

Free Business Plan Template

You can download a free shareware Business Plan Template called Exl-Plan. You can choose from different versions of the software based on the size of your business. Download it at www.planware.org/exldown.htm.

Every well thought-out business plan has these common elements.

- A description of your product or service
- An analysis of your competition
- A marketing plan
- A management plan
- A financial plan

A business plan can do something else. Just the process of thinking through all the elements of the plan will help you avoid mistakes and even uncover some hidden opportunities. The process of writing the business plan is just as valuable as the finished product. The very process of planning includes thinking about your business, discussing it with others, researching your market, and analyzing your competition.

Business Plan Tips

Writing a business plan is not easy. It takes a lot of time and hard work. It will take weeks—even months to write a good plan. So here are some general tips that can help you through it.

First, make a list of your new company's strengths, its weaknesses, the market threats and opportunities. Don't write a tome. Keep your plan short and to the point; no more than 20 pages or so. Then nail down your assumptions. Be realistic about your projections and base your assumptions on your market research and analysis.

Next, make a list of your business risks. Be honest with yourself. Every business has competition—decide who they are and how they will impact your business. List other risks such as potential changes in your market, personnel challenges, and technology risks. This shows that you've given thought to both the upside and downside of your business.

Free Business Plan Format

You can have a business plan template e-mailed to you free of charge. The format has been used to successfully raise capital for Capital Connections clients. Ask for it at www.capital-connection.com/freestuff.html.

Don't make statements you can't support. A good business is not built on wishful thinking. Back up your claims with research and analysis on your competition, your market, your business assumptions—and risks. Also, don't use highly technical terms. Keep the wording simple or if you must use technical terms, explain them fully in your plan.

Some good sources for business research on the Web are e-Marketer at www.emarketer.com, CyberAtlas at www.cyberatlas.com, CyberStats at www.zdnet.com, and InternetStats.com at www.internetstats.com.

Test Your Business Plan Skills

Want to experiment on someone else's plan before you write yours? You can. American Express has a business plan exercise that you can use at their Web site. You can test your skills on a fictional business plan and then be rated on how prepared you are to create your own. Check it out at home3.americanexpress.com/smallbusiness/resources/starting/biz_plan/try.

Finally a business plan is never finished. It's a living document that should be updated frequently as you move through your plan. You'll be surprised how many times you'll modify your activities when new market opportunities present themselves simply because you are in business.

One last thought. Should you hire someone to write your business plan? The answer is "No." Only you have full understanding of your business model. There are many companies that offer business plan writing services and there are a number of software packages on the market that claim to do the same. The truth is, the best they can do is show you a format to follow. You will have to do the research, think through the risks and opportunities, create the marketing hooks, and come up with your financial assumptions—that is, provide the bulk of the material for your plan.

Free Newsletter to Improve Your Business Plan

BizPlanIt.Com's free monthly e-mail newsletter provides subscribers with insights and useful business plan advice in every issue. Subscribe at www.bizplanit.com/free/newsletter1.htm.

Where to Find Sample Business Plans

Before starting on your business plan, it's a good idea to see what a plan actually looks like. Here are two Web sites that provide sample plans for your review. Just remember, these are just samples. They can only give you an idea of how a plan is organized and the type of materials that need to be included. Your business plan will differ dramatically.

Your first stop should be BizPlans.com at `www.bplans.com`. BizPlans is a very good resource not only for sample business plans but also for sample marketing plans. It also provides a Planning Spreadsheet Glossary that explains the details of a business plan spreadsheet. They provide this free service to attract traffic to their site to sell their business plan writing software package. By the way, giving something away to attract traffic to your site is a good thing to keep in mind for your online business.

Now let's discuss the sample plans. First, go to `www.bplans.com/sp/`. On this page you'll see a selection of more than two dozen sample business plans. Select a sample plan to view.

There you'll see the title of the business plan and a brief description of the business (see Figure 5.1). You'll notice that you can either view the plan step-by-step through your browser or download the plan onto your computer for viewing later.

Figure 5.1

Here's an example of a sample business plan from bplans.com, which you can download to your computer for viewing.

Can't decide which sample plan to view? Want to know which plans best match your business concept? Then BizPlans.com offers another useful service called the Plan Wizard at `www.bplans.com/pw/`. By answering just a few questions, their Plan Wizard recommends the sample plans on their site that match your business.

TIP

Create a Quick Mini-Plan

You can write a mini-business plan live on the Web to test your business idea—and it's free. The free process can help you test your business objectives, define its mission, analyze the market, and determine your break-even point. Check it out at www.bplans.com/mp/.

If you're looking for real plans—and top-notch ones to boot—then check out the business plan examples at the MootCorp Competition at www.businessplans.org/MootCorp.html (see Figure 5.2). They offer a library of different award-winning business plans. Each was a winner or a finalist in the MootCorp Competition. MBAs from the best business schools in the world were invited to present their business plans to a panel of investors who then chose the best new business ideas.

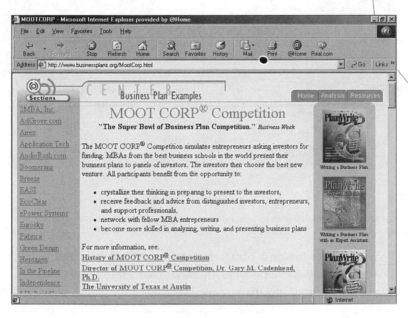

Figure 5.2

At MOOT CORP you can view award-winning business plans by topic—products, services, and Internet services.

Not only does MootCorp provide a selection of winning business plans, they also offer the best example of each specific business plan topic such as Best Executive Summary, Best Marketing Plan, Best Operations Plan, and so on.

Now that you have an idea of what a business plan looks like, it's time to write your own.

GREAT IDEA! BUT IS IT A BUSINESS?

Coming up with a business idea is relatively easy—it's the execution of it that's hard. A good business plan will go a long way in helping you execute your business idea. So, in this section I'll list the important elements you need to have in your plan, their purpose, and tips to keep in mind when writing each section. Also check out the Center for Business Planning (www.businessplans.org/plan.html) for links to general planning resources on the Net (see Figure 5.3).

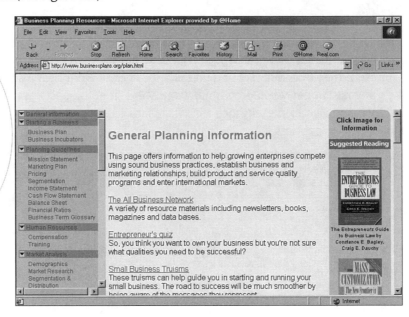

Figure 5.3

This library of resources contains links to sites offering research materials for every possible line of business.

When you write your business plan, remember to be succinct, to the point, and reader-friendly. Your plan should be no longer than 20 pages—including financials. Make it look professional. Use a word processor, have it bound, and have it proofread by someone other than yourself. Nothing looks less professional in a business plan than typos and grammatical errors.

If you're writing your plan for investors, be sure you tell them in your plan how their money will be used and how they'll be rewarded financially for their investment. For example, will their investment be used to fund the development of a technology or a product or information service? Would it be used to build a Web site or pay for rent and salaries? Be specific as to where their investment will go.

Then inform them in your plan how they will be rewarded for funding your online business. Are you planning to sell your business once it reaches profitability? Will you pay the investors back over time? Or will you go for an Initial Public Offering where your company goes public and sells it's stock on the NASDAQ?

An Online Business Plan Workshop

The Web can teach you how to write an effective business plan. At their site, American Express provides a Small Business Exchange Business Plan Workshop. The workshop actually provides a step-by-step process to create a business plan online. Check it out at home3.americanexpress.com/smallbusiness/resources/starting/ biz_plan/?aexp_nav=sbs_hp_bizplan.

My intent here is not to teach you how to write a detailed business plan. There are many books on the subject that can help you do that. The intent here is to show you the most important elements to include in your business plan.

The Executive Summary

Although the Executive Summary of a business plan comes first, it's the last section that you'll write. You should cull information from other sections of your plan to write it.

The Executive Summary is just that—a quick summary of your business, and it's potentially the most important part of your business plan. Keep in mind that if you offer your plan to investors, the Executive Summary is the first and probably the only part of the plan they will read. If it interests them, they'll read further. Others will read it first to get a snapshot of your business and see whether your business concept makes sense.

SBA Business Plan Outline

Want a quick outline of a typical business plan? The Small Business Administration (SBA) provides one on their site. Find it at http://www.sba.gov/starting/ indexbusplans.html

Your Executive Summary should be short—no longer than two to four pages and include

- A brief description of your company and what needs of the customer it will fill (for example—describe your Unique Selling Position).
- A description of the product or service you will provide.
- What your market is and how you plan to promote and sell your product or service.
- A short description of your key management.
- The type and amount of investment you will need.
- How and when investors will get paid back.

The Executive Summary is your chance to reach out and grab your readers and get them insanely interested in your business idea. Because this gives the reader the first impression of your business concept, let your friends and family read the summary first. Ask them if it makes sense. You only have a few short pages to pitch your idea, so it has to be clearly defined and easily understood.

Avoid these common Executive Summary mistakes:

- **Lacking focus**—You have just a few minutes to get your business concept across, and it should be loud and clear in the first few paragraphs of your Executive Summary. This is where your unique selling position should be displayed. Your USP is brief, to the point, and explains your business quickly and effectively.

- **Too wordy**—Most times, your Executive Summary is all that gets read. So, of course, you tend to explain as much as you can about your business opportunity. Don't! Keep each section of the summary as brief as you can. Just touch on the most important points of each part.

- **Reads like a preface; not a summary**—An Executive Summary is just that—a summary. It is not an introduction to your plan. Look at it as a mini-plan in itself.

- **No expression of a unique opportunity**—What's the opportunity? Why should anyone invest in your new business? What will investors receive in return for the risk they are taking? These questions should be answered in the Executive Summary.

- **Fails to generate excitement**—The Executive Summary should be more sizzle than steak. Although it should give the basic details of your business, it should also have a certain amount of hype to it. Remember that you're trying to get people to invest in your idea so make it sound exciting.

In summary keep in mind that the Executive Summary is not an introduction, preface, or abstract of your plan—it's your business plan in miniature. So be sure it touches on all the important aspects of your business idea.

Who and What Are You?

An effective business plan includes a clear idea of what your company is and does. You should have decided the type of business entity you are going to be. Is it a corporation (a separate legal entity that issues stock), partnership (a simple business agreement between one or more people), or sole proprietorship (owned by you and run by you exclusively)? State in your plan what business you are in. Are you going to be a retailer, distributor, or manufacturer?

You also should include a detailed description of the product or service you will offer. Here's where your unique selling position comes in. Your USP is your identity in the marketplace. It tells you and the reader of your plan in a concise manner who you are and what you do. You also should explain and support why your business idea will work.

The Macintosh evangelist, Guy Kawasaki and founder of Garage.com, a startup incubator, once said that the best business to start is one that eases a pain. If you can find a market in pain—and cure it—you'll have a successful business. So, be sure that you clearly state in your plan who's pain you'll be curing—that is, what market problem you are solving—and how you're going to solve it.

Finally, how will customers obtain your product or service? Will they buy it online, over the phone, via fax, through the mail—or a combination of all of them? What's your pricing strategy? Will you be the lowest or add value and charge more? And what about your competition? How you differ from them also should be included in your plan. And after your competition learns of your new business, how do you plan to stay ahead of them?

The answers to these questions will help you focus on your business and prepare it for what comes next.

What Is the Market and How Big Is It?

Socrates said, "Know thyself." In business, we say "Know thy Market."

Your business plan should reflect not only who your customers are, but also the size of the market they inhabit and its trends. From this information you should be able to estimate your sales revenues and company growth over time.

Next ask yourself where your market is. Is it national, regional, international, or local? You'll need to know the answer to that question when it comes time to create your marketing plan.

Make a List of Your Customer Characteristics

Want to identify the common characteristics of the people who will buy your product or service? You can download a customer profile worksheet at home3.americanexpress.com/smallbusiness/resources/starting/biz_plan/market/toolbox.shtml.

When considering a market's size, keep in mind the factors that affect market growth, such as social and economic trends, technology innovations, government regulations, and the trends in your particular industry. When selling a product or service online, many if not all of these will affect your online business.

For example, what improvements in Net technology will change the way you offer and deliver your product or service. Is your business positioned to take advantage of the relentless change of the Internet? Within a few short years, consumers will surf the Net with ever increasing speed. Is your business prepared to take advantage of the multimedia possibilities that will be available to the common Net user? What about government regulation? Will sales on the Net be taxed? You should consider how this will affect your online business.

As for sales projections, break them down to best case, worst case, and most likely scenarios. This way you can offer a spectrum of revenue projections.

How Will You Promote Your Product?

Once you know your product, know your customer, and know your market, you need to promote your business and market your product or service. To do this, your plan must contain a good marketing plan. A good marketing plan describes your target market (age, gender, geographic location, income bracket, and so on) and specific ways to market, promote, and sell your product or service to that market.

Your marketing plan should include a marketing strategy (how you will find your customers and how you will market to them), an advertising plan and budget (how you will get customers to buy your product and what it will cost to do it), and a public relations plan.

It also should identify what advertising and promotional vehicles you will use to reach your target market. For instance, what advertising mediums will you use to reach your customer? How often will each be used and what will it cost?

How about Public Relations, or PR as it's sometimes called?

Can you attract free PR? How will you do it? What's your PR plan? Will you do it yourself or hire an agency? Every successful PR program has an angle—that is what's press-worthy about your business.

Remember a strong marketing plan does double duty. It's a roadmap for you and lets a potential investor know that you not only have a good product or service but that you know how to sell it. The business world is littered with failures that had a good product or service and an identifiable market but little or no plan for how to sell into it.

Do You Have the Team to Do It?

It's said that investors invest in people—not ideas. This means that even a good idea has the potential to fail if the right team is not in place to execute it. A good management team can even take a mediocre idea and make it work. Your business plan must demonstrate that you have the right team to execute your plan or if you don't, you have identified the people you need and how to get them.

Investors are a picky bunch. They want to see a well-rounded team of professionals with experience in every function critical to the business. Your plan should clearly outline who on your team is responsible for carrying out which duties. Also, don't be afraid of having people on your team who have failed before. Most successful entrepreneurs failed at least once before, so look for people with experience starting a business, even if they've failed. And above all, try and find people that mix properly. Someone who is well skilled in their field may not be the best fit for your company "culture." Your team has to work close together, so chemistry and shared goals are key components to your startup.

Tips and Books for Startups

Nolo press publishes excellent books and tips for startups. Be sure to check out their book, *How to Write a Business Plan*. Find them at http://www.nolo.com/product/index.html.

Even if you don't plan to raise money with your business plan, you still need to give thought to your management team. Did you cover your bases? Who on your team has responsibility for executing which part of your business plan? Do you have the personnel in place to cover sales, marketing, procurement, accounting, customer service, and fulfillment? If not, who will? Your team should have an array of skills that complement each other.

Running Through the Numbers

The last element of your plan—and one of the most important—is your financials. This is where your numbers back up what you've been saying with words. The financials will tell the reader when you will turn profitable and how much money you'll need to reach that point.

Your financial plan should show revenue (your sales), expenses, your break-even point (when you stop burning money and turn a profit), and, most importantly, the financial assumptions on which you based your business. Another important part of your financials is cash flow. Cash flow, not profits, is the key to the survival of any business. You need to show in your financials how you will manage to cash and build a business that starts bringing in more cash than it spends as soon as possible.

Finally, it also should include a section about how you plan to use the money you raise from investors. This is called *use of funds*.

Although most financials go out three to five years (and in Internet time that's an eternity), they still are useful to track your assumptions and see how accurate they are after you open for business. As your numbers come in during the first few months to a year, you can review and redo your projections to get a more accurate reading on your first set of assumptions, changing them when necessary.

Remember: Your business plan is a roadmap, not a destination. It does and will change over time because your business will. You can count on it. After it's done, don't just file it way and forget about it. Update it regularly. Think of it as a process of a constant corporate self-appraisal. Assessing your business goals, strategies, and objectives by updating your business plan on a regular basis will keep your positioning fresh, your competitors at bay, and your business open to new and profitable opportunities.

GETTING THE DOUGH

In This Chapter

- Learn the different ways you can raise the money for your new business
- If you're going after venture funding, learn what venture capitalists look for in your business plan
- Learn where to look for venture funding
- Discover where to post your business plan for investors to see

Love might make the world go 'round, but if you're starting a business, it's money that you need. So where do you find it and how do you get it?

You first have to ask yourself a few important questions. How much do you need? What kind of financing is right for your business? Where will the dough come from? What will you be willing to give up for an investment in your company? These are all important questions and we will get to them in due time.

BRINGING HOME THE BACON

Are you ready for money? Who isn't, right? What I mean is—have you done your homework? Do you know how much money you need—and when? If you took my advice to heart in the last chapter and did a good job on your business plan, your financials will tell you how much you need and when you need it.

A One-Stop Source for Your Startup

Startup.com will handle your company office and operations, enabling you to focus on your core business. They'll supply everything from real estate and space planning to your technology infrastructure to payroll. Find it at www.startups.com.

You spent a lot of time researching your market, and now you need to spend time researching your financing options. This is important! You don't want to spend a lot of time chasing financing options that have little or no chance of success. You need to know what financing options are out there and which ones work best for your business.

How Much Do You Need?

The total amount of money you need depends on the size and type of business you have in mind. If it's a service business, your startup and continuing costs will not be as high as they'd be with a business that sells products. Selling products is very cost intensive. You might need to warehouse them and ship them. If so, your personnel needs will be high, adding another expense to your business.

The first step in deciding how much you need is to create a budget. You probably do that now with your personal and household bills. The process for a business is the same.

All-In-One First Year Budget Worksheet

Here's a quick and easy online calculator that figures your expenses and tells you how much financing you will need. Check it out at
www.ideacafe.com/getmoney/fgr_budget.html.

First figure what cost will be involved. While building your multimillion-dollar dream, you still have to feed your family and dog. So calculate how much you need for living expenses. Next, how much do you need just to open the doors of your new business? Will you start the business from home? If not, what are the costs to rent space? Even if you start from home you'll need a separate phone line and answering machine for business. "Daddy can't come to the phone right now" is not the response that a client or customer is looking for when they call.

Finally, you need to know how much your business will need to stay alive until you break even. You're going to burn cash at a certain rate and you'll need to know what that burn rate is.

Be realistic when you do your budget. Underestimate your revenue and overestimate expenses. When budgeting expenses, think of the unexpected: higher than expected phone expenses because of high personnel needs or higher customer service expenses because of more sales. It's these types of expenses that kill a budget quickly.

Also, run several revenue and expense projections. Look at worst case, best case, and several scenarios in between to get a good feel of what your budget should look like. And don't be afraid to test your assumptions with friends, family—and better yet—with professionals. Also, visit Working Solo (www.workingsolo.com) to sign up for their newsletter for tips on growing your business (see Figure 6.1).

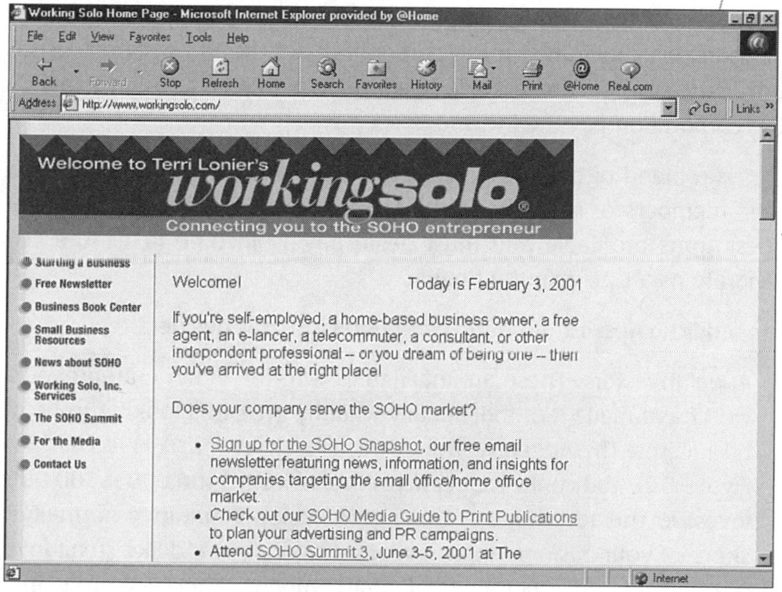

Figure 6.1

Working Solo is a great site for the self-employed or the small business owner.

What Type of Financing Is Right for You?

As they say, one man's meat is another man's poison. So it goes with financing options. Here are some things to consider.

Are you willing to give up a piece of your company for the money you need? How much? And are you willing to give up control? Giving up controlling interest in your company could lead to your removal from management if your investors think you're doing a shoddy job.

If you want to maintain control of your company, you'll either have to give away less for less money, dip into your own pocket, or borrow the cash. If you borrow the money, how much can you afford? You'll have to make payments on any loans. Your budget can tell you what you can afford and how much you can pay back over a time.

Finally, the structure of your company can place restraints on the type of financing available to you. If you decide to be a Sub-Chapter S, Standard C Corporation, or LLC (Limited Liability Corporation) these types of organizations place limits on the number and type of investors you can have.

For example, if you're looking for the big bucks from large investors or venture capitalists, you'll need to have a C Corporation to accept their investment. If you plan on raising a large amount of capital from a group of individuals, a Sub-Chapter S corporation is something to consider.

The main difference between a C and S corporation is who gets the tax write-off for the first few years of losses. In a C corporation, the business gets the write-off. In a Sub-Chapter S, the individuals investing in the corporation get the tax write-off. Usually, when a business starts to turn profitable, the owners elect to change from an S to a C corporation and let the corporation pay the income taxes.

An LLC is a blend of the two. It has all the personal protection of a corporation but also lets the members or investors in the LLC take the tax right-offs personally. But after the business turns profitable and must begin paying income taxes, the LLC might have to incorporate as a C to gain the benefit.

Here's a quick checklist of financing options for your business:

- Angel Investors—These are individuals who are either entrepreneurs like yourself who have made it or individually wealthy investors looking to help launch new businesses. The Angel Network (www.angelnetwork.com) is such an example (see Figure 6.2). You could expect investments from $100,000–$500,000 from an angel investor. The advantage of an angel investor is that they normally take a smaller share of your business than a venture capitalist—and like small investors—stay out of the day-to-day operations of your company. Angel investors understand that what they give you is not a loan but an investment. They don't expect to see the money repaid just some kind a fair return on their investment. That's why they call them angels—the perfect investors!

- About.com's, Judith Kautz (entrepreneurs.about.com/smallbusiness/ entrepreneurs/library/weekly/1999/aa052199a.htm), cites—The Small Business Administration estimates that there are at least 250,000 angels active in the United States, funding about 30,000 small companies a year. These investors are typically middle aged with at least a $90,000 annual income and a net worth of $750,000. They invest an average of $37,000 per venture and rarely invest more than a few $100,000.

- Since most angel investors do not invest in ventures far from where they live, they often work through regional networks. These can usually be found by conducting research on your favorite search engine. Sherbrooke Angels (www. sherbrookeangels.com) is an example of such a regional network. It is one part of a large network consisting of alumni from different universities throughout the nation. One can apply online within 30–45 minutes. No specific investment limit is mentioned, though the above guidelines will probably apply here. They promise that all information remains private and the entrepreneur must approve an investor before any information is given away. The network charges a $199 listing fee, as well as an undisclosed finders fee once an investor is found.

- A hybrid between angel investors and incubators (which are discussed later in this chapter) can be found at Redstone7.com. This company looks for start-up companies that will "address a recognized need in an addressable market." They provide seed capital as well as managerial support for introducing "innovative products." Their services are only for companies based in the New York City metropolitan area, but others are available nationwide. Once again, some research on your part will be necessary to locate this type of service in your area.

- You could expect investments from $100,000–$500,000 from an angel investor. The advantage of an angel investor is that they normally take a smaller share of your business than a venture capitalist—and like small investors—stay out of the day-to-day operations of your company. Angel investors understand that what they give you is not a loan but an investment. They don't expect to see the money repaid just some kind a fair return on their investment. That's why they call them angels—the perfect investors!

Keep in mind that almost all angel investor networks will require a presentation, personal appearances, and a substantial amount of written information about your business before investing any money. You will need to be able to express your idea in terms of what they stand to gain by helping you out. Most importantly, you will need to make it clear to them that you not only are an expert in your field, but also have the experience to be able to make your business successful.

- **Debt or Bank Loans**—If your balance sheet can support it and you can show that your projected revenue stream can meet a repayment schedule, then a loan—from either a bank or institution—is an option to consider. To get a loan, you must first be sure that you personally have a good credit history. Being a new business with little or no track record, you will almost certainly have to sign a personal guarantee on the loan. The amount of money raised with this option depends upon the size of the loan you can qualify for.

- **U.S. Small Business Administration (SBA)**—If you have trouble getting a loan, the SBA can help by guaranteeing your loan or a large portion of it. Their Web site at www.sba.gov contains a wealth of information on how to start, as well as finance a new business. You can download a startup kit to help you put together your business idea. There is also an SBA Classroom with online courses and resources concerning a variety of topics. Most importantly, there is a section on financing your small business. It contains lots of resources and ideas for coming up with the money to get started.

The main lending program of the SBA is the 7 Loan Guaranty Program. The gist of the program is that it guarantees the loan to a private lender. In other words, if you don't pay it back, the SBA provides assistance to the lender with recovering the loan. The SBA does not provide direct loans or grants to businesses.

To secure an SBA loan, the applicant must contact a local lender. Applications and information may also be requested from local SBA offices listed in the Web site. The maximum amount available is $2 million, and most loans are for $150,000 or less. In order to qualify for an SBA loan, you must have repayment ability from available cash flow. Other factors for consideration include: good character of the business leaders, management capability, personal or business collateral, and the owner's equity contribution. To help determine eligibility for your business, four factors are taken into consideration: the type of business, the size of the business, how you intend to use the loan funds, and other special circumstances.

Because the SBA is a government agency, the process is complicated and requires a lot of patience on your part. But if this is the only way to snag a loan, you might have to endure the bureaucratic red tape.

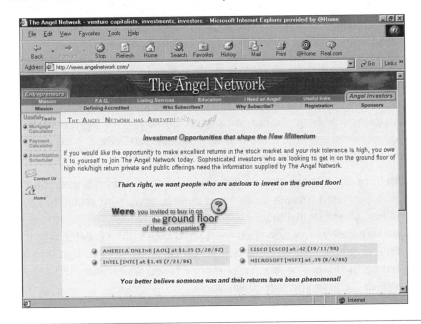

Figure 6.2

At the Angel Network, you can list your business and funding needs in hopes that Angel Investors will find you and invest in your business.

Good Resource for Raising Funds

Garage.com has a very good list of books about raising funds. Find it at
www.garage.com/resources/raisingFunds.shtml.

- **Private Placement or Seed Capital**—Individuals can be approached asking them to invest approximately $10,000–$25,000 apiece to meet the initial capital requirements of your company. If your capital needs are small in the beginning or if you can find a number of these small investors, this option might work for you.

- **Economic Development Programs**—This is another government-sponsored way to get money. These programs are found both on the state and federal levels.

  Nearly every state has available economic development programs for startup businesses. One example is the Economic Development Division in Washington state (edd.cted.wa.gov). This organization provides access to state and local business assistance resources throughout Washington. It also offers a variety of programs for technical and financial assistance for new and existing businesses. To find similar programs elsewhere, visit your state's government Web site or use a search engine to find programs available in your area.

  At the federal level, the Economic Development Administration provides this assistance. They are under the umbrella of the Department of Commerce and further information may be found on their Web site located at www.doc.gov/eda. Most of the federal programs are for the purpose of improving rural and urban areas with high unemployment or significant economic problems. Applying for one of these programs involves a lot of red tape and a lengthy consideration processes.

  You can get a free book, *The Small Business Financial Resource Guide*, that contains a comprehensive list of small business support programs by writing to the U.S. Chamber of Commerce Small Business Center at 1615 H St. NW, Washington, DC 20062.

- **Customer or Supplier Financing**—Here's another money option. Approach your best customers or even your suppliers. After all, they must like your business concept or they wouldn't be doing business with you. Ask them if they would like to invest in your business. You might be pleasantly surprised.

- **Venture Capital**—If you want to sit at the big table and get the big bucks, then the venture capital route is the way to go. But be warned. It's not easy and it has its disadvantages. The advantage is that you can raise ten, twenty, even a hundred million dollars for your new online enterprise. We'll cover the venture capitalist option later in this chapter.

- **Friends and Family**—Don't dismiss the possibility of family and friends as funding sources. They already know your capabilities and personality and if they're interested in your idea, they could be a ready source of seed funding.

ANTE UP, FELLA!

If after looking at the formal financing options I just described you've decided you're not ready for them yet, then self-funding is your first step.

If you don't want to tap into your savings—which you'll need to live on while you develop your business—look to your credit cards. Your credit cards are a ready source of unsecured loans. If your credit limit is $5,000 to $20,000 or more, you already have at your disposal a pre-approved loan. Another benefit of using your credit card is that they free you from having lenders and investors looking over your shoulder all the time.

Okay, so the interest rate is not so great and given the new bankruptcy laws that are being enacted, carrying a burdening credit card debt could place you and your family in financial trouble. But if you shop around, you'll find many banks offering short-term introductory interest rates at a fraction of the rates credit cards normally charge. If you have two or three credit cards, they could provide all the capital you need to launch your online business.

And here's another thought. Many credit cards offer rebates or perks of some kind. Find one that offers free air miles, rebates or credits towards products and services of some kind for every dollar you spend using their card, which is good for ways to pay for all those business trips.

TIP

Find the Best Rates on Credit Cards

BankRate.com's Bank Rate Monitor lists lots of frequently updated information on which banks and credit card companies are offering the best rates. Check it out at www.bankrate.com/brm/rate/cc_home.asp.

Another way to raise cash is to sell what you don't use. In the past, your friendly pawnshop would provide a quick and easy way to unload unwanted items around your house. The pawnshop didn't pay much, but it was a source of ready cash. Today there are better online options. Simply point your browser at eBay and auction off all that stuff gathering dust in your basement or garage. The money you raise can go towards starting your business.

HOW MUCH DO YOU LOVE ME? LET ME COUNT THE MONEY

In many cultures around the world, lending money to family members is an established way of life. But borrowing money from friends and family takes some courage. You're about to take their hard-earned savings and invest it in your online startup with no guarantee of success. Also, unless your uncle is Daddy Warbucks, friends and family are not the sources for large amounts of capital.

If you want to earn the trust of your friends and family, you should be risking most of your needed capital yourself. After all, if *you* don't have confidence in your new business by putting in the maximum you can why should anyone else? The downside to the friends and family option is that family members might show a sudden zealous hands-on interest in your business. When you bring family into your business it becomes by default a family business. If your business does turn into a family affair, then the Family Firm Institute at www.ffi.org is a good resource to check out.

Most importantly, are there any current frictions in your family? Will a business investment by them throw more oil on the fire? You don't want to be the cause—or the recipient—of more family flare-ups. To avoid this, be sure you inform all friends and family of the risks involved in your online business. Better yet, put it all in writing. Make it legal. Have a lawyer draw up a simple promissory note outlining the terms of the loan and how it will be repaid.

VENTURE CAPITALISTS

If you're willing to give up part of your company in exchange for the money you need to make your company grow, then venture capitalists—or venture firms—could be the way to go.

Before we explain the working of venture capital firms, let's put one concern to bed.

Many entrepreneurs fear showing their idea to a VC. They feel that if the VC does not fund it, they will steal their idea and do it themselves or find someone else to implement it. This rarely happens for two reasons. First, reputable VCs are honorable. Second, good ideas are everywhere. It's the passion, discipline, and knowledge needed to execute an idea that makes a new idea work. A good team with the ability to execute a good plan is what most VCs look for the most.

Venture firms differ in the ways they invest their money. Some invest in only highly profitable companies. Others look for fast-growing businesses, while some look for early to mid-stage ventures to invest in.

Venture firms raise capital from individual investors looking for 5, 10, even 20 times the return on their investment. Venture firms might invest in nine ventures that fail, but the tenth one will more than make up for the loss of the other nine.

Don't Pay to Find Money

Some companies masquerade as venture firms and ask you to pay them money to find investors. Forget it. Real venture firms won't charge you to look at your business plan.

Venture firms also specialize in particular markets and tend to invest in markets they know. Most look for companies that have proven their business concept and need a lot of money to exploit a market and move forward. Fast growth and explosive growth is what they look for. Think of a hockey stick. Venture capitalists want to get in just at that little flat part before the growth soars up the stick. If your company can show meteoric growth in a short amount of time, then you're venture material.

Find Yourself Good Professional Help

The first thing you need to do when you start your online business is to find a very good lawyer and a very good accountant that you trust. You'll be so busy running your businesss, doing what you do best, that you won't have time to be a lawyer and an accountant too. Finding this type of help early can mean the difference between success and failure at any stage of your company's growth.

Venture firms look to get their investment out in only a few short years so an IPO is usually their target. They do this because they want their money back fast. Most VCs are not in the business of building businesses. They are in the business of building quick wealth either through an IPO or by selling out to another company. Often this is counter to what someone like you would do who might want to stay, run, and grow your business.

Incubate Your Business

Another source of help for startups that is not so much money as support is Incubators. Incubators help small companies get started—especially those that help young companies by providing a shared space with experienced marketing, PR, accounting, and financial help. In some cities, these types of environments are publicly funded, which can also be a big help. It might not only be the funding that can be a big help in getting your e-business started, but also starting a business in a free space, with free or low cost, experienced legal, marketing, and financial assistance.

An Entrepreneur's Favorite Letters—I, P, and O

IPO stands for *Initial Public Offering*. In an IPO, shares of your company are sold to the general public in a stock offering. An online entrepreneur makes the big bucks when he or she sells the company—either to some other large firm or to the public in an IPO.

Funding Stages

There are several venture-funding stages to keep in mind when seeking venture capital. Your capital needs dictate the stage of venture funding you look for.

- **Early Stage**—Early stage funding includes the seed, startup, and first stage. The seed stage represents a small amount of money used to either prove a business concept or product development. Little initial marketing is done at this stage. Startup stage funding goes a little further than seed stage funding. Some marketing has been done, a management team is put in place, and the initial business plan is finalized but products have yet to be sold. First stage money is used for companies that have launched their business and are selling product.

- **Expansion Funding**—Expansion stage funding includes second stage, third stage, and bridge funding. After a company is launched and making sales, second stage funding is used to expand the company in size and market share. Although revenue is being generated, it might not be making a profit at this stage. In the third stage of funding, a company has at least broken even and needs funds to achieve profitability.

Cash Flow

The difference between breaking even and profitability is CASH FLOW. Companies with negative cash flow either need to dip into the funding market, or go out of business. A company with positive cash flow can stay alive as long as the flow is positive. Funding can be used to grow the biz, but cash flow is king in these stages.

This is the stage in which a business becomes a profitable working enterprise. Funds are used to expand the company farther into its market and build its growing infrastructure. Finally, bridge-funding financing is used to prepare a company for its IPO.

Hunting the Big Game

Finding a venture firm that would be interested in your business concept is not an easy task. Like the old saying goes, "You have to kiss a lot of frogs before you find a prince."

There are several venture-funding directories that you can use to try and narrow your hunt for funds. For example, vFinance.com lists many venture capitalist firms, but one of its best features is the ability to search for firms that invest in specific areas by using their Search by Industry Sector search box (see Figure 6.3).

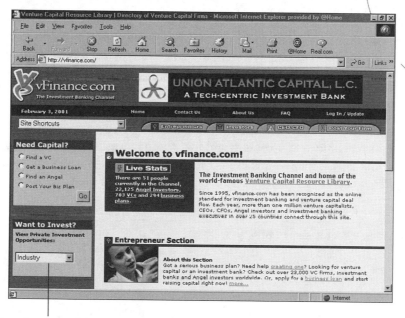

Drop-down search box

Figure 6.3

vFinance.com lists many venture capitalist firms. It is a destination on the Internet for companies seeking capital, as well as institutional and high net-worth investors seeking high growth companies.

Corporate Finance network at `www.corpfinet.com/vcapalph.htm` lists many venture capital firms, including the type of businesses they invest in, their location, assets under management, and what stage of funding they do. The InvestorLinks.com at `www.investorlinks.com/directory/service-venture-capital.html` lists a very large selection of venture capital firms with a description of what they invest in and the funding stages they support.

The Next Wave Stocks Web site at www.nextwavestocks.com/vcindex.html lists only those firms that specialize in investing in high-tech and Internet companies.

Then there's Garage.com at www.garage.com. More than just a directory, Garage.com does seed-level funding for high-tech and Internet startups. For investors, it helps find startup companies that match their investment criteria. For the entrepreneur, it introduces your business to venture firms and—if it likes your business idea—will even help you with your presentation to make it more sellable.

GETTING THE VENTURE CAPITALIST'S ATTENTION

After you've chosen a venture capital firm, how do you get their attention? What are the types of things that they look for? How can you improve your odds of being accepted by a Venture firm?

Venture capitalists look at these key things:

- **Can they make big bucks?**—If venture firms are going to risk millions of dollars on your business idea, they'll want to know what the big payoff is. They'd rather invest 5, 10, 20 million, or more in a $20 billion market than in a $100 million market. The bigger the market, the bigger the payoff if the business works. To get a venture capitalist's attention right away, show him a big market to exploit.

- **Do they invest in your specific market?**—Even if your idea is a good one, if you pitch your idea to a venture firm that doesn't invest in your market you're wasting your time. Venture firms usually specialize in one area. Make sure your business area coincides with theirs. Also, if you're looking for early stage capital, don't pitch to venture firms that only invest in late stage companies.

Here's Your Resource Library

Venture Capital Resource Library has the links to everything from locating a venture capital firm to details of security law and articles, all related to getting investors. Find it at www.vfinance.com.

- **Whose pain are you solving?**—You have to make very clear what market you will serve as well as what niche you're targeting. If you have a well-defined Unique Selling Position, you'll have a better chance of getting a venture firm's attention. Don't make claims you can't deliver. A venture capitalist will pick up on that real fast. Also, state your weaknesses. This shows the venture capitalist that you have thoroughly thought through your business concept.

- **Can you do what you say?**—When you pitch your business idea, be specific on why you can execute it. Remember, ideas are easy—the proper execution of them is the hard part. Be careful with terminology. Know the semantics of your market such as hits, unique visitors, and click-throughs. (We'll cover this terminology in Chapter 19, "Speaking the Language of Net Advertising.") Also, be sure you mention your competition—who they are and how you plan to stay ahead of them. Although there are few barriers to competition on the Net, speed and innovation are vital to an online business. Explain how fast you can execute your plan and how you will stay ahead of your competition.

- **Do you have the team?**—Venture firms say that they invest in people, not ideas. This tells you that the management team you've assembled or plan to assemble is of vital importance to a venture capitalist. Be specific in presenting their skills. The venture capitalist wants to know that you can deliver on the promise of your business idea.

Use KISS

Don't make the mistake of over complicating your presentation. If it's too complicated to explain, you'll lose a venture capitalist's attention post-haste. Practice the philosophy of KISS—Keep It Simple Stupid.

- **Do the numbers make sense?**—Do your homework. Be sure that your assumptions on your market, your expenses, and revenue are airtight—and be ready to defend them. Also, provide clear milestones to measure your success. When will you start to make sales? When will you break even and turn profitable?

Answer these questions to a venture capitalist's satisfaction and you will have their attention.

HELP INVESTORS FIND YOU

Instead of finding investors, have the investors find you. There are several sites on the Net that enable you to meet potential investors such as VentureDirectory.com (www.venturedirectory.com) or even post your business plan and will then match you up with investors looking for new business opportunities (see Figure 6.4). There's a catch, though. Many of them are not free. Prices and/or annual fees range from under a hundred dollars to a few hundred dollars.

Here's a list of such sites:

- Capital Match at www.capmatch.com ($200 annual fee)
- BusinessFinance.com at www.businessfinance.net (Free listing for 30 days)
- BizBoard at www.thebizboard.com (One-time $13.95/6 months or until funded)
- NVST.com at www.nvst.com (Free listing for 90 days then $39.95 a month)
- Venture Capital Finance Online at www.vcaonline.com ($30 for one year)

After your business concept is finalized and your business plan is finished, don't wait on funding to get started. Whether you need $10 million or $10,000, reach into your pocket and start your business today. You'll find that having an operating business—no matter how nascent—will help you raise money faster than just having a paper plan and an idea.

Figure 6.4

VentureDirectory.com is a great place to view and meet investors, angels, and other entrepreneurs. They even have a chat room where you can meet people and make deals.

P A R T II

SETTING UP SHOP

CHAPTER 7

GETTING STARTED—FIRST STEPS

In This Chapter

- Learn how to register your domain name
- Learn the e-commerce host essentials
- See what to shop for when you're choosing an e-commerce host

Now that you've decided to create on online business, whom do you get to host it? There are several options—host it yourself, host it at an ISP, or host it at one of the build-it-yourself services on the Web. How do you choose? What do you look for? What are the essentials?

> ### What's a Host?
>
> Creating a Web site on your computer does not automatically place it on the Internet. You need to find a home, or *host*. A host is a computer that is connected to the Internet. You can either provide that computer yourself—known as a *Web server*—or you can pay a hosting company to host your Web site.

Before you go charging off to create your new online business, there are a number of steps to perform and e-commerce elements to consider. Knowing this information upfront will help you later when considering where to host your site and what services to expect. Finding the right home for your site—one that offers the right e-commerce services—will help you successfully execute your business plan. So, it's important to know what the e-commerce site essentials are when considering a place to roost.

But first things first. Whether you host your site yourself, have it hosted elsewhere, or use one of the build-it-yourself Web-site services, you need to register a domain name.

REGISTERING A DOMAIN NAME

If you're serious about doing business on the Net you need to register a domain name. A domain name represents your company and is your URL. For example, Amazon's domain name is www.amazon.com and Wal-Mart's domain name is www.walmart.com.

> ### What's a URL?
>
> The URL is the site address that appears in the top window of your browser, such as www.yahoo.com. It's the way you find Web sites on the Net. The letters URL stand for *Uniform Resource Locator*, and it's sort of like a Web version of the house numbers on your mailbox.

When the brick-and-mortar company Barnes & Noble went online, they acquired a domain name. At first they used the long domain name www.barnesandnoble.com, then shortened it to www.bn.com and finally obtained www.books.com. That, by the way, was some coup. The books.com domain name was the property of another online bookstore. Barnes & Noble wanted it, so they bought the bookstore!

This raises a problem for you. Many of the most popular domain names have been taken. You will probably find that someone has already registered your business name or business type. Creating a unique domain name could be quite a challenge. That is unless you have the deep pockets of a Barnes & Noble to buy an already assigned domain name. The fact is, grabbing a great domain name that reflects your business type or even your business name is getting harder to do.

But what if you want to use a domain name that's already registered? Check out Glenn Sobel's article at www.domainnameadvisor.com/acquisition.htm. He explains the different ways to acquire a domain name owned by another party.

Finally, when choosing a domain name, keep it short and memorable. A long domain name with two many letters or with hyphens is hard to remember. Also, make it easy to spell. Lastly, try to choose a name that relates to your core business or business name.

Psst! Wanna Buy a Domain?

Looking for a really good domain name? The one you want is already taken? Then check out the Great Domains Web site. It's a brokerage site that enables you to buy and sell domain names. Find it at www.greatdomains.com.

Where to Start

First, find out whether that nifty domain name you thought up is available. To do that, head over to Network Solutions at www.networksolutions.com (see Figure 7.1). Registering a domain name is not free, and the annual fees you pay depend on how you plan to use it. More on that later.

A Silver Lining?

One of the good things coming out of the DOT-BOMB collapse is that some really nifty names are becoming available again. Who knows, maybe even eToys.com will be available some day.

When you arrive at the Network Solutions site, you'll see a search box near the top of the Web page with the words "Register a Web Address" above it. Type the domain name you would like to use to see if it's available. Notice that there's a drop-down box next to the search window. The drop-down box defaults to .com but there are two other choices. One is .org and the other is .net. There are also several new domain extensions called .tv, .cc, and .ws. The .tv extension was added for those businesses that want to show that their business is not only on the Web but on television too. But keep in mind the .tv extension is basically a marketing gimmick. When you register your Web site as a .tv you are registering your business on the island of Tunavasu which sold their right to the Internet country code 'tv'.

The .cc and .ws extensions are alternatives to a .com extension. They're useful if you can not find the name you want with the .com extension. To add even more to this alphabet soup, ICANN, The Internet Corporation for Assigned Names and Numbers, has authorized three new extensions named .biz to designate a business; .info for news and information sites and .pro to designate a professional services Web site like .cpa.pro for certified public accounts, .law.pro for law sites, or .med.pro for medical sites.

Because you are setting up a business on the Net, the extension you will use is the .com one. The .org extension is for organizations like the United Way and the .net is for networks on the Internet. When you search, make sure the .com choice is in the drop-down window.

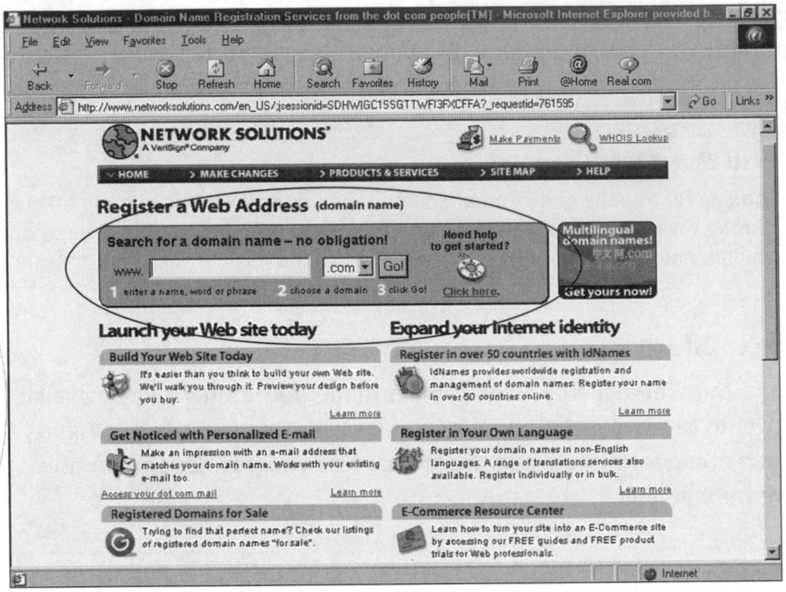

Figure 7.1

The Network Solutions site will walk you through the process of choosing and registering a domain name for your business.

Get Help Creating a Valid Domain Name

Here's a very useful site to help you choose a domain name. Just enter a few words that represent your domain name and E-gineer's Domainator will create a valid domain name from those words. Try it at www.e-gineer. com/domainator/index.phtml. Another helpful site is Network Solutions (www.networksolutions.com) itself. Their NameFetcher also helps you find available domain names.

After a quick search, Network Solutions will tell you if that domain name is taken or not. Be prepared to try several variations on your domain name until you find one that has not been registered. You can search as many names as you like—it's free. After you find the domain name you want and it's available, you can proceed to register it at the Network Solutions site.

Discounted Domain Registration

There are some companies on the Web that promise to register your domain name for less than what Network Solutions charges. Bizland at www.bizland.com is one such company. You need only have a small spot at the top of your page for advertising Bizland. Be sure you read the fine print in these discounted services and be sure that you can be both the 'administrative' AND 'technical' contact. I still prefer to go straight to the horse's mouth and register with Network Solutions. That way you know you have total control over your domain name.

Here's the Process to Follow

At the Network Solutions home page at www.networksolutions.com, click **Need Help to Start** next to the domain name search window.

You will be brought to a page where you can enter your available domain name to start the registration process. Enter your available domain name and click **Go**.

After your domain name is accepted, you will be told what other Web address for your domain name, if any, is available. These are the .net and .org extensions of your same domain name. Click the **Continue** button to ignore these and continue.

Be Sure You Are the Administrative Contact

You will be asked to name both an administrative and technical contact when you apply for a domain name. It is very important that you name yourself, not an employee, as the administrative contact. The administrative contact is the *ONLY* one who can make changes to your domain registration. Don't be caught having to chase down someone who no longer works for your company to make future changes to your registration.

Next, you pay the piper. You have two choices. If you do not have a place to host your site yet, you can reserve your name for when you do. If you've chosen a place to host your Web site, then you need to know your hosting company's *domain name server (DNS)* and *Internet protocol (IP)* information. You will get these from your host provider.

To reserve a domain name for future use, the cost is $119 per address for the first two years. The cost to register a domain name when you have a hosting server is $70 per address for the first two years. You must pay with a credit card to complete your registration.

And that's it. Network Solutions will send you an e-mail to confirm.

Finally, there are a number of Web sites on the Net that will register your domain for you. Some will add their fee on top of the fees that Network Solutions will charge you for registering your domain name and others are cheaper than Network Solutions. For a good unbiased list of registrars visit DomainNameBuyersGuide.com (www.domainnamebuyers-guide.com). They rate the different registrars and tell you where you can get the best deal.

Register Your Misspelled and Alternative Domain Name

Why lose potential customers because they misspelled your URL? Register the obvious misspellings of your domain name and redirect them back to your site. Also register alternative spellings of your name. For example, take a company called One Minute Shopper.com. You would register under the names oneminuteshopper.com, 1minuteshopper.com, and minuteshopper.com. To further protect yourself, you might consider registering your domain name not only as a .com, but also as a .net, .org, or even a .tv.

FINDING A HOME

After you have secured your domain name, it's time to consider finding a home for your new online business. This is called finding a host. A *host* is a computer, or server, on which you place your Web site. The host's server is connected to the Internet, 24 hours a day, 7 days a week. This is how your customers find you and shop at your online store.

Whether you host your pages at free community sites such as AOL, GeoCities, Tripod, or Angelfire, use the do-it-yourself Web-site builder services of Yahoo Store or BigStep, or host at a commercial ISP—or even host your site on your own server—you need to consider some e-commerce site essentials. Later, I'll cover the different types of hosting options in Chapter 8, "Hosting Your Store for Free," Chapter 9, "Hosting with an ISP," and Chapter 10, "Be Your Own Host."

No you don't need to register a domain name. But if your are in business on the Net and want to look professional, you should consider having your own domain name and not just an extension of a free site URL such as Lycos.

A lot of thought should go into choosing a home for your online business. If your business existed in the real world, you wouldn't set it up in the most expensive part of town and pay exorbitant rent. Nor would you place your store at the end of a pothole-ridden dirt road and expect customers to come to you. You'd also expect the lights to stay on and the police and emergency services to be in the area making it safe for commerce.

So it is with your online business. Your Web site *is* your business and you should expect that wherever you host it, the basic essential services should be available.

E-COMMERCE HOST ESSENTIALS

Your e-commerce host requirements will vary with the size and type of business that you have. But there are three important criteria that you must address no matter what the size of your online business. They are

- Costs
- Bandwidth
- Tech support

Cost

What you pay for is what you get in the e-commerce game and what you get depends on how much control you want over the look and feel of your online store and the services you want to offer the online shopper.

The more elements you want to include in your online business, the higher the cost of creating and maintaining your site—elements such as these:

- Product reviews
- Special sales sections

- Discussion rooms
- Live customer service
- Personalization
- Gift reminder services
- Multiple e-mail addresses
- Frequent buyer programs
- Interactive marketing features

The first question to ask yourself is whether you will buy a server and host your site yourself or outsource it to a hosting service.

Outsourcing

If you're on a budget, you can host an online business for free at community sites such as AOL and Tripod, but you'll have little more than a catalog page or two offering a few products that must be purchased through the mail. In addition, because the community sites control the advertising, you'll have no control over the ads placed on your pages. You might well find a competing product advertised on your site.

Don't Skimp on Hosting

Go with the best hosting company you can afford—*not* the cheapest. Look for OC3 (OC stands for Optical Carrier—a standard for fiber optic transmission) connections or T3s (a T3 telephone line can deliver information at 44.736Mbps—the equivalent of 28 T1 lines). Don't use a commercial hosting service that has only T1 connections.

Another outside hosting option is the all-in-one store such as Yahoo! Store. They provide a basic e-commerce site where you can create an online store complete with product pages, shopping cart, and order form. No software is needed, there is very little to learn, and you can do it all through your Web browser. The cost for these types of hosting services ranges from $100 to $500. The downside is that services here are limited. Content and community elements such as product news and reviews or chat rooms and discussion boards for customer service—even more than one e-mail address—are normally not available.

Hosting Yourself

If you want to create your e-commerce Web site yourself, then you need to look for a commercial ISP who will host your site on his server. CNet at webhostlist.internetlist.com lists a large number of Web-hosting companies (see Figure 7.2). Costs can range from as little as $7 a month to whatever the market will bear. If you create and maintain your own site, you might be required to do your own programming for a shopping cart, product database, and other essentials for your e-commerce site.

- Setup fee
- Monthly cost

- Disk space
- E-mail accounts
- CGI access
- Domain registration

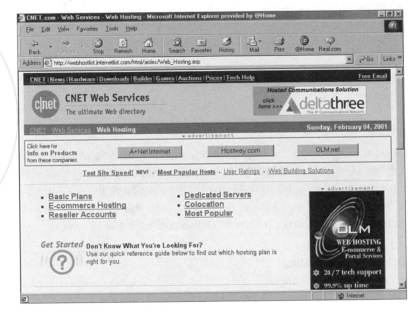

Figure 7.2

CNet has an A-Z list of Web hosting companies.

Finally, even if you host your site on your own server, you need to connect it to the Internet. You can have either a telephone or cable line run to your business and connected to your server, or you can place your server at a hosting service connected to the Net. Costs will vary depending on how fast your connection is and how close your server is to the backbone of the Net.

This brings up the issue of bandwidth.

How Fast Is Your Connection?

Want to check the page loading time of your Web site? Surf on over to Virtual Stampede and use their Load Time Check service. Find it at www.virtualstampede.com/ tools.htm. You might also ask friends and family who are online to check your connection speed.

Bandwidth

For your business to be a success, you want your customers to have a good experience. The customer's experience of your site will either make or break your online business.

The first thing a customer experiences when he or she visits your site is how fast it appears in their browser. A slow loading Web site will probably not be visited again. So a fast download time is essential.

CAUTION

Let Your ISP Know Your Marketing Plan

Planning a big marketing push that's going to generate a lot of traffic to your site? Launching a major marketing initiative and not telling your Internet Service Provider could bring your whole site down.

The time it takes to download and view your pages depends on the bandwidth available to your host. The ideal scenario is that your host provider should run his own network rather than buy a network connection from some larger host provider. Your hosting service also should have a good caching system in place and be close to the Internet backbone—the main telephone lines that carry the Internet.

Also, does your host provider have a standard agreement with you to provide additional bandwidth automatically and on demand when unforeseen peaks in traffic hit your site? It's important that it does.

JARGON

What Is Caching?

Caching is the process of storing Web pages on a server so pages download more quickly.

If you're hosting your own site with your own Internet connection, you must have at least a T1 line connected to your server, a cable connection or even a DSL or ISDN line that may be available in your area. As your business grows, keep in mind that you'll need more bandwidth requiring larger pipes to handle the traffic coming to your site.

Tech Support

What good is your store if it can't stay open? In the real world, staying open for business requires only some personnel and an unlocked door. On the Internet, however, the reliability of your host server and your Net connection is critical to your business.

When shopping for a host, be sure they offer and deliver technical support 24 hours a day, 7 days a week, all year 'round. Can you reach your provider's tech support personnel? Does your provider have a tech support telephone number? Can you ask questions via e-mail?

If you're doing self-hosting, you have to ask yourself who will reboot your server at 2 a.m. when it goes down. Do you have personnel always available to fix any problem that develops?

TIP

Protect Your Backups

It is a good idea to back up your Web site each day, but where do you keep the backups? Leaving them on site is just as bad as not backing them up at all. Consider using a remote storage facility company to pick up your backups each day. Check you local yellow pages for companies near you.

And how about a disaster recovery plan? Your entire site can go down due to something as simple as a disk crash or worse—a fire, earthquake, or hurricane. Does your host provider backup your Web site regularly and do they keep the backups off-site? If your site does go down, how long will it take your host provider to get it back up and running again?

If you're self-hosting, do you have the resources set aside to deal with these recovery problems? I guarantee they will happen.

Your Shopping List

Cost, bandwidth, and tech support might be the essential elements to consider when hosting your site, but there are additional items to add to your shopping list when considering a host provider—regardless whether you host through an ISP or self-host your site.

To generate a serious amount of sales at your site, you'll need to accept and process credit card payments. You must have a secure e-commerce server to take orders and process credit cards, one that encrypts card numbers when sent over the Net. Over the last few years, the media has had a field day telling horror stories about credit cards being stolen while buying over the Net. The truth of the matter is that there has never been a documented case of any individual having their credit card number stolen while sending their information to an online merchant using a secure server.

Credit Card Scare Tactics

Simson Garfinkel, author of a book on good privacy encryption software called *PGP: Pretty Good Privacy*, says that sending your credit card over the Internet is no big deal. "By law, if there is no signature, the customer is liable for nothing. If there's a signature, they're liable for $50. The reason the credit-card companies want cryptography is to limit their own liability. It has nothing to do with protecting the consumer."

But consumer concerns do not fade quickly. So, whether you're hosting through an ISP or hosting yourself, you must have a secure encryption system for credit cards. Shoppers will be looking to see whether your site is secure before they feel comfortable giving you their credit card number. Besides, accepting credit cards at your online store will increase sales dramatically.

While we're discussing security, check to see what kind of security systems your host has in place to prevent break-ins into your server. Ask about their *firewall* protection. A firewall keeps sensitive information on your server out of the reach of hackers and pranksters at best, and credit card thieves at worst.

Your provider should also offer an electronic shopping cart service to your customers. A good shopping cart system gives you control over your products and services *and* makes shopping easy.

What's a Firewall?

A *Firewall* is a security barrier set up between a company's server and the outside world. Firewalls are designed to keep hostile visitors out—a way of protecting the company's internal information.

Be sure your provider offers an easy, Web-based way to add and subtract items from your product database. A good database not only enables you to manage your merchandise but it also connects to your shopping cart, changing prices and deleting products from inventory as they are sold. The Database also should be able to calculate and add shipping and handling costs to an order and calculate sales taxes that are required by law.

Your hosting service should provide site and traffic analysis reports on a daily basis. These reports are very important and are used to manage your business. They should include, at the very least, the number of site visitors, the number and type of pages viewed, where visitors are coming from, how long they stayed on your site, and the URLs that referred them.

How many e-mail address and mailboxes does your hosting service provide? Can they add new e-mail boxes quickly? To run an average size e-commerce site, you need more than webmaster@mysite.com. You should have e-mail addresses for sales, customer service, order status, and general information at the least.

With these items on your shopping list, you're prepared to go out and find a host for your online store.

CHAPTER 8

HOSTING YOUR STORE FOR FREE

In This Chapter

- Learn how to sell products and services from a free personal Web page
- Discover the different ways to set up an online storefront on the Web using only your browser
- See how to add a complete online store on your site with no programming to do, no inventory to handle, and no order processing or customer service concerns

You say you want to sell on the Net but have no programming or technical experience. You want to set up an online store but funds are limited. Or perhaps you have a nice content or community site that attracts a good number of visitors each day and you'd like to turn those visitors into customers.

Well, you're not alone. Thousands of people like you are setting up shop each day on the Net with little or no funds and even less technical know-how. They're using their own personal Web pages or the new free online storefront builders to share in the benefits of the e-commerce revolution. And it's all being done on their own PC through their own Web browser.

No special hardware is needed. There's no software to learn. There's no technology to buy. With just a few minutes of your time you can be selling products and services on the Web like the big boys.

SELLING FROM A PERSONAL WEB PAGE

Soon after the Web became popular, a number of Web site hosting companies emerged offering free home pages to anyone who would join their community. The price was right—free—and soon hundreds of thousands of cyber-surfers became cyber-squatters. Using the simple tools of the Web-page hosting services such as GeoCities, cyber-squatters set up personal home pages by the millions.

At first, they were simple one-page sites for friends and family. But as the personal Web-site hosting companies grew and competition increased, new features and services were offered to those building personal Web pages. In addition, it didn't take long for these people to see that along with offering pictures of their family or acting as a fan site for the Spice Girls or Madonna, you could sell products or offer services over the Web.

It proved to be an inexpensive way to open shop on the Net. Of course, selling from a personal Web site is not the same as having an online store. On the plus side, hosting is free and you can build a Web page quickly using the service's page building tools. On the minus side, there is no shopping cart or a way to take credit card orders. In addition, you can't use a registered personal domain. You must use a cumbersome URL that the Web-page hosting company provides.

For instance, instead of having `www.myshoebiz.com`, you have to use `www.angelfire.com/biz/myshoebiz/index.html`—a URL that's long, obscure, and hard to remember. Another trade-off is, whether you like it or not, the company hosting your site for free will place advertising on your site. After all, selling ads on your site is how they make money so you can have a free Web site.

Still, selling from a free personal Web page is a great way to test the e-commerce waters. Whether you have a personal Web page or e-commerce site, you still have the same challenges of drawing traffic to your site and making the sale. On little or no budget and with no out-of-pocket costs, selling from a free Web page could be the best way to test your e-commerce idea.

> **TIP**
>
> **Free Web Page Directory**
> FreeWebspace.net is the place to find a comprehensive list of free personal Web-page hosting sites. You can even search by the amount of free space each offers. Find FreeWebspace.net at `www.freewebspace.net`.

If you want to set up shop at one of the personal Web-site hosting services then these are the ones to check:

- America Online
- Yahoo! GeoCities
- Lycos Angelfire
- Lycos Tripod

America Online

The granddaddy of all personal Web-page hosting services is America Online (AOL). It boasts over 12 million members and is still growing. Many of the AOL members sell products or offer services from their personal Web pages.

AOL calls their Web-page hosting service AOL Hometown (see Figure 8.1). You can find it at hometown.aol.com/hmtwnpromo/build/index.htm. As an AOL Hometown resident, you get a free home page, up to 12 megabytes of space, and free special features such as a personal chat room.

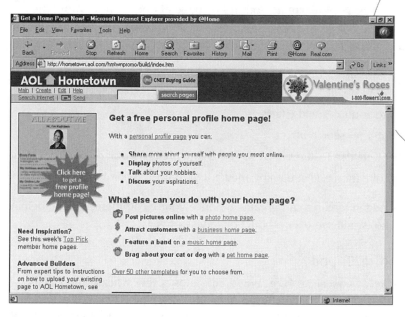

Figure 8.1

By using AOL's Hometown Home Page Builder you can create a personal home page in minutes.

TIP

How Much Space Do You Need?

A simple Web site of several pages and a few graphics will fit within 5MB of space. Text takes up very little space, but graphics files are a memory hog. Five megabytes of space should be more than enough if you are selling a product or two, or describing a service. If you plan to have a large number of pictures or graphics on your Web site, then look for hosting services that provide more free space. If not, you might have to pay for the additional space.

Do you need to be a member of AOL to join AOL Hometown? Surprisingly, no. If you use one of AOL's Web-based services such as Instant Messenger, Personal Finance Web Center, or My News, you can use the screen name you have to create your AOL Hometown Web page. You can join one of these free services and create a screen name at publish.hometown.aol.com/_cqr/createsn.adp.

Unfortunately, many of AOL's other free Web site building services are available only to AOL members.

GeoCities

If AOL is the granddaddy of personal Web pages, GeoCities is close behind. GeoCities was the first public membership such service to hit the Web and quickly grew into the largest personal Web-site hosting service on the Net. GeoCities was so successful that Yahoo! bought it. You can find GeoCities at `geocities.yahoo.com/home/`.

At GeoCities, you can create your home page at one of 40 or more themed communities and have up to 15 megabytes of space to do it. Using the Yahoo! Page Builder, you can build your page in a matter of minutes just by using your browser. You also can add

- Free clip art
- News headlines
- Stock quotes and charts
- Internet search boxes
- Interactive features such as forms and a guest book
- Animation and streaming media and more

These added features can greatly enhance your e-commerce site by helping to draw visitors who would see your product or service offer.

Angelfire/Tripod

Angelfire at `www.angelfire.lycos.com` adds a few whistles and bells to this mix. Like GeoCities, a big portal purchased Angelfire. This time it was Lycos. Besides a generous 50 megabytes of space for your Web site, you can also get what other hosting services all lack—a personal URL. Instead of a URL that reads `www.angelfire.com/biz/mysitename/index.html` you can have a URL that reads `www.mysitename.angelfire.com`—a much better URL for business.

As with other personal Web page services, you can build a free Web site using Angelfire's online page building tools and free clip art. Or, if you use Microsoft FrontPage or Office 2000 to design your Web pages, you can easily upload them to Angelfire. In addition, you can enhance your Web site with Angelfire's easy to use JavaScripts and polls.

Angelfire has a program that enables you to acutely earn money from their participating merchants. It's called "Commission Central." You can join any number of merchant affiliate programs through Commission Central. You can join as many of them as you want for free with just one form. Just pick the products you want to sell, place the merchant links on your page, and the merchant processes and ships the orders placed by your customers.

Angelfire also has a site traffic program that tells you how many visitors you have and where they're coming from.

Another Lycos-owned personal Web-page hosting service is Tripod at `www.tripod.lycos.com`. Because the same company owns both Angelfire and Tripod, many of the services offered for personal Web pages are similar.

QUICK AND EASY ONLINE STORE BUILDERS

Suppose you've tried selling from a free personal Web page and now want to set up a fully integrated Web storefront. You have little capital in the bank and—even if you had the dough—setting up a secure server and a functional database of products can be technically intimidating. This is a very common situation but easy to overcome.

Beyond the personal Web-page hosting services are the Commercial Service Providers. As e-commerce has heated over the last few years, a host of these Commercial Service Providers have arrived to give you a pure and simple way to open shop on the Net. These Commercial Service Providers can provide you with an integrated browser-based Web storefront, including an online catalog, shopping cart, support for real time credit card payments, advertising, and customer support.

How much do their services cost? Why, they're free!

BigStep, FreeTailer, and FreeMerchant are three examples of Commercial Service Providers where you can set up and maintain an online store for free. These services give you the opportunity to design and build fully featured, integrated commerce-enabled Web sites, including a host of supporting services.

These free sites offer sophisticated yet easy to use site building through your own browser, and many eBusiness essentials such as an online catalog with built-in shopping cart, marketing help, credit card clearing, customer communications, comprehensive reports, online customer support, and, of course, site hosting.

BigStep

BigStep at `www.bigstep.com` offers you all the features you need to start and run a small business online. (See Figure 8.2.) And like the personal Web-page hosting services, your URL reads `yoursitename.bigstep.com`. But if you don't want the word *bigstep* to appear in your URL, you can also register your own domain name and use it on their service.

BigStep offers a flexible system that allows you to build a Web site as original as your company. They give you complete control over your site's layout, colors, fonts, images, and content. They also give you the ability to make unlimited changes at any time. In addition, they offer

- Search engine and directory submission.
- A resource page that connects you with other Web resources that helps you find customers.
- Personalized e-mail newsletters.
- A customer database to keep track of your customers and their e-mail addresses.

- A catalog or portfolio of interlinking pages that allows you to put photos and descriptions of your catalog items, artwork, or services on the same page and even add shopping-cart capabilities.
- Help securing a credit card merchant account.
- Statistics about your Web site that tell you which and how many pages your visitors look at when they come to your site, and which Web site they came from.

Figure 8.2

Here's an example of a Web store created using BigStep.

The entire service is free to you. So how does BigStep make money? Will they run ads for other merchants on your site like the personal Web-page hosting services? Nope. BigStep intends to generate revenue from advertisements placed on its own BigStep.com site and through a series of Premium services that will be offered to you to increase your online business.

FreeMerchant

FreeMerchant at www.freemerchant.com (see Figure 8.3) offers pretty much the same free e-commerce services as BigStep offers, including

- Internet Store Hosting with no preset limits
- Secure Shopping Cart
- Internet Store Builder Catalog Importer
- E-mail Account

- Shipping Calculator
- Tax Calculator
- Coupon Creator
- Real Domain Hosting
- Traffic Logs
- Inventory Control
- Payment Gateway Interfaces
- Map Maker Store Templates Discounted Corporate Services
- Offers Customer List Manager for up to 10 people

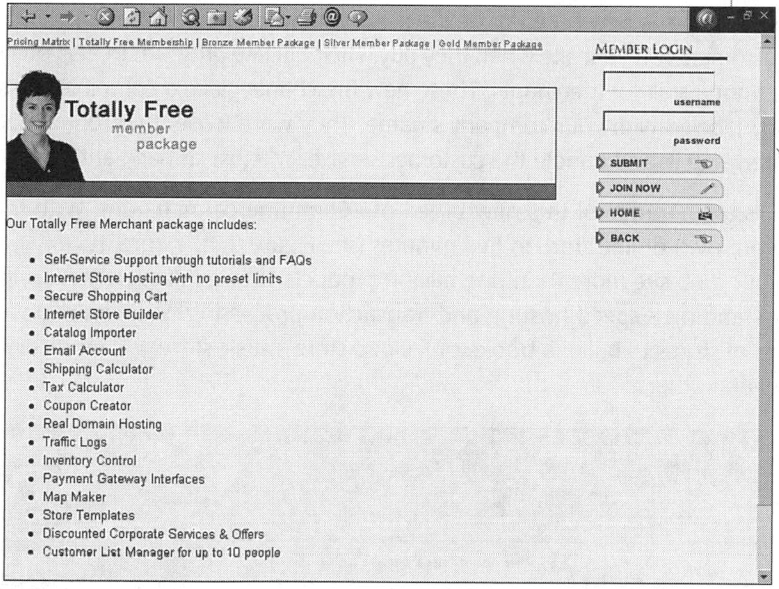

Figure 8.3

FreeMerchant lives up to its name—look at all the free services for your free Web store.

One drawback is how FreeMerchant makes its money. It makes money by selling and placing banner ads on the bottom of your FreeMerchant site.

E-COMMERCE: ENABLE YOUR WEB SITE FOR FREE

Personal Web-page hosting services and Commercial Service Providers are a good solution if you don't have an existing site. But what if you do? What if you already have a nice content or community site and want to set it up for e-commerce? Better yet, suppose you want to sell a wide variety of products without the hassle of holding inventory, processing the orders, getting a credit card merchant account, shipping the merchandise, and handling customer service?

> **TIP**
>
> **The WebPage-O-Matic**
>
> Build professional looking Web sites quickly and easily using an awesome free Web-site construction tool called the WebPage-O-Matic. Simply fill out a few fields, click a few buttons, and that's it. WebPage-O-Matic creates, uploads, and even promotes your multipage Web site for you automatically. Download it at http://www.webpageomatic.com/.

You can quickly and easily e-commerce enable your Web site by joining one of the hundreds of merchant affiliate programs out there on the Net. The problem is, as with most affiliate programs, you have to send your site customers off to the merchant's site and—voilà—they become the merchant's customers, not yours. That's the problem with most affiliate programs today.

But there's hope. A new breed of online merchant has appeared that keeps your traffic—and your customers—on your site when they buy. Their affiliate program treats you like a true partner and not a shill for merchants. These new merchants place a complete store on your site, privately labeled with your company's name. They warehouse the product you sell, process the order, ship it, and handle the customer service. You just sit back and collect the money.

VStore is an example of this new breed of eCommmerce merchant. With Vstore you can open your own online store in five minutes (see Figure 8.4). Vstore at www.vstore.com can offer your Web site more than one million products to sell, full customer support, order fulfillment, and high-speed hosting and transaction processing. You can choose any number of types of stores to build: a bookstore, video store, music store, gift store, electronics store, and several others.

Figure 8.4

Open a virtual store on your site with Vstore and you have hundreds of products to sell immediately.

Vstore does all the work and takes full responsibility for your customer's purchase. And here's the best part. All products are sold at a discount from list price. And because your store is private labeled with your company name, your customers stay your customers. Vstore does not compete for your sales. You make a commission on each and every sale. Commissions range from 5% to 25%, depending upon the product.

> **Beyond Affiliate Programs**
>
> Envision this: A visitor to your site is reading a review of a printer and right next to it is a small icon that says Buy It. And do it without ever leaving your site? They can now. It's called *embedded commerce* and Pop 2 It is doing it. See it at www.pop2it.com.

Another example of this type of program is the 'store within a banner' (see Figure 8.5). When visitors come to a Web site, they may see a large banner advertising a selection of products or services of an online merchant.

Figure 8.5

CD Now is an example of a 'store within a banner' that would reside on your Web site.

At first glance, the banner looks like a traditional affiliate banner link. But instead of being whisked off to another Web site or even another page on your Web site, when clicked on by the visitor, products appear for sale. The original page still appears in the background, so when the visitor is finished reading the offer—or even completing a transaction—your visitor still remains on your site.

As you can see, there are a variety of ways that you can enter e-commerce without spending any money at all!

CHAPTER 9

HOSTING WITH AN ISP

In This Chapter

- Set up an online storefront for less than a dollar a day
- Learn the difference between Internet service providers and e-commerce hosting companies
- Learn what e-commerce services to look for in a hosting company

Sooner or later (sooner if you have the money in the bank to do so) you'll want to consider running your own e-commerce Web site. The free sites are fine to start with if you have limited funds. But to become a real online business you need more than what the personal Web page providers and commercial service providers can offer.

Let's face it, as a real business you have a number of e-commerce needs that a person with a personal home page does not. And selling other merchants' products has its limitations. Free hosting is fine but generally a poor choice if you're going to generate your own transactions and sell your own products on your site. In addition, eBusiness services such as customer wish lists, gift certificates, advanced search capabilities, gift reminder services, personal shopping agents, and one-click ordering are not normally available at the free hosting sites.

When you're ready to become a full-fledged e-business, you need to ante up and pay the piper.

ALL-IN-ONE HOSTING SERVICES

There are several All-In-One hosting services on the Web to host your online store. An All-In-One hosting service is similar to the free hosting services in that no programming knowledge is required to set up your Web site. You build your store on their server through your browser, following a series of quick and easy steps. You don't need to know any HTML or have any prior experience setting up an online storefront—and there is no server to buy.

Although not free, these services offer low-cost, one-stop solutions for e-commerce. And all claim you can build a store and start taking orders in minutes. Orders are accepted securely and you can retrieve your orders securely whenever you want. All management of your online store is done through your browser and you can add, delete, or change products whenever you please.

Costs vary. Some of these hosting services charge a flat rate based on the number of products you sell whereas others charge for the amount of server space your store takes up. None of the services listed here charge a transaction fee per sale. Steer clear of any service that does.

Here's a list of the largest All-In-One hosting services:

- Yahoo! Store (`store.yahoo.com/`)
- eBiz Builder (`www.e-bizbuilder.com`)
- Earthstores.com (`http://home.earthstores.com/i`)

You need to decide which plan is best suited for you depending upon the size of your store and the services you would like to provide.

Yahoo! Store

Setting up an online store at Yahoo! Store at `store.yahoo.com` is quick and easy (see Figure 9.1). You can even test drive your store before you decide to commit to the Yahoo! service. There are no startup costs, no minimum time commitments, and no transaction fees per order. You pay a flat fee per month depending upon the number of products you offer in your store.

- A small store (up to 50 items for sale) is $100 a month.
- A large store (up to 1,000 items for sale) is $300 a month.
- Larger stores cost $300/month for the first 1,000 items, plus $100/month for each additional 1,000 items.

You can either use the Yahoo! Store domain for your online store such as `store.yahoo.com/yourstore/` or you can use your own domain name. Yahoo! Store even helps you transfer it to their servers.

An advantage that the other All-In-One hosting services can't offer is the inclusion of your store in the Yahoo! Shopping Search engine. The products in your store are searched and displayed to cyber-shoppers who are looking for the type of products you sell. Ordering through a Yahoo! Store is 100% secure. Credit card orders are encrypted when they're placed online and encrypted when they're sent to you. Yahoo! Store also submits your store to the most popular search engines (check out Figure 9.1).

You can retrieve your orders in four ways. View them on the Yahoo! server through your browser, retrieve them as a database file to your computer, have them faxed to you, or if you have your own secure server, have the order posted to it in real-time. You can update your store as frequently as you want and you have control over the look and feel of your site to make it unique.

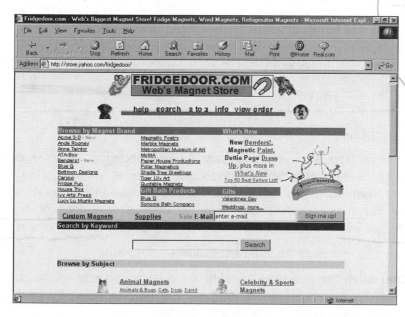

Figure 9.1

Yahoo! Store created a Web store for the Fridgedoor.com.

Yahoo! Store even supplies you with a set of sophisticated site traffic tracking tools including the number of page views, where your visitors came from, what they searched for, and the click paths they used to navigate your site. There's also a Repeat Customer Detector that analyzes each order, which enables you to recognize repeat customers without requiring them to register.

What about the speed of your connection? You should have little worry about bandwidth. Your site downloads fast for your customers because you have the same network connection as Yahoo! itself. After all, your store is residing on their servers.

> **CAUTION**
>
> **Credit Card Authorizations**
>
> When you take a credit card order and get an authorization, keep in mind that an authorization is just an indication that a card is valid and the customer has enough open credit to charge the sale. It is not a guarantee that you have a valid sale. For example, the card might be stolen.

Finally, Yahoo! Store has a relationship with Paymentech for credit card processing. If you already have a merchant account you can use your own to process credit cards online. If you don't have a merchant account, you can easily set one up at Paymentech. Yahoo! Store also supplies you with a set of merchant resources such as how to sell online, site design tips, and a monthly newsletter.

> **TIP**
>
> **This Could Be z-Place**
>
> Amazon has put a different spin on the All-In-One shop. Although not a real store, you can list your products for sale or for auction at their zShops. You pay $39.99 per month to maintain as many as 5,000 items. Find it at `s1.amazon.com/exec/varzea/subscription-signup/`.

eBiz Builder

eBiz at `www.e-bizbuilder.com` offers many of the services that Yahoo! Store provides (see Figure 9.2). It offers three service plans to choose from: eCom Basic, eCom Solutions, and eCom Professional. Its cost structure is a little different from that of Yahoo! Store. You don't pay per month for the number of products you offer but the amount of server space your online store uses. There are setup charges for each plan but no transaction fees.

Here are descriptions of the three eBiz Builder service plans:

eCom Basic—This plan gives you 5MB of space and uses eBiz Builder's URL subdomain name such as `www.e-bizbuilder.com/yourstorename`. The cost for this plan is $19.95 a month with a $35 set up fee.

eCom Solutions—With this plan you receive 20 megabytes of space but you can use your own domain name. The cost for this plan is $35.95 a month with a $75 set up fee.

eCom Professional—This plan gives you 50 megabytes of space but you can use your own domain name. The cost for this plan is $59.95 a month with a $100 set up fee.

eBiz Builder has a very good comparison chart of their services at `http://www.e-bizbuilder.com/services/content/service_plans.html`.

In theory, you could offer an unlimited number of items for sale on eBiz Builder. The only limitation would be the server space that you pay for in your plan and the performance of your site. All the plans have these features in common:

- Unlimited Inventory
- Personal Search Engine

- Shopping Cart
- Product Sales Receipt
- Customer Tracking System
- Customer E-mail Receipts
- Integrated Shipping and Sales Tax System
- Credit Card Account Set Up
- Accepts Visa and MasterCard
- Real-Time Card Processing
- Secure Credit Card Transactions

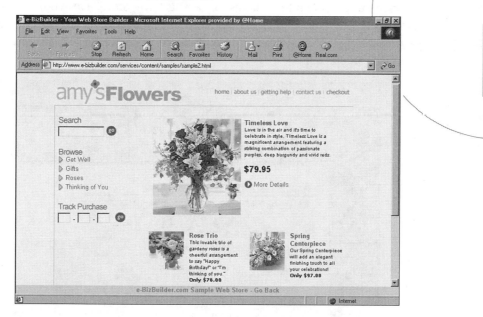

Figure 9.2

eBiz Builder was used to create an online flower shop complete with site search functions.

The eCom Basic plan does not offer an e-mail account, total Web site statistics, or Web-based reports. Costs and server space for each plan vary.

eBiz Builder sets you up with a credit card merchant account. It's quick, fast, and automatically installed and integrated into your eBiz Builder Web site. Your Web store can also be configured to accept COD orders, Checks, and Money Orders.

Earthstores.com

Like Yahoo! Store, you can test drive an online storefront through Earthstores.com. Earthstores.com at www.earthstores.com/, offers many of the services of the other three

All-In-One Hosting. You can build an online store in minutes, take orders securely, make changes to your storefront, track customer sales, and choose from a variety of store layouts. You can even use your own domain name.

You can use Earthstores.com's professionally designed templates to create your store. Earthstores.com's shopping cart system lets your items have any properties you want, not just size and colors. It has built-in support for monograms and inscriptions, supports quantity discounts, and will recalculate unit price and subtotal on the fly as quantities change. Also, the tax and shipping charges on purchases are calculated automatically, so shoppers know right away what they are being charged.

The cost of ShopBuilder's hosting service starts at $25 a month for a Bronze Store. This enables you to offer up to 25 items for sale. Its Silver Store gives you up to 100 items for sale for $50 per month, and the Gold Store up to 1,000 items for $100 per month. There are no setup fees for the Bronze Store but there is a $100 set fee for the Silver and Gold Stores (see Figure 9.3).

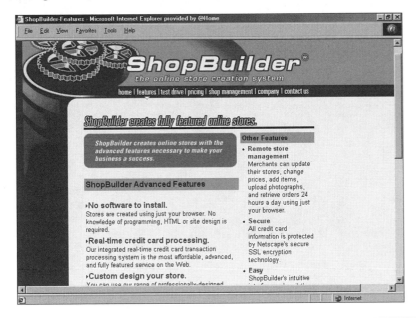

Figure 9.3

Credit card orders are processed in real-time on their secure server, and an e-mail receipt is automatically generated and sent to each customer.

More Is Not Necessarily Better
You don't have to sell hundreds upon hundreds of product to be a successful e-tailer. Many e-tailers have been successful selling only a dozen or so well-defined products to a niche market.

CHOOSING AN ISP HOSTING SERVICE

If you have dreams of becoming the next Amazon or CDNow, the All-In-One hosting services will not get you there. You're still constrained by the necessities of these types of hosting services. Sure, you can offer the products you want, take and process a credit card order, have an e-mail account, and use your own domain name. But to be a real e-commerce player you need to take charge of your own destiny and build your own online store.

In addition, if you're planning to raise a large amount of capital from investors or venture capitalists to realize your e-commerce dream, you'll need the flexibility—and credibility—to execute the type of eBusiness that will compete with the large established e-commerce sites on the Net.

Locating an ISP

To start your hunt for an ISP, check out Yahoo!'s list of regional ISPs at dir.yahoo. com/Business_and_Economy/Business_to_Business/Communications_and_ Networking/Internet_and_World_Wide_Web/Network_Service_Providers/ Internet_Service_Providers__ISPs_/ and the Definitive ISP Buyers Guide at thelist.iworld.com/.

That kind of flexibility and credibility comes only with the control and design of your own site. In Chapter 11, "Building Your Web Store," the essentials of building your own e-commerce Web site are covered. But first you need to learn how to choose the proper Internet service provider (ISP) to host your site.

Why host on an independent Internet service provider? Why not host your site yourself?

ISPs stand between you and your customer. They are the primary providers and the managers of the servers and other hardware that link the threads of the Web together. Like a fine weaver, they knit together the many diverse pieces of the Internet. If you had to bring all these elements together on your own it would be a costly and—if you're not technically skilled in the ways of the Net—a frustrating experience.

Not any Internet service provider will do. If you're in business, you need a dedicated Web hosting company. Dedicated e-commerce hosting companies do one thing and one thing only—they host businesses on the Web. They don't normally offer dial-up accounts to individuals. If you use a dedicated e-commerce hosting company, your customers won't have to compete for bandwidth to access your online store with online Doom players or people surfing NSync fan sites. Nothing frustrates a customer more than a slow download time.

Locating your Web site on a qualified ISP's server could take less time than pulling together the necessary services to quickly and safely take sales at your online store. The right ISP can provide your e-business with a turn-key e-commerce package that gives you fast credit card processing, end-to-end customer service, a high-speed connection—and gets you up and running in a matter of days.

The Interactive ISP Chooser

Use ClNet's Interactive Host Chooser to help you zero in on what you need from an ISP. It's a quick and easy way to locate ISPs that meet your site and traffic size requirements, pricing, and technology needs. Find it at www.builder.com/Servers/ Publish/Business/ss01a.html.

The Nature of the Beast

Your first task in selecting an appropriate ISP for your online business is to learn about the nature of the beast. You'll find ISPs all over the map—literally. You'll find them in different parts of the country. They have different prices and services.

At the very bottom of the food chain is the very small ISP. Believe it or not, you can find a person who has set up a server in his basement or spare room that hosts Web sites. Any person can build or buy a Web server, install a T1 line in the back, connect to the Internet, and become an ISP. If you are serious about business, leave these people to hosting family and friends, and the sites of lawyers and real estate salesmen.

Small ISPs might be cheap in the short run—and they are—but cost you a lot more in time and frustration later on. You're looking for a reliable business partner, not a hobbyist.

You might find that many Web site developers host the sites they design for clients on their own servers. Although these people are more professional and business focused, the downside might be price and a smaller, slower connection to the Internet.

Next up the chain is the dial-up ISP. As I stated before, hosting with a dial-up ISP can have its problems. You need a hosting service that understands business—not Net surfers. If the focus of the ISP is its dial-up customers, the eBusiness services you need might be minimal or even non-existent. Still, there are a few large ISPs that have separate divisions for Web-site hosting and dial-up customers and they might be useful if they are nationally based (see Figure 9.4). Following the dial-up ISP is the business Web hosting ISP. These ISPs take eBusiness seriously and focus only on Web business hosting. Prices are competitive, service is good, and technical support for your business is on call when you need it. They also give you dial-up access to your site, usually via FTP to make site changes and additions.

Finally, there's the large business or industrial strength ISP. If your Web site attracts a large amount of traffic, you're going to need one of these ISPs sooner or later. These ISPs offer few bargains, but you can expect to have maximum reliability, 24-hour in-house technical support, mirror sites on both coasts, and a redundant connection to the Internet.

Figure 9.4

TopHosts.com offers a directory of hosting solutions for your Web site. Each month they rank the top 25 hosting services.

ESSENTIAL SERVICES

Having to change ISP horses in midstream can be a costly and time-wasting affair. After your online business is up and running, switching ISPs definitely disrupts your business.

So how can you ensure that you're making the right choice?

First, make a list of the site hosting essentials you'll need for your online store. (We'll get to those in a minute.) Next, try to get referrals from satisfied business people. Referrals are always the safest way to shop for anything.

If you are using a Web site developer to create your Web site, ask for his or her advice. The Web site developer probably has a few ISPs that he or she would recommend. But keep in mind that even his advice may be a bit tainted if a close friend or relative is an ISP. That's why it's important to take your list of ISPs that seem to have e-commerce experience and send them your site hosting essentials asking them which ones they can supply. Ask for a written response—and references to Web stores they host—and give them a deadline to do it.

Here are the essential questions to ask an ISP.

Connection Speed

How fast can your customers access your site? Be sure your ISP is using at least T1s or T3s to connect to the Internet. A T1 can carry up to 1.5Mbs (megabits per second), whereas a T3 can carry 45Mbs. Make sure that the ISP is not using a fractional T1 or an ISDN line or buying access from another larger ISP. This affects the download time for Web pages.

JARGON

What's an ISDN?

ISDN—or Integrated Services Digital Network—is another way to connect to the Internet. Using an ISDN card and an ISDN connection, your connect speed to the Net is five times faster than a dial-up modem. ISDNs require special telephone lines that cost more than normal phone lines.

Another thing that can affect your download speed is the number of clients your ISP has on the server that your site is on. The more Web sites that are on your box, the more hits it gets and the slower your Web pages download. This can happen even if your ISP has a fast connection to the Net. Even if there are just a few Web sites on your server, if one of them is a high-volume site with lots of traffic, it, too, can affect the download speed of your Web pages.

Your hosting contract states how much bandwidth you will be paying for (how much of a T1 you will be using). If you exceed that amount of bandwidth at peak times, will the ISP automatically increase it to match the traffic? What will they charge you for the increase? And when it's time to increase your bandwidth, know up front what the incremental costs will be.

TIP

Check Your Page Loading Time

Want to see how fast your connection is by seeing how fast your page loads? Surf on over to Virtual Stampede and use the Load Time Check program. It's free. Find it at `virtual-stampede.com/tools.htm`.

Finally, ask the ISP about its downtime guarantee—what percentage of the time is its service up and will it guarantee that percentage. A few dollars refunded to you as a downtime penalty cannot make up for lost sales. And while you're at it, ask about technical and customer support. Is it 24 hours 7 days a week? It should be. Is the support done over the phone? Through e-mail only? Both? The more channels of communications that are open to you, the faster you will have your technical problem solved.

Space and Site Requirements

An ISP assigns you a certain amount of space on its computer for your Web site. This space allotment usually starts at 5MB and is enough to house the text and graphics of a small to medium e-commerce site. One thing to ask is whether log and mail files are counted in the space allotted to you. If not, you need to ask for more. Mail files are the number of e-mail messages that you can receive or store on the server space allotted to you. The log files contain the day to day traffic numbers that your Web site generates and are kept as a log on the server. If you want to do an analysis of how many visitors come to your Web site, where they come from, and what they do on your site, the log files will tell you this.

Next, ask if the ISP will move the domain name you have registered for your business for you and do all the necessary paperwork for InterNic (Network Solutions). This could be quite a hassle if you're new to the mysterious ways of InterNic (Network Solutions).

Unlimited E-mail Addresses and Auto-Responders

Having one personal e-mail address is nice. Having one or two more on Yahoo! or Hotmail is cool. But neither will do if you're in business. Ask your ISP how many e-mail addresses you are allowed. You need more than one. Your business should have several e-mail aliases for your domain name for different departments of your business.

Be Sure You Have at Least These E-mail Aliases

You'll need more than one e-mail address for your e-commerce site. Offer at least these e-mail addresses to your site visitors.

- info@yourcompany.com—for those requesting general information.
- service@yourcompany.com—for customer service requests.
- orders@yourcompany.com—for order status questions.
- sales@yourcompany.com—for suppliers to contact you.
- feedback@yourcompany.com—for general feedback on your site or service.

And remember to check their e-mail addresses daily!

Make sure that the ISP can provide you with aliases. Also, make sure that each alias can be forwarded to the company e-mail address of the person responsible for that department.

Finally, ask whether the ISP can provide e-mail auto-responders. You can use these auto-responders to automatically reply to certain e-mails asking for information. For example, when a customer contacts you with a problem, you might create an auto-responder that states you have received his e-mail and his request is being processed. Another type of auto-responder would be an e-mail confirmation of the customer's order and another when his product is shipped.

cgi-bin Access

If you'll be using a shopping cart on your site, generating e-mail messages sent out by Web page forms, or running programs such as polls or surveys, you need access to the ISP's cgi-bin. This is a place on the server that hosts your site where you can run the programs that you have written.

cgi-bin access is critical in supporting a shopping cart application for your online store and you might want to seek out the advice of a professional Web development service to help you with this.

What Is Telnet?

Telnet is an Internet process that lets you connect your machine as a remote terminal to a host computer somewhere on the Internet.

Be sure you ask if the ISP enables Telnet access to a cgi-bin directory.

Mailing List Programs

In a short amount of time, you will need a way to contact your customers. You might want to create an e-mail newsletter for them to opt into, or e-mail a special offer to a segment of your customer base, or even send an e-mail to all your customers thanking them for their business.

These are all good ways to keep your business in front of your customers and prospects. By communicating periodically with your prospect and customer base, you increase their likelihood of returning to your site to make future sales. If this is your goal—and it should be—then your ISP must provide you with a mailing list program.

One such mailing list program is called Majordomo. At first glance it looks like the name of some Japanese officer but it's really an automated e-mail management program. For example, suppose you want to set up an e-mail discussion group or an e-mail newsletter list. People who visit your Web site can subscribe to your discussion list or e-mail newsletters from a page on your site. Their e-mail address is automatically entered into the Majordomo database and when it's time to send a message, you just compose it and paste it into an e-mail message. Majordomo then sends it to everyone on the e-mail list.

The Majordomo FAQ

Still not clear on Majordomo? Everything you need to know about Majordomo can be found at the Majordomo FAQ. Find it at www.visi.com/~barr/majordomo-faq.html.

In addition, if someone wants to unsubscribe from the list, she can return to your Web site and ask to unsubscribe. Majordomo automatically does it all without any action on your part.

Other Considerations

Most ISPs provide you with unlimited FTP access to your site. You need this to upload your site after it's created and then to make changes when needed. If you're in the software business and want to let customers download demos or if you want to offer some free information for download, you need to have an anonymous FTP capability. This differs from your normal FTP access, which requires a username and password. An anonymous FTP does not.

What Is FTP?

FTP stands for *file transfer protocol* and is the process you use to send and receive files from your computer to the server your Web site resides on. To do this you will need to have an FTP software program.

An ISP also should supply you with a statistical package that can tell you how many people visited your site and from where. (This can tell you which marketing efforts worked and which did not.) The package should tell you the number and types of pages they visited and the path they used to click through your site. (This can help you improve your site navigation.) It should tell you which are your most frequented pages and which are not. (This can help you see which products are popular and which are not.) Finally, if you're taking credit card orders, be sure the ISP provides a secure commerce server running a *Secure Socket Layer* or *SSL*. This is the standard for credit card security over the Net. If you plan to use some kind of back-end database for your Web site, be sure that the ISP's operating system is compatible with the system you use to maintain the database.

What Should You Expect to Pay

The price you pay for an e-commerce hosting service varies with services that you need. A typical site with multiple e-mail alias, cgi-bin access, and a T3 connection to the Internet can run anywhere from $20–$40 a month. If you add SSL security to that you can expect to pay up to $75 a month. If you have a high-volume site, you might be charged additional fees for peak periods of bandwidth.

Remember, ISPs are very competitive. If you like an ISP but its prices are too high, ask if it is possible to match the competitor's price. You never know.

CHAPTER **10**

BE YOUR OWN HOST

In This Chapter

- Discover how to switch ISPs
- Learn what hardware and software you need to build your own Web site server
- Learn whether you should hire a professional to design and build your Web site

Your online business is humming along. Traffic is up, sales are great, and you have Jeff Bezos in your crosshairs. You've gone beyond what an e-commerce ISP or All-In-One hosting service like Yahoo! Store can give you. You're ready to hunt the big game. You're ready to become an Enterprise Site—you're ready to own and maintain your own Web server.

You might be a candidate for an Enterprise Site if

- You're getting tens of thousands of hits a day and your pages are getting slower and slower to download.
- Your hits are crashing your ISP's servers.
- You need access to sophisticated programs such as one-click ordering, advanced product search capabilities, or personal shopping agents that your ISP won't install.
- You need to access and update a customized or large database of products and customers—or even direct access to a mainframe computer.

Deciding to go it on your own by owning your own Web server is a serious choice. The costs of building and maintaining an e-commerce Web server are not to be taken lightly. If you do it for ego or at the insistence of some computer systems person who wants a new toy, you could greatly damage your successful business.

Are there ways to reduce the risks as you move toward being an Enterprise Site?

Yes, there are. You could co-host your server before you bring it in-house. But first things first. You have to move your site from your current ISP—and that is a challenging task.

MOVING YOUR WEB SITE

In the realm of e-commerce headaches, moving your Web site to another server ranks right up there with having your site crash. Transferring your Web site to a new server has the potential to disrupt your business, and could cause you to lose sales—and even customers—if not done correctly.

Unfortunately, when you move a site, you must expect the worst to happen. Don't assume anything—just be prepared in case something—or everything—goes wrong.

First—and most importantly—where are the pages that represent your Web site? Do you have a copy of them on your PC? If you're going to move your site, you must have possession of your Web site pages to transfer them to your new server. If your store is currently running on an All-In-One service like Yahoo! Store, then you have a much larger problem. Because there is no Web site to call your own, you'll need to build one from scratch.

Second, any programs or scripts that you're running on your current ISP need to be moved—or if the ISP provided them for you—replaced or amended to work on your new server. In addition, all the data on customers and products that you have created and stored must be transferred as well. This in itself can be quite an undertaking. Be sure that you maintain a copy of these databases on your computer system.

Third, you have to move your domain name. Sounds simple, right? Not quite. A number of things can go wrong here. First of all, the people at InterNic are nearly impossible to speak to personally. At InterNic you can set up a domain name in a matter of minutes. Making any changes to it can take months!

Here's the problem. InterNic accepts changes to a domain registration from only the Administrative Contact. When you registered your domain name, you were asked to supply an Administrative and Technical Contact. You can see this information at Network

Solutions site at www.networksolutions.com/cgi-bin/whois/whois (see Figure 10.1). The Technical Contact is usually someone in technical support at the ISP where your domain resides.

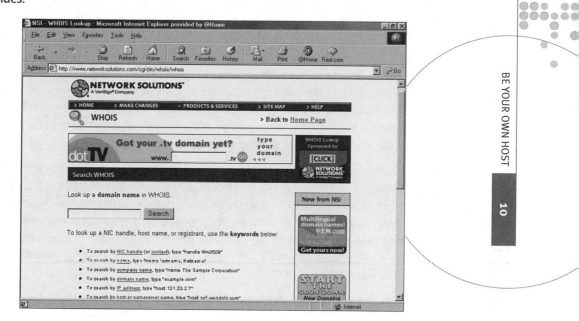

Figure 10.1

Check Network Solution's Whois to view your domain name registration file. When you enter your URL, InterNic brings up your file.

Most people make the mistake of having that person be their Administrative Contact as well. If you do that, you won't be able to make changes to your domain registration—such as moving it to your new server—without the Technical Contact's permission. And only he can do it. Even worse, if the Technical Contact is an employee of the ISP and has left the company, he might be nowhere to be found. So be sure that you are always the Administrative Contact—not one of your employees.

Here's something else to prepare for when you move from an ISP. Service goes from good to poor in a matter of minutes. After the ISP loses you as a customer, he has little motivation in helping you move. After all, you're not his customer anymore, why should he service you? Don't assume your old ISP will cooperate with you—and even if he does—don't assume he'll stick to your timetable.

You might consider withholding any funds due your ISP until the transfer is complete, but I don't recommend it. They could lock you out of access to your site.

To avoid this problem, don't shut down your ISP until your new site is up—and fully functional—on your new server. In fact, run both. When you're confident that your new site is running the way it should, then and only then contact InterNic and point your domain name to the new server. If you're the Administrative Contact on your domain registration, pointing your domain name to your new server takes only a few days and about a week or so for the Internet to update its records and point your traffic to your new home.

IN-HOUSE, CO-LOCATED, OR DEDICATED HOST SERVICE?

Having your own Web site server is the premier Web hosting solution. It gives you complete control over your Web site, the flexibility to execute your eBusiness plan, and your site visitors are the only ones using your server. Once you've made the decision to use a dedicated server, the first thing you need to do is connect your server to the Internet. You have three choices. Do it you yourself with your own dedicated server and connection in-house, use a dedicated host service, or use a co-location service.

But no matter which type of service you use, you have to decide which software platform you're going to use to run your site. About Guide Gordon Whyte has a Web Store Software Selector at ecommerce.about.com/finance/ecommerce/library/blsw.htm that can help (see Figure 10.2). Of all the software choices you make for your Web server, the most important will be your software platform—or operating system (OS). Other than DOS, you're probably not too familiar with Web server operating systems. The two most popular are Unix and Windows NT.

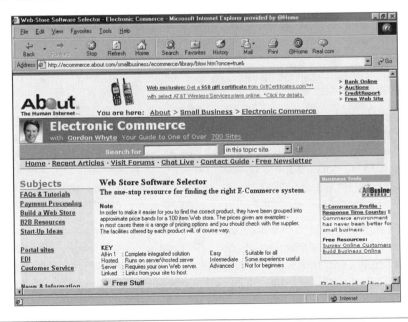

Figure 10.2

About Guide Gordon Whyte has created a Web Store Software Selector to help you choose the right e-commerce software system.

The oldest of the Web server operating systems is Unix. Unix was developed in 1969, and, up until several years ago, was the first choice of server operating systems. Its popularity stems from the fact that it was designed to be a multiuser/multitasking operating system that is perfect for Web servers. But unlike Windows, it is not a graphical OS—it's more like DOS.

Unix or NT?

Top Host has a very good article that describes the pros and cons of Unix and NT. Find it at http://www.tophosts.com/pages/articles/ntis.htm.

Microsoft has been very aggressive in promoting its Windows NT Web server and many businesses have adopted this operation system. Which OS you use will depend upon the advice and knowledge of the Web developer you consult with.

Hosting your server in-house at your business location is expensive. Not only is there the cost of the Web-serving hardware, but also there's the cost of administering the system in-house. It can take a staff of technical people just to keep the server up and running. You need to lease a T1 line, buy routers to connect to the Net, and build firewalls to keep out unwanted guests. Costs for this can start at $20,000 and go up—way up—from there.

For the Do-It-Yourselfers

The ZDNet Developer site is probably the best Web site design resource on the Net. Find everything from shareware to online classes in HTML. Find this site at www.zdnet.com/products/iu/designers/.

Co-Location Host Services

If you don't want to incur the costs of connecting your server to the Internet, you should consider a co-location service provider. This is a good option if you're confident you can maintain a server but don't want the hassle of bringing in an Internet connection in-house. Your server is kept at a high-grade facility that the co-location host provides.

A definite advantage to this type of service is that a co-host's Net connection is usually faster than a simple T1 that you could provide. A co-host will most likely have a T3 line or even a fiber-optics line connected to the Net. It also solves the physical security problem and reduces the chance of the server going down due to power failures.

As for support and service, that's still your responsibility. The co-location host service provider's main job is to connect your server to the Net. When your co-location server goes down, it's up to you to fix it—or pay someone to do it. Are you willing to leave your warm bed at two in the morning to coordinate the repair of your server when it goes down?

Choosing a Web Server

Looking for a good source for help on choosing a Web server? Check out the links at About at http://compnetworking.about.com/compute/compnetworking/cs/webservers/index.htm.

As for costs, they're higher than a dedicated hosting service. First you have to buy a server. A low-end server will set you back about $4,000 and a mid-range server about $9,000. Next you need to place your server in a rack. A rack contains a number of servers that are stacked one on top of another. A half-rack costs about $500–$700 a month to rent at the facility. Finally, you have to purchase a router that connects you to the Internet. All total, and assuming you invest in a low-end server, you're initial outlay to get up and running will be about $7,500—not including personnel time for set up and configuration.

Dedicated Host Services

If you still want your own dedicated server but don't want the costs incurred in buying one, setting it up, and connecting it to the Net, then a dedicated host services company is your ticket.

The dedicated host services company supplies your server—fully configured and ready for your site—the rack space, the connection to the Internet, a large bandwidth, back up power, and 24/7 monitoring of your site. One advantage of using a dedicated host service is the speed at which you can add hardware to service unplanned business needs. For example, suppose your site is the subject of a story in *USA Today* or the focus of a TV news story. This news would draw a large number of unexpected visitors to your site.

Check Your Site Performance

Is your Internet provider delivering the speed and service it promised? Then give your Web site a tune up. Use WebSite Garage to measure your site's performance, optimize your graphics, and analyze your site traffic. Check it out at websitegarage.netscape.com/.

If you co-located, you would have to quickly add additional hardware to your site—hardware that was not originally budgeted for. But because the dedicated host company provides all the hardware, upgrading your system to meet the unplanned need would be easy and much less expensive.

In addition, if the traffic subsided, you could simply cancel the use of the new hardware. If you co-located, you would now own an unused piece of hardware. These considerations are very important for an e-commerce site because as the Internet grows, an eBusiness must be prepared to move quickly and add new hardware as the market demands.

Costs for a dedicated hosting service are far less than the co-location option. Because you don't need to buy a server or pay to connect to the Net, your initial costs are very low. You just pay a start up fee of about $900, which includes your server's configuration, and a monthly fee of about $900 a month for the service.

Hosting Requirements

When choosing either a co-location or dedicated hosting service, you should keep a number of requirements in mind.

Free Server Uptime Check

Want to sleep better at night? Here's a free service that checks to see if your server is up and running. It runs a check every 15 minutes. You're e-mailed if your server goes down. Check it out at uptime.arsdigita.com/uptime/.

- Are they insured?
- Is the physical computer environment secure? Are the necessary security precautions in place?
- Is the environment kept clean?
- Are their technical people knowledgeable? Do they have knowledge of computers and telecommunications? Both are necessary.
- What kinds of technical support will they offer? Are they easily reachable? Do they offer the support 24 hours a day 7 days a week? Your online store doesn't close and neither should they.
- Can they provide references? What other companies can you talk to that use their facilities? What kind of experience have they had with the service?
- Will your site be backed up? How and how often? Do they have a disaster recovery plan in case of a fire or explosion? Do they keep their backups offsite?
- What happens if their primary power goes down? Do they have an uninterruptible power supply (UPS)? Can you install a UPS for your own Web site server on site?

Finally, your decision to either go with a co-location or dedicated hosting service—or do it in-house—depends on the monetary and technical resources you have at your disposal.

SHOULD YOU HIRE A PRO?

Being your own host means that you're serious about building a large business. Designing and building a large e-commerce Web site is no easy task. It's no shame that as a businessperson you might need help with the project.

Check Your Site Performance

Advertising Age's Business Marketing leads you step-by-step through the process of choosing a Web developer. It is quick and easy and directs you to actual developers that meet your needs. Find it at http://www.businessmarketing.nikusource.com/.

So, when should you outsource your Web site to a professional?

- When you don't have the technological and design skills in-house.
- When you need a professional looking Web site that can compete in looks and credibility with your biggest competitors.
- When speed is of the essence—and it always is on the Net—and you want to leverage your limited time and dollars.

It's rare to find a business person who also has good technical skills. You not only must know how to write in HTML to create Web pages, but know how to program in Perl, C++, and Java. And then there's graphics for your site—your company logo, navigation elements, and the look and feel of your online store. Creating graphics from scratch requires a good working knowledge of Adobe Illustrator and PhotoShop.

Sure, designing your site yourself saves you money, but if you're going to host it yourself and swim with the big boys, you're going to need professional help. Check out About Guide Jean Kaiser's site at `webdesign.about.com/compute/webdesign/library/designers/bldirectory.htm` (see Figure 10.3) to find a Web designer in your area. Even if you have a site and are moving it to a new server, you still need help transferring files and reprogramming your site to get it ready for business.

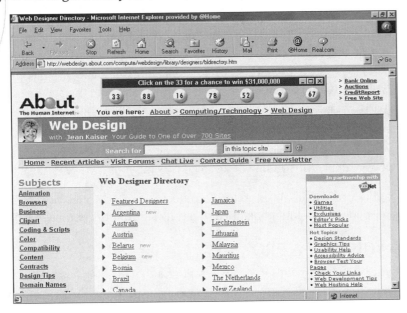

Figure 10.3

If you're looking for a Web designer, About Guide Jean Kaiser has a directory of designers from all over the world.

What's It Cost?

So what can you expect to pay? That all depends on what you want in your online store and how big it will be.

If your business is small, expect to pay up to $10,000 or more to set up an online store. This gets you a pretty good-sized site with a shopping cart. A medium-sized business might spend $10,000 to have its Web site designed, and this doesn't include additional costs for custom graphics and CGI programs such as chat rooms, discussion boards, and polls. These could run thousands of dollars more.

What Should I Pay?

The Web Price Index Card gives you the average rates for programmers and Web designers to compare against the proposals you receive from Web developers. Find it at `http://www.btobonline.com/cgi-bin/article.pl?id=3050`.

The sky's the limit when designing an e-commerce Web site. Large businesses have been know to spend up to a million dollars or more for all the previously mentioned items—and then more to add animation, audio, and streaming video to attract shoppers to their site.

Time Is Money

There's another reason for outsourcing to a professional—time.

The Internet moves fast and the Web is littered with companies that did not move fast enough. Speed of execution is critical on the Net. There's a joke that goes, "If you want to pull ahead of your competitor—give him a computer." Don't get bogged down in technology. Go to the people who know. In the real world, time is money. If you're to succeed on the Net, spend money—not time.

CHAPTER 11

BUILDING YOUR WEB STORE

In This Chapter

- Learn the basic essentials of your e-commerce Web site
- Discover what software and graphics tools you need to create and maintain an e-commerce Web site
- Learn the most important things you need to have on your e-commerce Web site

If you've ever built a new house or purchased one, you know that finding a home is just the first step. You still have to furnish it. That goes double for an e-commerce Web site. Whether you've chosen to host your Web store on a free personal Web site service, an ISP, or your own server, you now have the challenge of making your Web store inviting and useable.

So, before you rush out and hastily toss together a catalog of products or services and place them on your server, you have to consider some basic Web site essentials and the tools to provide them if you want your eBusiness to be a success. Knowing these site essentials will prevent you from building fatal errors into your site that are sure to be shopping turnoffs.

These Web site essentials are important if you want to make your customers' shopping experience easy, convenient, enjoyable, safe, and reliable. Good e-tailer sites make this look effortless, but don't be fooled. A lot of hard work and planning go into creating a successful online store. Just putting up a personal Web page on Yahoo! GeoCities or even using one of the free online store builders at Yahoo! Store is not enough to make your e-commerce enterprise a success.

WEB SITE ESSENTIALS

Like it or not, your Web site is your "brand." If you can create a positive image—a strong brand—that is memorable, online shoppers will not only be attracted to your site but also return to it over and over.

On the Net, a brand is more than just a graphic design such as the Nike swoosh or McDonalds' golden arches. It represents an interactive experience and the online consumer gets this experience through your Web store.

What makes a good online brand? The same thing that makes a good interactive Web site—a good user experience.

Your brand must target a specific audience or market niche. You did that when you created your Unique Selling Position. But just as important, your brand—that is, your Web site—must be useable. A pretty logo is not a brand on the Web. It's the overall user experience your shopper has with your site. This includes the look and feel of the site and its ease of navigation. For some good tips on Web site design, check out About Guide Jean Kaiser's Web site at `webdesign.about.com`. It also includes before, during, and after sales support (see Figure 11.1).

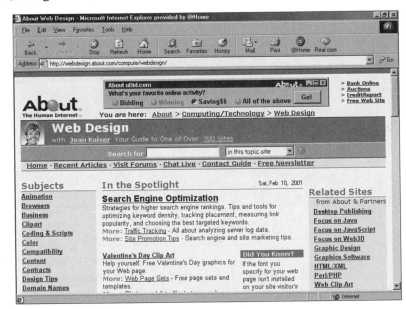

Figure 11.1

Just about everything you need to know about Web design can be found at About Guide Jean Kaiser's Web site.

SETTING UP SHOP

PART 2

It's easy to create an adequate e-commerce Web site. What you want to do is create a great online brand that customers will enjoy shopping at and come back to again and again. And to do that you need to keep a set of Web essentials in mind.

And here they are:

- Make your pages load fast
- Make your Web site reflect your business
- Keep the number of images to a minimum
- Write for the Web
- Make your Web pages easy to find

Fast Loading Pages

There's an old saying: "You can always tell a pioneer by the arrows in his back." Using the latest technology to differentiate yourself from the competition is not the best idea for an online store. In fact, it can be fatal.

If you remember one thing and one thing only in designing your e-commerce Web site, remember that the fastest way to drive a customer away from your site is to confront him with a lot of flashy animation, slick Java applets, or require plug-ins to view your site. In other words—stay away from the bleeding edge of Web site design. Even if you include all the proper Web site essentials to your online store, they will be all for naught when your customers are driven away in the first few seconds of their visit.

So, before you move mouse to browser to design your site, keep this in mind. There are millions and millions of potential customers who are still cruising the Web at 33.3kbs—many even at 28.8Kbps! All that work you did finding and choosing a good Web hosting provider with a fast connection to the Web will be irrelevant if you design a technology blotted site that takes the average Web surfer several minutes to download.

JARGON

What's a Kbps?

Kbps stands for *kilobits per second*—the amount of bytes of data that a modem can send in a second. It's a way of measuring a modem's speed. Most modems today run at 28.8Kbps to 33.3Kbps and in theory up to 56Kbps.

Let the other guys stand on the bleeding edge. Forget all the fancy stuff. Forget streaming video, animation, and live audio. Keep your site simple and make it load fast. You only have a few seconds to grab a shopper's attention.

Remember to address the technological level of the audience at your Web site. e-Commerce will continue to explode over the next 10 years because of the growing number of Internet users. But as the number of new users increases, their level of technological sophistication decreases. Security, good prices, great customer service, easy site navigation, detailed product data, and simple ordering are far more important than cool techno-tricks on your site.

The Right Look and Feel

Your Web site should reflect your Web business. Are you selling products at a steep discount? If so, your site design and look might have more of a warehouse or superstore feel. Or perhaps you're selling unique or made-to-order creative items. Your site then might have a boutique look and feel to it. If you're running a service business, then a design that displays a professional image would be more appropriate.

The wording you use on your site, the graphic images you choose, the navigational icons you provide—all should reflect the look and feel of your eBusiness. You have only a few moments to get your visitor to look at your site. Your home page—the first page of your Web site—should inform your visitors of not only what you sell but also the type of shopping experience they are to expect. Your visitors must be able to quickly determine if you have anything that interests them. Your home page must be designed to entice the shopper inside your online store.

CAUTION

Is Your Web Site Sick?

Does your e-commerce Web site suffer from debilitating diseases such as Clarity Constriction, Image Inflammation, Monitor Myopia, Frames Fixation, Background Blemish, Button Bloat, and Navigation Neuralgia? If so, check out www.wilsonweb.com/articles/7diseases.htm for the cure.

Keep your home page short, fast loading, and to the point. Be brief on you first page. Give the customers enough information to interest them in making a purchase. Then direct them to pages that have more details of your offer.

Finally, try looking at your Web site through the eyes of your customer. Read your Unique Selling Position. Are you targeting the right customer? Does your home page let your customer know exactly what you sell? Does it reflect the other pages on your site? Does it direct the shopper straight to your product offers? Do all your Web pages reinforce the purpose of your site? If the answer is No to any of these, make changes.

Photos and Graphics

Although a picture is worth a thousand words, too many graphics on your site will slow the download of your pages. Make sure you use a graphics person that not only is a good graphic designer but also understands the needs of the Web. He should be skilled in the art of creating good looking but small graphic files for fast downloading.

Image size should be kept small. Nothing is more frustrating to a shopper than to watch the little blue bar at the bottom corner of her screen inch along at a snail's pace. The total amount of graphics on a Web page should not exceed 40K. Try to stick with the basics and use only 256 colors. Use *interlaced* graphic images to keep your visitors' attention while the graphic loads in to their browser.

One solution to the download problem that photos and graphics pose is to create two versions of your site. If the products or services you sell must be displayed with lots of images (screen shots of a software program, for example), then offering a link to a text version of the site might be a good solution. It would take more time and money, but the payoff could be more sales.

> ### What's an Interlaced GIF?
>
> Interlaced GIF images help keep your customer's interest as the graphic gradually displays over four passes. Although the download time is the same as non-interlaced GIFS, your customer gets to see it slowly form on the page and might wait instead of clicking off your page.

JARGON

Keep in mind that graphics are there to complement your sales copy—not replace it. They are there to reinforce your sales offer. It's your sales copy that will ultimately sell your product—not the graphic. If you must use a large graphic—such as showing more product detail or a product in use—then place a thumbnail of the picture next to the copy (see Figure 11.2). The page will load quickly and if the customer wants to see a larger image of the product, he can click the thumbnail to expand the image. ValuePrint Pro or Firehand Ember Ultra are two programs that will create thumbnails for you. You can find them at download.com.

There are two types of image formats. One is called the GIF and the other the JPEG. GIF images can be viewed by all Web browsers and work best with graphic images. One downside to GIFs is that they are much larger than JPEGs and can take longer to download. If you're going to use product photos, then JPEG images are best. They will load much faster than a photo image created as a GIF. Another graphic type to consider is the transparent GIF. These types of images have a transparent background. This is useful if you want the edges of your image to blend into the background color of your page.

Basic Page Elements

Reading off a monitor is tough enough. Don't make it more difficult for your customers by having them scroll through page after page of a product description. Use language that's concise, short, and to-the-point. A Web site is different from a printed catalog page. Don't just dump the product specification sheet on a Web page.

People don't read a Web page—they browse it. Use headlines and subheadlines that describe the product or service concisely. Then follow the headline with supporting copy in more detail. Use short sentences—even bullet points—to make the information easy to read and understand. You're not writing for *Vanity Fair* here. You're trying to make your sales offer as compelling and concise as possible. Use this same formula for other pages on your site, such as Customer Support pages, Company About pages, and so on.

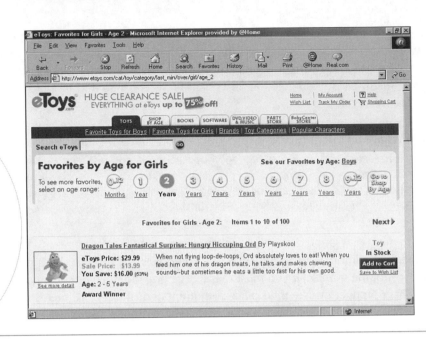

Figure 11.2

This is a good example of the use of thumbnails on a Web page. Click the thumbnail and a large version of the picture appears.

Is there a place for long Web pages? Yes there is. You might want your customer to download technical information on a product for future reference or an instruction sheet that might go with a product that you've created yourself. You could instruct the customer to either wait for the page to load, and then print it, or make it so the customer can download the page as a file to his or her computer. And suppose you need more than one page to describe your product or service offer? Then consider using multiple shorter pages that are linked together.

If you have many products or services in several categories, you should consider listing the categories, then the products or services in text format until the shopper arrives at the item he or she is looking for. At that point, yon can display the image of the item and other graphics that are appropriate to sell the product or service.

Each of your Web pages also should have the following elements at the top of the page:

- Page title
- Page description
- Page keywords

The page title resides at the top of your Web page. You can find the title of each Web page in the <TITLE> tag on a page that looks like this:

```
<TITLE>Your Page Title</TITLE>
```

Why is it important to title your pages? Because the top line of your Web page often shows up in search engines such as AltaVista (`www.altavista.com`). By making your title descriptive, people will know right away what's on that page and be more willing to visit your site.

Page Description

The page description normally follows the page title. The page description is what's called a *meta tag* and the code on a Web page would look like this:

```
<META NAME="description" CONTENT="Your page description here">
```

Some search engines display the page description tag in their search results. So, a good page description will entice potential customers to view your page and visit your site.

Get the Scoop

Here's your chance to hear what successful professional Web designers have to say about creating a top notch Web site. Check out their interviews at http://webdesign.about.com/compute/webdesign/cs/interviews/index.htm.

Page Keywords

Following the title and description tags you'll see the keyword tag that looks like this:

```
<META NAME="keywords" CONTENT="Your keywords'>
```

Page keywords are very important! This is the primary way that most search engines find your Web site. The right choice of key words will make your site rise to the top of a search engine's search results. Because most search engine users only go as far as the first page of search results, its important that your Web site show in the first 10 results or so. We'll talk more on this in Chapter 18, "Marketing Your e-Business."

Web Page Forms

Finally, the Web is interactive and your Web site should be too. An essential element of your Web store should be the ability to capture information from your customers. That's how Web page forms are used. Customers or site visitors simply fill out a form on a Web page, press the **submit** button at the end of the form, and the information is immediately e-mailed to you. Or, if you have access to a programmer, he or she can set up a database that you can access to retrieve the information.

Web page forms can be used in a number of ways. One use is "Requests for Information." Shoppers can use this form to request further information on your products or service or ask a question about your service guarantee. Customers can use this form to find out about the status of an order or ask to return a product.

Another use for Web page forms is for a Guestbook or Newsletter sign-up. You can ask potential customers to sign your Guestbook or subscribe to your e-mail newsletter, and in the process, collect certain information that you could use to market to them later. If you don't have a shopping cart software application on your site, you can use Web page forms to take an order right online. Even if you have a shopping cart program on your site, you could still make this form available to those who want to fill it out and fax their order to you or mail it in with a check.

Now you're ready to build your Web store and to do that you'll need a set of Web site tools.

WEB SITE TOOL KIT

Like any successful builder, the right tools can make the difference between a mediocre outcome and an excellent one. Whether you build your Web store from scratch or maintain it through one of the online store builders, you'll need a specialized set of Web site tools to make it happen. By the way, many of the software programs mentioned here can be downloaded free from download.com (see Figure 11.3).

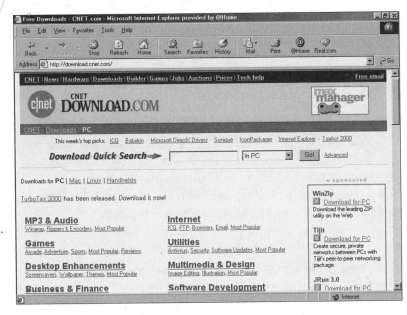

Figure 11.3

At C/Net's Download.com, you can download many of the programs mentioned either for free or as a trial version.

Your Web site toolbox should consist of

- An HTML Editor
- Graphic tools
- FTP software

An HTML Editor is used to build your Web site from scratch and then edit and maintain your pages after they go live. If you're using an online store builder such as Yahoo! Store, an HTML Editor is not necessary. You create and make changes to your Web store HTML pages right through your browser. And even if you use a Web page builder provided by the personal Web page hosting services such as Yahoo! GeoCities, if you're serious about having a real business online, you would want to create your own Web pages and upload them to the service.

HTML Editors only help you create the actual HTML text pages and Web site structure. You still have to create or find and modify the site graphics you need, such as product images, company logo, and navigational icons. For this, you need a graphics design program.

Finally, after you have your site completed, you need a way to upload your pages to your host server. You need an FTP program to transfer the files on your computer to the server that is hosting your Web store.

The following sections introduce the different software packages available to you, starting with the HTML Editors.

HTML Editors

There are two ways to create or edit a Web page. The first way is to use an HTML Editor. The second is to use a text pad such as Notepad for the PC. Why use a text pad instead of an HTML Editor?

Text pads give you ultimate control over the layout of your Web page. Unlike the HTML Editors, you code your Web page using raw HTML. That means you must be very familiar with HTML and understand how to use and apply the mark-up language. The HTML Editors, on the other hand, work more like a word processor—some more, others less. In these cases, little to no knowledge of actual HTML is required of you.

Many developers like to build their pages and Web sites using an HTML Editor for the ease and speed of execution and use a text pad to edit the pages later. That way they are not constrained by the HTML Editor when making upgrades or edits.

Free Site Design Templates

Need help designing your site? Then how about some free site design templates? There are hundreds of these to choose from and many of them are free to download. Find them at toolsforthe.net.

The process you use really depends on your knowledge level of HTML and your own personal preferences. For those of us that prefer to use an HTML Editor, here are some of the most popular.

- **Macromedia's Dreamweaver**—Dreamweaver at www.macromedia.com/software/dreamweaver/. This is a premier WYSIWYG (what-you-see-is-what-you-get) HTML editor. Because is acts like a word processor—that is, WYSIWYG—you would think it would cater to beginners. Unfortunately, it does not. Dreamweaver is designed specifically for the professional Web site developer.

- **Homesite**—Homesite at `www.allaire.com/products/homesite/` is a more user-friendly HTML Editor. It has an easy-to-use interface and also has a WYSIWYG feature that can be turned on or off.

- **Adobe Pagemill**—As a visual HTML Editor, Pagemill at `www.adobe.com/prodindex/pagemill/main.html` also has a WYSIWYG interface and includes a simple drag-and-drop interface. Easy to use and full-featured, this is a good choice for beginners. It also integrates with current office and graphics applications, such as Microsoft Word, Corel WordPerfect, Microsoft Excel, Adobe Photoshop, and Adobe Illustrator.

- **Hotmetal Pro**—Hotmetal at `www.hotmetalpro.com/products/` is again for the professional. Its editor offers page creation wizards, and visual and source code editing.

- **Microsoft Frontpage**—Microsoft Frontpage at `www.microsoft.com/frontpage/` is an HTML Editor designed for nonprogrammers. It's easy to use and integrates fully into the Microsoft Office family of products.

- **NetObject's Fusion**—NetObject's Fusion at `www.netobjects.com/`, a high horsepower WYSIWYG, is a Web site creation and management tool for building small business solutions or your first site.

Ask Doctor HTML

Submit a single Web page, and Doctor HTML will check it for errors. He'll check spelling, syntax, forms, and table structure—even verify your page links. Find him at `www2.imagiware.com/RxHTML/`.

- **Sausage Software's Hot Dog**—Sausage Software at `www.sausagetools.com/` offers a series of editors for both the novice and advanced HTML programmers.

- **Arachnophilia**—Arachnophilia at `www.arachnoid.com` is a pretty cool HTML editor for the PC to weave your Web site. And it's free.

Graphics Tools

Let's face it. The Web is a graphical medium. If you want your Web pages to look like more than gray pages of text, you need more than just an HTML Editor. Sooner or later you have to add graphics.

As with HTML Editors there are two approaches to the problem. First, you download and use the multitude of free clip art that's on the Net, or you can create the graphics yourself. Creating graphics or manipulating photographs takes more skill than writing a Web page. Unlike the HTML Editors, there are no simple graphics design programs. To learn how to create graphics will take quite a learning curve and much of your valuable time.

Unless you plan to use the ready made Web templates available on the Web or the free downloadable clip art, it's best that you find yourself a good graphic designer who knows how to use the following graphic tools.

Fill Up at the Web Diner

The Web Diner offers tips, tutorials, and Web page templates and a cool set of alphabet icons. All free to download. Find it at www.webdiner.com.

- **Photoshop**—If you're going to have pictures of your product on your Web store, then this is the program to use. Photoshop at www.adobe.com/prodindex/photoshop/main.html gives you the tools to import, crop, retouch, and edit any picture that you would like to use on your site.

- **Adobe Illustrator**—Illustrator at www.adobe.com/prodindex/illustrator/main.html is the premier graphics design program. Any designer worth his or her salt uses Illustrator to create graphic images from scratch.

- **Paintshop Pro**—Paintshop Pro at www.jasc.com/ has many of the same features as Photoshop but is far less expensive.

- **Fireworks**—This is Macromedia's contribution for creating Web graphics. Fireworks' code at www.macromedia.com/software/fireworks/productinfo/contents.html integrates seamlessly into Dreamweaver and other leading HTML editors.

- **CorelDRAW**—Corel at www.corel.com/draw9/index.htm has been around almost as long as Adobe Illustrator and includes a complete suite of graphics tools.

Finding Free Graphics Online

If the thought of learning to use a professional graphics program is too much too bear, then consider using free clip art that's available for use on your Web pages. There are many places on the Net where you can find and download graphics for use on your site. There are hundreds of sites that offer all kinds of images, pictures—even photos—that you can use for free on your site (see Figure 11.4).

The types of free images you can find on the Net are

- Animated GIFS
- Backgrounds, borders, and textures for your Web pages
- Navigational bars, icons, and control pads
- Web page templates
- Stock photography, royalty free photography, and public domain images
- Clip art, icons, and buttons

You can find links to many of these sites at two About.com Guide sites. Jean Kaiser, the Web Design Guide, can point you towards dozens of free image sites at webdesign.about.com/compute/webdesign/mlibrary.htm and Bobbie Peachey, the Web Clip Art Guide, at webclipart.about.com lists just about every conceivable resource for finding clip art specifically made for Web sites.

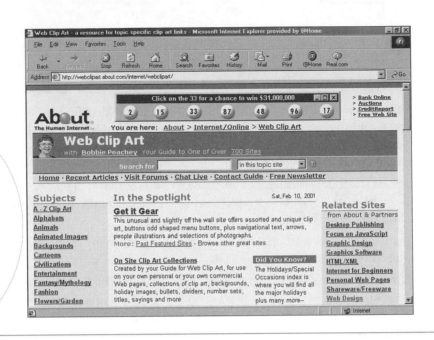

Figure 11.4

If it's free Web clip art you're looking for, visit Bobbie Peachey's About.com Web site. You'll find free images from A-Z for your Web site.

FTP Software

After you have your site designed and edits made on your computer, you have to upload your Web site files to your hosting server. For that, you're going to need an FTP software program. An FTP (File Transfer Protocol) program is quite simple to use. You simply take the complete directory structure of your site that you've created on your personal computer and duplicate it on your hosting server by transferring it over the Net.

Here's an important thing to remember. After you transfer your Web site files to your hosting server, your Web pages go live immediately. So, make sure that you've reviewed, proofread, and tested your pages before you FTP them to your hosting server.

One nice thing about FTP programs is that many of them are *shareware*. This means that you can download and use them for free! Finding them is easy. Just go to C/Net's Download.com, choose **Internet** from the menu page, then **FTP** from the menu page after that. Choose a free FTP program and download it to your computer.

THE SIX MOST IMPORTANT THINGS YOU NEED TO HAVE ON YOUR SITE

Great creative, catchy copy; good graphics; perfect coding—all these are necessary for a well-designed e-commerce site.

But there are some important fundamentals that must be on your Web store. These fundamentals have more to do with business than design and technology. They are an important element in assuring that your customers quickly know your product offers, have their questions answered, and feel comfortable buying from your site. In other words, it goes back to brand.

Like I mentioned before, your Web site is your brand and your brand is the experience your customer has with your Web store. The quality of the experience an online shopper has with you while visiting your Web store has a lot to do with whether they make a purchase and whether they'll buy from you again. You might get them to enter your store, but potential customers must have sufficient trust to actually buy from you. So keep these six important fundamentals in mind and you will go along way toward turning window shoppers into customers.

- Start them shopping right away
- Let them know who you are
- Give them the FAQs
- Provide full contact information
- List a Privacy Policy
- Provide shipping and handling costs

One: Shop Now!—Start Them Shopping Right Away

If you want the site to sell, (and that's why you're building an e-commerce site, right?) then sell potential customers right on your home page by sending them to your shopping areas from the home page as seen at www.outpost.com (see Figure 11.5). Place your best products in the front of your store—on your home page—and then direct them right to the product page to buy.

Create opportunities on your home page for impulse buys with a button or icon that says "Buy Now!" That's an important element of sales. Any salesperson worth their salt will tell you to always "Ask for the sale." Also, change your home page frequently. Just as news sites offer fresh content each day, you should offer fresh "content" in the form of "Today's Special" or promote seasonal items on your home page.

At the very least, you should integrate and link to holiday products and timely gift guides from your home page to reflect

- The Christmas holiday season
- Winter fun—skiing, skating, and clothing
- Mother's Day
- Father's Day
- Graduation

- Summer fun—beach, BBQs, and vacations
- Back to school
- Halloween
- Thanksgiving
- Special events—births, birthdays, anniversaries, and weddings

Although your home page should reflect who you are and what you can do for the online shopper, be sure that your home page sells.

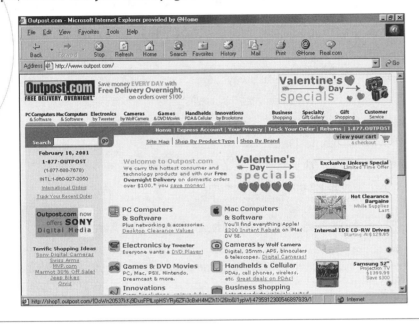

Figure 11.5

Outpost.com's home page offers impulse buys and holiday specials right on their home page.

Two: About Page—Let Them Know Who You Are

Shoppers would like to know from whom they're buying. Tell them. Have a section linked from your home page that provides a history of your business, who's involved, your business philosophy, and vision. Here's a chance to tell them your Unique Selling Position and sell the customer on why he or she should buy from you and how you're different from your competition.

Inform the window shopper how you do business, what values you hold, and what's important to the customer. Remember selling on the Net is not about you—it's about the customer. So make sure your About Page reflects this fact. The customer is not interested in you; only what your company will do for him or her.

Finally, you might consider adding a picture of you and your staff and some brief bios on your About Page. Online or off, people still want to do business with other people.

Three: FAQs—The First Place Your Customer Turns To

FAQs, or Frequently Asked Questions, are the first place shoppers will go to if they want quick and easy answers to their questions. A FAQ on your Web store is essential and will save both you and your customers a lot of time (see Figure 11.6).

The object of a FAQ is to list as many questions and answers a shopper might have as possible, such as

- Who are you?
- Where are you located?
- How can I contact you?
- What's the cost of shipping?
- Do you ship overseas?
- What are your return policies?
- How do I do a return?
- What are your product warrantees?

If you're selling certain categories of products that need a technical explanation, you can include those in your FAQs too.

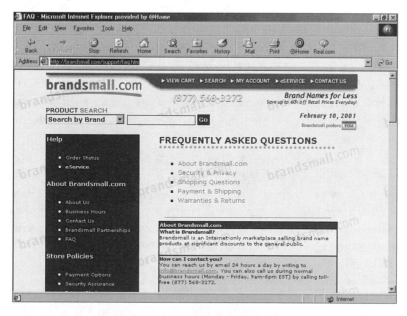

Figure 11.6

BrandsMall has a good example of what an e-commerce FAQ page looks like.

When organizing your FAQ page, list the questions at the top of the page and link them to the answers on the same page. Shoppers can read all the questions up front, find what they are looking for, and jump right down the page to the answer with the question included. If you have many questions you might consider breaking the questions up into categories, then creating a menu page of these categories as the main page of the FAQ.

Make sure that you link to your FAQs from your home page. A well-written FAQ will be one of your most popular pages, so make it easy to find.

Finally, link your answers to your questions to other pages on your site where appropriate, such as a map to your offices or links to products mentioned in your answers.

Finally, update your FAQs frequently from questions you receive via e-mail from your shoppers and customers. You can really cut down on the time-consuming effort of answering these e-mails by including your responses to these questions while updating your FAQs.

Four: Full Contact Information—Address, Phone, Fax, E-mail

Shoppers want to know that you have a real business. One of the best ways to show that is to give them a variety of ways to contact you. An e-mail address is not enough. In fact, it could be suspect. Here's the minimum amount of contact information you should have on your contact page:

- **Company address**—Display your full company mailing address. If you run your business out of your home and don't want to use that address, get a private mailbox at one of the commercial pack-and-ship businesses, such as Mailboxes Etc (MBE).
- **Phone numbers**—Provide your business phone and fax numbers. If working from your home, install a second line or business line. Connect an answering machine to it with a professional sounding message or hire an answering service for after hours or when your line is busy. Also list your fax number on your site.
- **E-mail addresses**—Provide different e-mail addresses for each department or function of your business. At the very least, have a different e-mail address for customer service.
- **Toll-free customer service number**—Your credibility as a business increases dramatically when shoppers see that you can be reached through a toll-free customer service number. These are not expensive and are worth the small investment. Publish the toll-free number on your contact page. If you'd rather not staff a customer service phone line, then outsource your 800 number to a service company that will answer your calls on a cost-per-call basis.

A good contact page can help build a level of trust in your business.

Five: Privacy Policy—Get on the Right Side of the FTC

Next to credit card security, privacy issues are second on the list of customer concerns. It's becoming vital that eBusinesses post their Privacy Policy on their site. Your customers want to know what you intend to do with the personal information you collect when they place an order on your site.

FTC Is on the Prowl

The FTC has made it known that if Web sites do not take the initiative in creating good Privacy Policies, it might intervene. If that happens, be prepared to follow government rules and pay the fines when you break them.

In a survey of 1,400 Web sites examining the privacy practices of commercial sites on the World Wide Web, the FTC found the vast majority of privacy policies on Web sites to be woefully inadequate.

What does this mean to you?

The FTC will be scrutinizing Web sites to see how they adhere to protecting consumer privacy, so it's important that you have a privacy policy on your site. And there's an easy way to do it.

The Direct Marketing Association has a section on their Web site with an easy-to-use Privacy Policy Page creation form at `www.the-dma.org/library/privacy/creating.shtml` (see Figure 11.7). Simply answer the questions and click the **submit** button and the DMA will send you a Privacy Policy Web page to post on your site. The Generate HTML Page button will allow you to see a copy of your statement onscreen as soon as you submit the form.

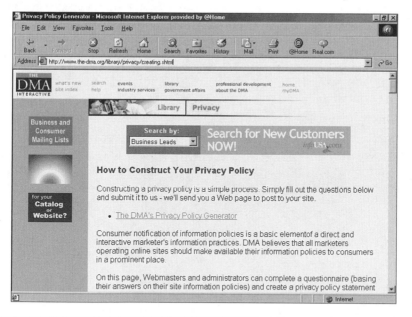

Figure 11.7

At this Direct Marketing Association's Web page you can create a Privacy Policy page for your Web site.

After you get your page, edit the page as needed. You might want to clarify some aspects, add your company name to the title of the page, or make other modifications to make the policy fit in with your site.

That's all there is to it. One last thing: Don't forget to make sure your company abides by your stated policy! The FTC will be checking.

Six: Shipping Policies—Tell Them the Full Cost of Shipping and Handling

Currently, up to 80% of all online shopping carts are abandoned by shoppers before reaching the final check out page. This number is appalling. Picture going to your local grocery store and seeing that 80% of the people filled their shopping carts with food and then left the store, leaving the carts in the aisles! That's what's happening to many online merchants today.

There are a number of reasons for this. Either the customers didn't feel they had enough information about the product to make a buying decision or they still had questions about the credibility of the merchant. But another reason for abandoned online shopping carts is that customers don't like surprises. One of the worst is being surprised with the true cost of a shipped product at the very end of the transaction.

Your customers need to know before they complete their transaction what the total amount of their order will be including shipping, handling, and applicable taxes. Customers should have the opportunity to see the changes made to the total transaction cost, such as changes to shipping methods and gift-wrapping charges, before they check out.

If you want to surprise your customers, surprise them with good offers and great service.

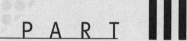

PART III

E-COMMERCE BASICS

CHAPTER **12**

THE 3 C'S OF E-COMMERCE

In This Chapter

- Learn the successful ingredients of an e-commerce site
- Learn how content can help support your online offer
- Discover how helping your visitors and customers interact with one another will increase repeat visits to your site
- Discover the different types of revenue streams that you can generate from your Web site other than selling a product or service

If you think that a successful Web store is just an electronic catalog—think again. Just slapping together pages and pages of product connected to an online shopping cart might get you sales, but customers don't live on offers alone. Along with the big C of commerce there are two other Cs you must consider to make your online store a success:

- **Content**—Selling your product and service in a context that's relevant to your target audience
- **Community**—Creating an online environment in which site visitors and your customers can participate in and feel a part of
- **Commerce**—The actual offers and revenue generating streams of your Web site

That's the e-commerce site equation—Content builds community, which establishes credibility, which generates sales.

CONTENT—TURN YOUR SITE INTO A LEARNING FOUNTAIN

Content is King on the Net. People use the Net to learn. That's what drives visitors to a Web site. Content can consist of information and community participation and even your e-commerce offers are considered content. Your site's content—whether it be information, community participation, or a product or service offer—must be interesting enough to make visitors come to your site, stay, and keep them coming back for more.

Encourage Contributions

Offer a way for visitors to submit articles, allowing their experiences to be included on your site or in your newsletter. Not only do you get free help in building your site content but you also gain long-term repeat visits from people whose content is included on your site.

Keep in mind that your content does not have to be closely related to your product, but to your prospective customers' needs and desires. To do this you need to make your Web store not only a place to buy things, but a Learning Fountain, too. That's what Paul Siegel recommends.

Paul Siegel is an author, an Internet marketing consultant, trainer, and speaker. He is the originator of the Learning Fountain at `learningfountain.com` (see Figure 12.1). His Learning Fountain is a Web site that influences visitors by helping them learn. He is known for saying "A Learning Fountain is a Web site that attracts prospects—not merely visitors—by helping them learn. While learning, they linger and buy." You should take a leaf out of his book and do the same for your Web store. By the way, his site is a good resource for building your online business.

According to Siegel, the top five popular sites are Learning Fountains. Yahoo! at `yahoo.com` is a Learning Fountain. The Motley Fool at `fool.com` and Consumer World at `consumerworld.org`—even `Amazon.com`, an e-commerce site—are all Learning Fountains.

Your e-commerce site should be a Leaning Fountain, too. Siegel divides the content of Learning Fountains into four types: Referrer, Informer, Advisor, and Context Provider.

The Referrer

No one knows the product or service you're selling better than you do. So use this knowledge to help your visitors understand all aspects of the product or service you sell. You might not have all the information they need, but with a little research, you can create a directory of sites on the Net that can provide the information they need and refer them to it.

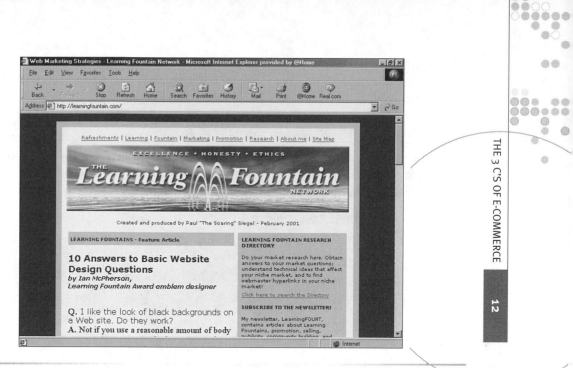

Figure 12.1

Paul Siegel's site is a great resource if you want to turn your site into a Learning Fountain.

For example, suppose you sell computer products. On your site you could provide a long list of product reviews comparing one product you sell to another. That would be a very time-consuming task. You could refer your customers to sites that specialize in these reviews, such as ZDNet at www8.zdnet.com/products/ and TechTV at www.techtv.com. Or suppose you sell tools for the do-it-yourself home improvement. You can refer customers to ImproveNet at improvenet.com where they will direct your customer to design ideas and project estimators.

Another idea is to refer shoppers to places where they can find free stuff, such as at Free Forum Network at www.freeforum.com or Free-Stuff.com at www.Free-Stuff.com. Shoppers will come to your site just to see your latest links to free stuff on the Net. If you get into the habit of refreshing your links, shoppers will return again and again for fresh referrals.

The Informer

Providing regular updated information on your site that is of practical use to your visitor will bring him to your site and entice him to make repeat visits. Include access to the latest news—even news on your product area—articles, and reminder services.

TIP

Add a Calendar Service to Your Site

Sign up for SuperCalendar's affiliate program and offer a calendar to non-techie users who have to manage lots of events. In addition to receiving a co-branded calendar, you also have the opportunity to generate revenue when your users sign up for SuperCalendar. Find it at www.SuperCalendar.com.

---

iSyndicate at iSyndicate.com aggregates free content from over 500 different providers in categories such as Top News and Weather, Sports News, Business and Finance, Entertainment and Lifestyles, Technology, and Health News—even Fun and Games. News providers include CNet, *Rolling Stone* magazine, CBS Market Watch, and *Sporting News*. And most of the content is free to use on your Web site.

A similar site to iSyndicate is Screaming Media at screamingmedia.com (see Figure 12.2). With Screaming Media, you can display news stories based on any keyword that you choose. The story headlines and full stories are integrated into your site pages.

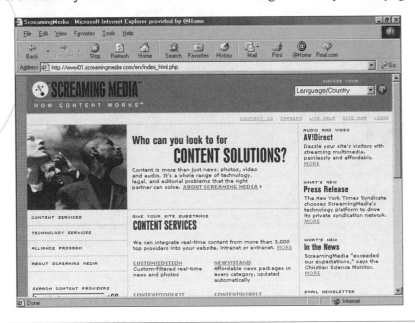

Figure 12.2

Screaming Media has a very simple interface and a quick and easy way to add news content to your Web site.

> **TIP**
>
> **Offer a Free Notification Service to Your Site Visitors**
>
> People have busy lives and there are lots of things to remember to do. You can offer a free personalized, practical e-mail notification service to your site for visitors to use to keep track of their daily, weekly, monthly, and yearly things to do. Find it at www.lifeminders.com.

The Advisor

Many shoppers need advice to make a buying decision. By making product advice available to your shoppers, you increase the possibility of making a sale. For advice to work, it must be trusted and credible.

A good example of this kind of advice can be found at Amazon.com. They pioneered the concept of reader reviews for the books they sell. Anyone who has purchased and read the book being offered for sale can write his or her own review. A peer review looks more objective to a potential customer and increases the possibility of a purchase. Shoppers trust other consumer's opinions more than the advertisers. Amazon.com also sells videos and customers who have bought a video also can review it on Amazon's site.

Although not real peer reviews like Amazon.com, CDNow at `cdnow.com` offers CD reviews from noted music critics and writers. c|Net at `www.computers.com` will not only review hardware products, but advise you on the best places to buy them. TechTV at `www.techtv.com` will also give you help on how to use your computer once you've brought it home.

Consumer Opinions on Your Site Pay-Off

According to Forester Research, 65% of community users rate the opinions of other consumers as important or somewhat important influences on their buying decision.

Written reviews are great to attract and retain customers and they generate longer visits, helping customers get more familiar with you and your products. If the thought of page after page of reviews on your site would add too much of an expense, think about using a quick numeric-rating system next to a product—such as one out of five stars. Your shopper can then just pick a rating and that rating could show up next to the product on your catalog page.

The Context Provider

Providing informational tools to shoppers to help them make a buying decision is another important content feature for your Web store. Consider giving the shopper the capability of solving a problem or determining their shopping need in the context of your site using online tools, such as checklists, calculators, evaluators, and simulators.

Let Your Shoppers Find the Exact Time Around the World

If shoppers need to contact a merchant or order by phone he or she should know which time zone they are in. Place a link to World Times on your site and offer this service. Find it at `www.hilink.com.au/times/`.

Context-specific information could be either product specific of shopping specific.

First, let's look at the product-specific tools. Suppose you had a mortgage brokerage service on the Web. To help shoppers of your service make a buying decision you might offer them a mortgage calculator on your site. They can calculate their monthly mortgage payment based on the type of mortgage they want, the interest rate, and any other options that would be available with the service. An example of this kind a shopping tool can be found at `www.bloomberg.com/cgi-bin/ilpc.cgi`.

Investors that visit The League of American Investors at `investorsleague.com` can run a simulation game that teaches a potential investor how to invest wisely.

Your context-specific information need not be product specific. You could offer several shopping tools at your site that make the shopping experience for consumers more helpful. You could offer some useful general tools at your Web store, such as links to currency exchanges, international holiday listings, and a world time calculator.

Free Currency Converter

A great little service to add to your site is an international currency converter. This way shoppers from anywhere in the world can see what the price of your products is in their currency. Find it at www.xe.net/currency/.

One of the best shopping tools that you can provide your customers is a link to a package tracking service, and the FedEx Web site has an excellent one. From their MultiCarrier Trace Page at grd.fedex.com/cgi-bin/rmt2000.exe?func=entry, a customer can track their package after it has been shipped by you by using any shipping company you choose. A great service tool to offer your customers is called LifeMinders at www.lifeminders.com. The LifeMinders program enables Web site visitors to sign up to receive timely, relevant tips and reminders each week about their home and garden, family, auto, entertainment, personal finance, personal events, health, and pets.

MAKE MONEY HOSTING CONTENT ON YOUR SITE

Wouldn't this be nice? Point your customers to content on the Web—and get money for doing it!

There are a number of companies on the Web today that offer all kinds of content that could fit well on your Web site and these companies will pay you for the privilege! Why would they do this? To acquire customers and increase revenue. They do this by creating tiny content packages that you place on your Web site. In return, you feed traffic back to their site. Their give-away content is a link back to full content hosted on their site. And here's the best part. This valuable content is FREE and there is no cost to join their affiliate program.

These affiliate programs come in many flavors and there's a very good chance that one of them would fit your e-commerce site. You can find content sites that provide

- News of all types
- Articles on many subjects
- Web search services right from your site
- Local news, weather, entertainment, and events
- Sports and stock information
- Downloadable music, photos, and Webcasts
- Auctions
- Even consumer reviews and opinions

News and Features

If your online business serves a local market you could consider joining an affiliate program that offers Local news, weather, entertainment, and events. AOL Digital City's affiliate program (`home.digitalcity.com/chicago/affiliate/`) lets you offer guides to local restaurants, clubs, attractions, live music, museums, art and cultural events, movies, and more. You just add one of their local content boxes on to your site, and every time someone clicks on that box, you get paid $.03 (see Figure 12.3).

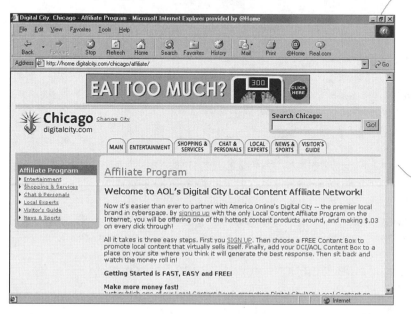

Figure 12.3

Digital City offers local content for your Web site.

For more general news, affiliate programs from InterestAlert! and Strategy.com can fill the bill. InterestAlert! (`interestalert.com/remote/siteia/affiliate.html`) lets you put news headlines and summaries on your pages. Categories include top news stories, women's news, political news and commentary, sports news, a stock index, and a large variety of industry news. Your site gets paid $.0025 per paid view on the news pages they serve.

There's also an affiliate program for one of the biggest content sites on the Web. When you join About's affiliate program (`affiliates.about.com/index.htm`), you can take advantage of a wide range of quality content from more than 700 of their expert Guides (see Figure 12.4). Each Guide specializes in one area and provides in-depth information about his or her subject. You can link to an individual Guide's content that is relevant to your company's interests. You also can add the ability for shoppers to search exclusively within your topic area, or search the entire About network. About will pay a standard rate of $0.01 for each qualified click-through from your site to About.

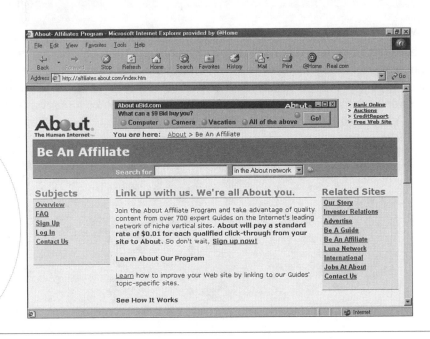

Figure 12.4

About offers affiliates access to hundreds of thousands of pages of content in more than 800 categories of information.

Web, Media, and Consumer Opinion Searches

There are several Web search affiliate programs that you can join to add a Web search service for your customers to use right from your site.

AltaVista's program (doc.altavista.com/affiliate/) offers more than just a search service to your site visitors (see Figure 12.5). Not only do they offer normal Web search capabilities right from your site, but your visitors can also search for up to the minute breaking news from around the World, multimedia images, audio/MP3 and video files, and even stock quotes, stock news, research, and analyst opinion. In addition, your visitors can search local indices or search Web pages in your users' native language. AltaVista has two payment programs. A Standard Program that pays $.02 every time a user clicks on their search box or uses any of the other available features from your site, and a Premier Program that pays $.04 per click.

> **JARGON**
>
> **What's a Webcast?**
>
> Webcasting is the process of delivering media content—voice, film, video, animation—on demand over the Internet.

Global Music Network's program (ap.gmn.com/) not only offers downloadable music, but the news headlines plus story extracts from music world, Webcast features that offer the latest in online streaming audio and video with a new Webcast featured every day, and features and photos of popular artists. You're paid $.05 each time someone clicks on a link to Global Music Network from your site.

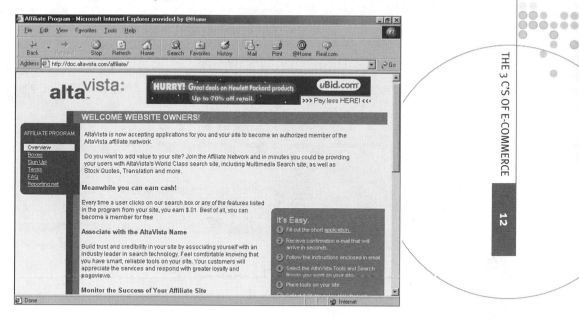

Figure 12.5

With AltaVista's affiliate program, you can place its search services on any page of your Web site.

Another entertainment affiliate program content provider is Boxerjam (`www.boxerjam.com/affiliate`), a game show content site. Game Show entertainment is hot right now, leading the ratings on TV and is the number one reason new users are flocking to the Web. Boxerjam provides a game link that launches free games and chances to win thousands of dollars in cash and prizes from your site. One popular game is a puzzle called KnockOut! and offers original, new content each day. With games like Boxerjam on your site, you can increase traffic to your site and keep them coming back for more. As an affiliate, your company can earn $0.75 for every person who clicks through to a Boxerjam game or banner on your site, signs up for more fun, or plays a free game show at Boxerjam.

All-in-One Content Programs

Besides the affiliate programs already mentioned, there are three multiple content programs that you can offer visitors to your Web site.

With CNET's program (`www.cnet.com/webbuilding/0-2633572.html`) (see Figure 12.6) you can get access CNET's award-winning news headlines, price comparison services, tech question and answer service, and the largest free software download library on the Internet. Each time you pass a user along to CNET, your company earns $.02.

When your company becomes an affiliate of Lycos (`www.lycos.com/affiliateprogram/`), you can choose one or more of its dynamic Lycos Network Content Boxes. There are several Content Boxes to choose from. Each contains useful information from around the Lycos Network and the kind of information that can help bring users back to your site. You can offer your visitors a general search service, a Safe Search for Kids service, access to small business articles that help users run and build their small business, in addition to sports scores, a people finder, stock information, software downloads, news, and TV listings. Your site can earn up to $.03 every time someone clicks through.

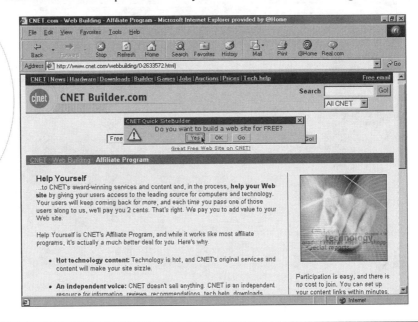

Figure 12.6

Add CNET's news headlines, price comparison services, tech question and answer service, and the largest free software download library on the Internet when you join their affiliate program.

GoTo.com (www.goto.com) offers two affiliate program that are designed to increase your Web revenue and encourage repeat usage. The first is a Web search service that pays you $.03 each time your visitors search the Web using GoTo.com from your site. The second, is an integrated auction service search performed on your site, through which you can earn $7.50 for every 1,000 auction searches. The search results are customized and are integrated into your Web site.

COMMUNITY—BUILDING AN INTERACTIVE COMMUNITY

Siegel had one more important Learning Fountain—the Learning Community. People go online not just to be informed but also to interact with other people. Filling this need at your Web store will help you turn shoppers into customers and customers into repeat buyers.

Content can attract shoppers to your site. But to generate a continuous flow of repeat visitors, you need to provide access to an interactive community.

Community is just as important as content when planning an e-commerce site. If done properly, community features on your site will increase the number of page-views per visit, giving you opportunities to offer merchandise to your shoppers.

Community features can be used to encourage customers to return to your site. Establishing a Learning Community can help shoppers develop expertise through the interaction with other shoppers who visit your site. Asking questions, discussing problems, raising issues, and the general camaraderie that develops in an interactive community breeds a kind of loyalty that is beneficial to the success of your Web store. And loyalty breeds repeat visits.

Another benefit of an interactive community is that it can add content to your site. Discussion boards and forums, chat rooms, and discussion lists can provide content because they generate information by their very nature. You can take a short quote from one of your forums or discussion lists and post it each day on your site as fresh content to generate interest in your product or offer. This type of content can act as a traffic magnet, bringing continuous visitors to your site.

Communities can build your business. Think about it. The more times a shopper visits your site, the more familiar they are with it. The more familiar they are, the more comfortable they might get making a purchase from you instead of some unknown merchant a mouse click away. Look at it this way. Communities are sticky. Visitors tend to spend longer periods of time at your site than before. The stickier they are, the more loyal they get. Loyalty builds trust and trust is the currency of business.

TIP

Build Your Community with No Programming

"Build Your Own Community" offers software to buy that lets you build guest books, discussion forums, polls, and many more great interactive features, including start pages for visitors that direct them right to your site. Find "Build Your Own Community" at www.buildacommunity.com.

You should include as many interactive community tools as possible on your Web site. The major tools of the interactive community are discussion boards or forums, chat rooms, discussion lists, and newsletters.

Discussion Boards or Forums

Everyone has an opinion and most people want to know that their opinions are taken seriously. Some enjoy helping other people and others have a desire to learn more about a subject, issue, or product. These desires cause people to gravitate to online communities. As word gets out that serious discussions are going on at your Web store and if you can promote those discussions on your site, shoppers will come back on a regular basis to see what's discussed next.

Discussion boards and forums—or *message boards* as they are sometimes called—provide a bulletin board of threaded discussions. They start with a series of subjects or questions that readers can post their comments or answers to. Later readers read the posts and add their two cents to the thread of postings—either to the original subject or in response to a reader's posting—until the discussion dies out after available feedback is exhausted.

Visitors to your site are allowed to read any and all posts. But if they want to participate in the discussion, they usually need to register and get a username and password. When they register, this gives you an opportunity to collect some demographic and interest information for marketing uses.

Discussion boards need to be programmed. But if you don't mind using a message board service, you can add a discussion board to your site for free! A free discussion board service and one that offers many options is Delphi Forums at `Delphi.com` (see Figure 12.7). Using their Web interface, you can create a customized message board that resides on their server but links to it from your site—and they also provide a free live chat room for your site's use.

Figure 12.7

Set up a free customized message board on your site with Delphi Forums.

Chat Rooms

The stickiest interactive community tool of all is the live chat room. Having a live chat room on your Web site can keep visitors on your site for hours at a time. That's a lot of face time for one Web page. During this time, you could place offers on the chat discussion page pitching your products or service. You could even join in the chat about your product or product category, identifying yourself as the merchant and offering to answer any questions about your company, its products, and the types of products it sells.

There is a downside to chat rooms. Unlike discussion boards where you can read all the messages posted there and remove any that are deemed unfit for your board, chat rooms are open free-for-alls. To supervise them would take a staff of people monitoring them 24 hours a day. To solve this problem, you could open the chat room at certain times of the day when monitoring is available.

Like discussion boards, you don't need to set up a resource-demanding chat room on your server or your hosting company's server. There are many free chat services on the Net that you can use by providing a link from your site to the chat services server. As mentioned before, one such service is Delphi at `Delphi.com`. Another free chat service is FreeChat at `www.sonic.net/~nbs/unix/www/freechat/`. You can download the free chat software from their site and install it on your server. After installation, users of your chat room need not download any software. The chat room can be used through their Web browser.

Hello? Is Anybody There?

Nothing kills a chat room tool like people dropping by and asking, "Is anybody there?" and having no response. That is why a chat moderator should always be present when you have your chat room open.

Here's another use for chat. How about real-time customer service? Lands End at `landsend.com` provides live customer service through a chat interface. If you need help with a product, you click the **Live Help** button and it opens a chat window and initiates a chat session with a live customer service representative.

Discussion Lists

Although discussion boards and chat rooms require that shoppers visit your site, there are other ways to build a community with shoppers that do not require a site visit, yet build loyalty and keep your Web store in their mind. One of the best and least expensive ways to build community is through the use of an e-mail discussion list.

A discussion list is a discussion board via e-mail. Subscribers to your discussion list receive e-mails on a regular basis containing comments that are echoed to every other subscriber on the list. Every subscriber on the list receives every post to the list. All posts to the list are done via an e-mail message sent to the list. In a typical discussion list, the listserver software enables a member to send his or her message to the list address, and then broadcasts or echoes that message out to all the list members—all within a few minutes.

A well-executed discussion list can gain wide visibility and a very good reputation for your business and for the products or services you sell. Members of a popular discussion list could number in the thousands and offer a great opportunity to sell your product or service.

Drop Your Programmer—Install Programs Yourself

A multitude of free cgi scripts are readily available on the Web. One such site is Matt's Script archive. He has guest books, counters, discussion boards, and forums—even search engines for your site. Check them out at www.worldwidemart.com/scripts.

You might use a discussion list as a communications platform for customers who use your manufactured product. If you sell other company's products, you can use the discussion list to inform your subscribers about your product's category. For example, suppose you sell collectible first-edition books. You could form a discussion list for collectors to exchange ideas about collector books. You could participate and answer their questions about first edition books, showing off your knowledge of the market and building trust in the eyes of your subscribers for your business.

And where do you get the listserver software to run a list? Do you need to place a program on your site? No. You can use one of several free—there's that great little word again—listserver services on the Net. One is MSN's ListBot at `www.listbot.com` and another is Yahoo! Groups at `groups.yahoo.com/` (see Figure 12.8).

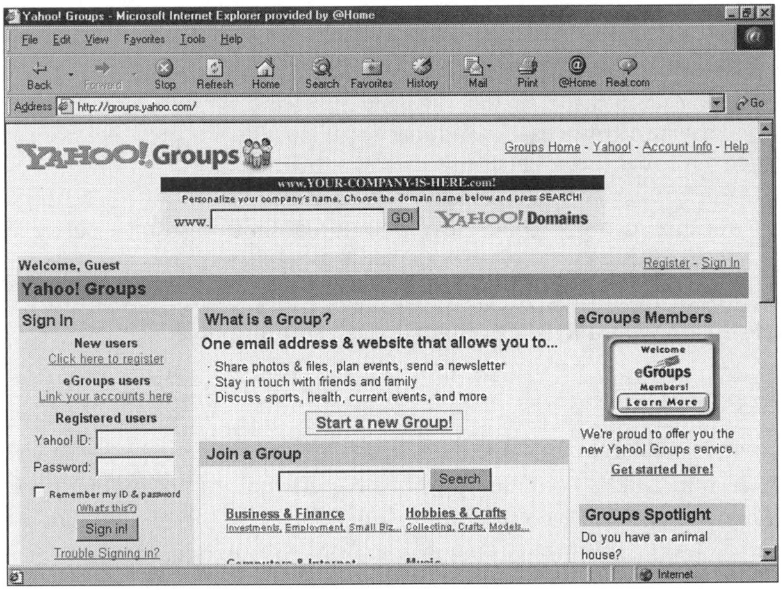

Figure 12.8

With Yahoo! Groups you can set up your own private discussion list for your shoppers. Your shoppers can send and receive e-mails, schedule meetings, share files and photos, or have private group chats.

There are three types of discussion lists:

- Unmoderated discussion lists
- Discussion list digests
- Moderated discussion lists

An unmoderated discussion list sends all messages received out to all members of the list. If the number of members on the list were small and not very active, then this would not be a problem. But if the list is large and very active, it could generate hundreds of messages a day and swamp the users of the list.

One solution is to create a list digest. The digest collects all the messages sent to the list first, then bundles them, and e-mails them—in one e-mail—to the list members. The digest can be either daily or weekly.

Another way to cut down on the number of e-mails to the list is to have a moderated discussion list. You'll find that the free listserver services only provide what's called unmoderated discussion lists. That means that all posts that are sent to the list appear without any review. If you want to control what is said on the list or the number of posts sent to the list, you need to bring the listserver software in-house.

Web Marketing Today (`www.wilsonweb.com/reviews/free-lists.htm`) has a good review of free mailing list programs. They review eGroups (now Yahoo! Groups), `OneList.com`, `Topica.com`, and `ListBot.com`. The review explains the main features and points out differences and advantages of each.

Newsletters

Unlike discussion boards, chat rooms, and discussion lists, a newsletter is a one-way communication device that does not allow interaction. But it's a very good way to stay in touch with your visitors and keeps your company in the front of their minds. With the typical newsletter, members can subscribe and unsubscribe freely. You need a listserver software such as Majordomo (`www.greatcircle.com/majordomo`) to manage the list and send out your electronic newsletter.

An electronic newsletter can be used in a number of different ways.

The most basic use of a newsletter is to keep your subscribers informed about what's new on your site. You can announce new features, new products, or new promotions that can be used to drive subscribers back to your site on a regular basis. Use your newsletter to nurture potential customers until they're ready to purchase a product from you or sign a contract.

Or you can use your newsletter to send out information that subscribers can use, such as movie, book, or music reviews or upcoming updates to the software they've purchased. You also can enhance your reputation—and get business—through well-written articles in your product or service subject area. You also can archive these information-type newsletters on your site, adding more content for shoppers to view when they visit.

How Long Should Your Newsletter Be?
If you have valuable information to say in your newsletter, don't be afraid of your newsletter's length. Give people valuable information on a topic they're passionate about, and they'll read every word.

There's even a revenue-generating opportunity with electronic newsletters. If your newsletter is unique and offers information or even support that consumers can't get anywhere else, you can solicit paid subscriptions. Or you can ask the manufacturers of your products to sponsor your newsletter, in effect, selling advertising space.

Finally, don't be shy about asking visitors to your site to subscribe. One of the best ways to obtain subscribers is to ask visitors to sign up when they first enter your Web site. Place your subscription offer on your home page and tell them what they'll receive as a subscriber. You also might want to offer an incentive to sign-up, such as a $10 discount coupon or perhaps a free demo of your software.

COMMERCE—ADDING MULTIPLE REVENUE STREAMS

The Net not only evolves quickly, it also quickly evolves those that are on it. Take Yahoo! for example. Only a few short years ago it was a simple search engine. Then it added e-mail, games, investment information, white pages, and other services, and became a portal. In its latest incantation it has added online store hosting and has evolved into an e-commerce site. The other portals, such as Excite at www.excite.com/, Hotbot at www.hotbot.com, and AltaVista at www.altavista.com, have done the same.

Even e-commerce sites have evolved. Amazon.com sold only books. Now they're selling movies, CDs, electronics, toys, games, and a variety of other products chasing the commerce dream. And what dream are they chasing? It's called *multiple revenue streams*. Multiple revenue streams goes beyond simple product sales. Adding as many of these streams to your site will leverage your site traffic and generate additional income.

Here are some multiple revenue stream possibilities:

- **Product or Service Sales Income**—This is the main revenue stream of your Web store. It's what you built your eBusiness around and should be your prime focus. It's the bread and butter of your business and should be your top priority.

- **Advertising Income**—After you've built up traffic to your site, you can consider turning some of that traffic into revenue. Advertisers are always looking for ways to get their product or service message out to potential customers. They know that placing ads on Web sites that cater to shoppers that might buy their product is a wise way to spend their advertising dollars. Banner advertising can generate $5 to $75 CPM (cost per thousand per impression). That means you could earn anywhere from $.005 cents to $.075 cents each time an advertiser's banner ad is shown to your site visitor. It might not sound like much at first, but if you had thousands and thousands of your site visitors viewing an ad, the dollars add up fast.

- **Referral Income**—Another income source is to refer your shoppers to another company's Web site. These are the affiliate programs that we discussed earlier. You might consider referring your shoppers to a non-competitive merchant in exchange for a paid click-through or a percentage of the sale. Income can vary from five cents to $1 per click-through or from 5% to 20% of sales.

Develop several of these income streams simultaneously and you can grow your site revenue beyond your product or service offers.

STAYING UP TO DATE IN E-COMMERCE

The Internet can help keep your online business on top of what's happening in the e-commerce world with current market intelligence. Not only can you do research on your particular market space right from your PC, but you can also gather market intelligence about your competitors.

Web sites such as eMarketer (`e-land.com`) are a comprehensive, objective, and easy-to-use resource for any business interested in the Internet. And the information on their site is free to all. eMarketer provides statistics, news, and information on all aspects of the Internet. They aggregate, filter, organize, and analyze data from hundreds of leading research sources and put the information into handy, easy-to-read tables, charts, and graphs and provide analysis, statistical estimates, projections, and long-term trends for the evolving Internet marketplace. Their e-reports offer a comprehensive and accurate picture of the Internet marketplace.

Another free information source for market research is WebCMO research (`webcmo.com`). The marketing information they offer is not about what people have bought, but why people choose a product and the different market segments to which they belong. Their research is not only about the past market activities but also about future market changes and explores winning Web-marketing strategies. You can also subscribe to their free *Journal of Web Marketing Research,* a weekly publication about Web-marketing research and strategy. Topics in the Journal include online branding, effectiveness of Web business promotion, targeting demographically online, one-to-one marketing, market segmentation, advertisers' preferences, and other subjects relating to market research and strategy. And don't be put off by the statistical semantics of these topics. The Journal reports are all in plain English.

Free Demographic Reports

Get up-to-date free demographic data to target your market from the Right Site (`easidemographics.com`). Use their search interface to narrow your search by geography (ZIP Codes, regions, and so on) and type of data (quality of life, income, and so on) for detailed market-specific statistics and reports (see Figure 12.9).

But the flow of information and market intelligence doesn't stop here. There are many other Web sites that provide valuable resources too. They include

- **Cyber Atlas** (`cyberatlas.internet.com/`)—Gathers online research from the best data resources to provide a complete review of the latest surveys and technologies available.

- **NUA** (`nua.ie`)—Offers a compendium of news articles, reports, and surveys on all facets of the online world.

- **Deep Canyon** (`www.deepcanyon.com`)—Provides market research to help companies on the Net make informed strategic decisions.

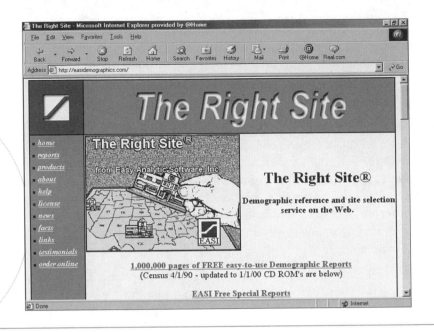

Figure 12.9

Get up-to-date free demographic data to target your market from The Right Site.

And what about your competition? Where on the Net can you conduct competitive-intelligence research on them? The first place to start, of course, is the search engines. Just type in your competitor's name and visit their site. There's much that can be gleaned about their business model by just perusing their Web site. Next, financial data on public companies has always been available but now is even more accessible on the World Wide Web.

At Hoover's Online (`hoovers.com`) you can find the income statements and balance sheets of nearly 2,500 public companies. The service is not free, but Hoover's Online lets anyone download free half-page profiles of 10,000 (mostly public) companies. Another free source is Inc. Magazine. *Inc. Magazine*'s own Inc. Top 500 database (`inc.com/500`) lists the fastest-growing companies in the country and provides information about thousands of privately held companies that have made the list in the past eight years. This information includes revenue information, profit-and-loss percentages, number of employees, and Web links (see Figure 12.10).

Go to their home page at `www.freedgar.com` and you are presented with an alert box that says little of what they offer is free anymore!

You can also find the latest news on your competitors at NewsDirectory.com (`www.NewsDirectory.com/`). This site lists more than 2,000 newspapers, business journals, magazines, and computer publications. You can search any number of periodicals to locate news stories on your competitors. Some of the periodicals are more easily searched than others, and some charge fees.

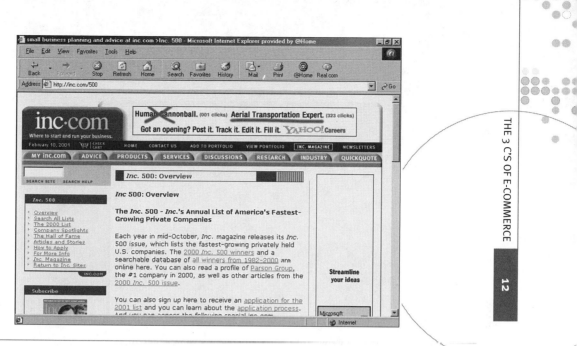

Figure 12.10

You can access more than 11,000 public, private, and international companies from Inc.com.

And don't forget the online grapevine. The Net can give you a good opportunity to listen in on conversations about you or your competitors. This might represent one of the best market research values on the Web. The grapevine I'm referring to is mad up of the newsgroups and discussion groups around the Web. Online consumers are always talking about products, services, and the companies that provide them in these community gabfests. One of the best places to listen in on these conversations is Deja.com's Usenet Discussion Service (www.deja.com). At Deja.com, you can search keywords such as the name of your competitor or the product or service that you offer and see what the Web community is saying about them. Other places to check out include Remarq (www.remarq.com) and Liszt (www.liszt.com), searchable directories of e-mail discussion groups.

Finally, are you contemplating filing a patent or want to know if your proposed business methodology has already been tied up? Then check out the Patent and Trademark Office Web site (uspto.gov). There you can get a good idea about whether or not someone has filed a patent on a product or business methodology that you are considering.

 A Caveat!

When reading posts on any discussion board or newsgroup, keep in mind that what's posted there may or may not be accurate. After all, these are posts from people whose credibility and motivation is unknown to you. So be sure to check the information posted when you can.

CHAPTER 13

MEETING THE CUSTOMER'S EXPECTATIONS

In This Chapter

- Learn what customers expect from a Web store
- Learn the Big Five of online shopping—selection, price, service, convenience, and security—and how to apply them to your online store
- Discover how to build confidence in your customers so they will buy from your online store
- Learn how to sell to the world

To paraphrase President Clinton, "It's the customer, stupid."

Shoppers don't care about your site, your business, or your life. What they care about is themselves. When they come to your site they want to see if there's anything there that interests them. They want to know, "What's in it for me!" They come to your Web store with a certain set of expectations. Your job as a Web merchant is to meet those expectations.

Your customers expect to find what they came for, a fair price, a good selection of product, great service, and a secure and safe place to shop. In other words, they're looking for the Big Five of online shopping. And if they're from "out of town"—that is, another county— they're also looking for a site that talks their language!

THE BIG FIVE OF ONLINE SHOPPING

Everything on your site should be about the customer and designed from the customer's point of view. Your customer not only needs a reason to buy, but to buy easily and safely. They want to know right away if their visit to your site is going to save them time and money and if their shopping experience will be a pleasant one. Can they find what they want easily? Can they place an order in a variety of ways? Can they find your customer service pages, shipping and handling fees, and return policies without spending a large amount of time digging through your site looking for them?

These are the customer's expectations and you have to meet them if you want your online business to be a success. If your site is designed with the Big Five of online shopping in mind, you'll provide your customers a pleasant shopping experience and a reason to buy from your online store again.

The Big Five of online shopping are selection, price, service, convenience, and security.

Selection—Do You Have What They Want?

Shoppers come to the Net for the vast selection of product and services that are available at the click of a mouse. Whether shoppers find you through search engines, store directories, or through your own marketing and promotion, after they arrive at your site they want to know you have what they're looking for. Don't build an impression in the shoppers' mind that you sell computer software or have an online bookstore then offer only a small selection of titles.

JARGON

> ### What's a Search Engine?
> Web surfers use search engines—or Web site directories as some of them are called—to find particular Web sites that they're looking for. Yahoo! at `yahoo.com`, AltaVista at `altavista.com`, HotBot at `hotbot.com`, Lycos at `lycos.com`, and Go at `go.com` are some of the larger search engines and Web directories.

When building a small to medium-sized business you need to focus your product or service offering. Look at your unique selling position. If done correctly, it tells you the market you're targeting and the unique product or service you're selling. If you've done your homework and created a compelling unique selling position, the shopper will feel that your Web store offers the best selection on the Net.

Offering a good selection to shoppers is not necessarily a numbers game. The quality of your selection is much more important for a small Web business than the quantity. The following are some good examples of small sites that work in large product categories yet deliver a good selection of product offerings for their market.

Music Stores

You don't have to be a CDNow.com or an Amazon.com to be successful selling music CDs on the Web. Acres of Historic Videos & CDs at `stores.yahoo.com/ggroup` (see Figure 13.1) sells hard to find CD sets. Shoppers that come to their Web store will find a good product selection specializing in hard-to-find classic music CD Sets. They organize their offerings into 3-CD sets focusing on subjects like Jazz, Disco, Country, and Pop.

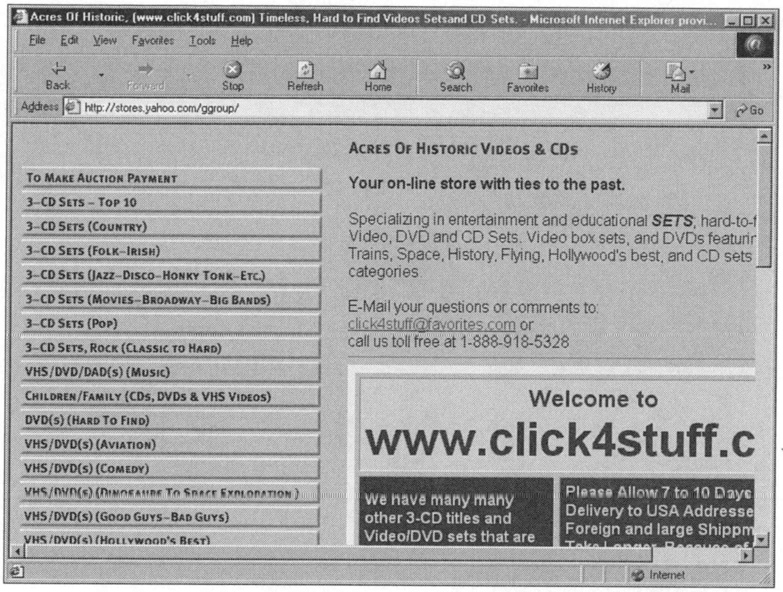

Figure 13.1

Acres of Historic Videos & CDs has carved out a unique niche in the online music sales channel.

Aramusic at `stores.yahoo.com/ara-music` sells Arabic music CDs from Lebanon, Iraq, Syria, and Egypt. And Harmony Marketplace at `stores.yahoo.com/harmonymarketplace` carries the best in barbershop music on CDs.

Software Stores

You don't have to be a NECX (`necxdirect.necx.com`) or CompUSA (`compusa.com`), to competitively sell software on the Net. You can offer a specialized selection of software to shoppers and still give them a good selection in the category you choose.

AccountingShop at `stores.yahoo.com/2020software/` sells only accounting software whereas Bargain Bin Software at `stores.yahoo.com/bargainbins/` sells software starting at $12.95.

Pet Stores

The large pet stores on the Net like Petco (`petopia.com`) and PetsMart (`petsmart.com`) carry a wide variety of pet supplies for all kinds of pets. But a small store like BunnyLuv-Essentials (`stores.yahoo.com/shopbunnyluv`) offers a nice selection of rabbit care supplies, toys, hay, food, and grooming tools. A shopper who comes to their site would be pleased with the selection of product in that subject area. Houndz in the Hood at stores.yahoo.com/houndzinthehood (see Figure 13.2) offers only coats for Dachshunds, Mini Poodles, and Italian Greyhounds.

As you can see, you can run with the big dogs of e-commerce if you choose your product or service well and deliver the best selection in that category.

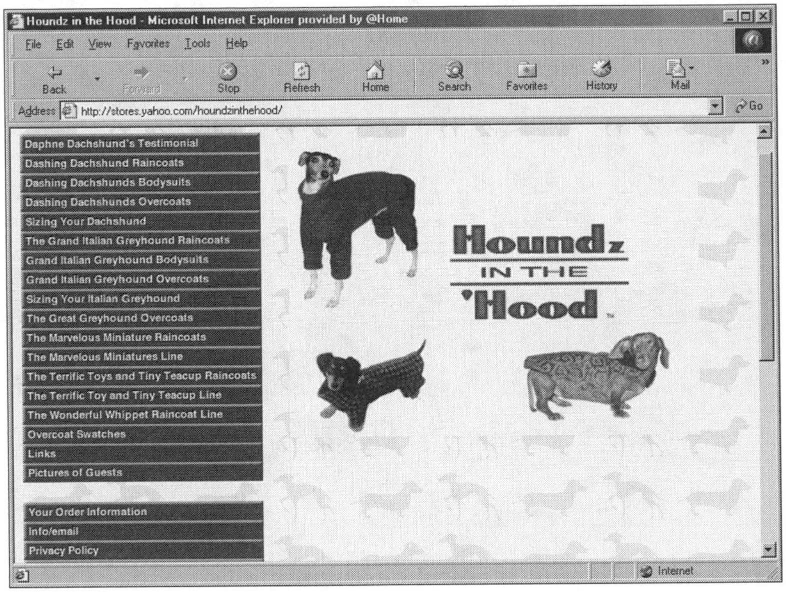

Figure 13.2

The ultimate in niche marketing to a large audience—coats for Dachshunds.

Price—Is Your Price Right?

What kind of price animal is your e-business? That's a question you need to answer. And after you answer it, your Web store must demonstrate it.

Do you sell products or services at a discount? Do you want to be a low-cost leader in your market niche? Or are you a value-added reseller? Do you add additional value to products in the form of some kind of service charging a higher price? Do you set the price of the products and services you sell—or does the consumer? What did you decide on as your pricing model back in Chapter 4, "Creating a Unique Selling Position?"

Whatever pricing model you decide on, you need to make it very clear to the shoppers that come to your site. Consumers do not like surprises. If you promoted your site as the low-price leader, your prices should show it. If you're a boutique shop and charge better than average prices then show the value you've added to your products or service. Make it very clear what you charge and why and be sure it fits the expectations of your site visitors.

Money Talks—Baloney Walks

If you claim to be the low-price leader, put a shopping bot on your site to prove it. Comparison shopping sites like mySimon at `mysimon.com` allow you to place their shopping bots on your site for your shoppers' use.

Another important thing is not to hide your prices. Nothing annoys a shopper more than going through the process of ordering from you, entering their credit card number, and then being told what the total shipped price is. Be sure that you give your shoppers all the information they need to make a buying decision—upfront—before they buy. A site that does a good job of informing its customers about shipping is DVD Empire at `www.dvdempire.com` (see Figure 13.3).

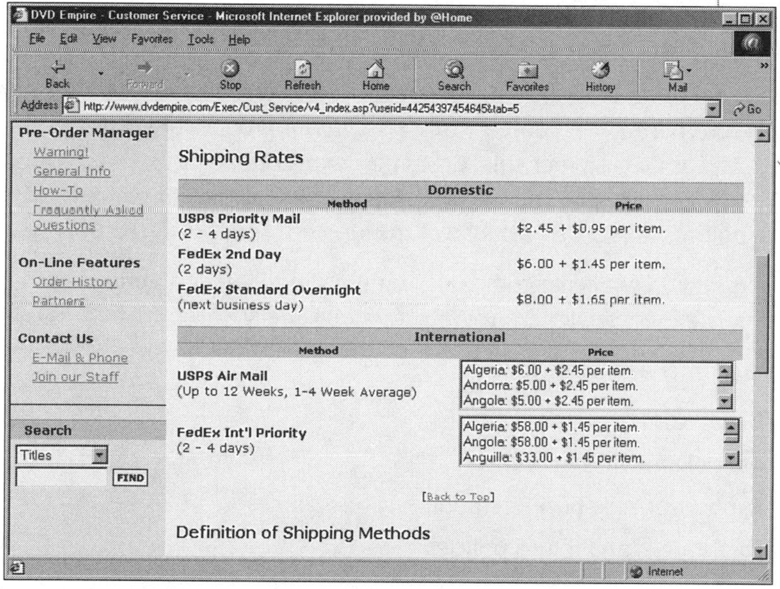

Figure 13.3

DVD Empire does a good job of telling the shopper before he orders what his shipping and handling charges will be.

Don't draw the customer into the buying process with low prices then surprise them after they place their order with exorbitant shipping and handling charges on the order confirmation page. If you want to see a shopper bolt for the door, this is the way to do it.

What About International Surcharges?

DHL Airways, the U.S. arm of DHL Worldwide Express will soon let companies go to DHL's Web site and learn what government-imposed charges exist in any country in the world. You can direct consumers to their site to know in advance what the total international surcharges will be. Find it at `www.dhl-usa.com/bs`.

So how do you inform the shopper of your shipping and handling charges? You can do it in one of two ways.

- Provide an easy-to-find section on your site that lists and easily explains your shipping and handling charges.
- Present an order confirmation page to the buyer that lists the price of the product and all applicable shipping and handling charges. Give the buyer the total shipped price before you request their credit card number.

I suggest that you do both. That way the shopper fully understands the total amount of the sale before he or she completes the purchase. Don't forget to include any and all applicable taxes in the total of the sale.

Service—How Do You Measure Up?

You've put a lot of effort into building your Web store. You've created a good selection of product for your market category and priced your product or service to sell. But that's not enough to earn a customer sale. Customers expect to be serviced so customer service is a top priority for your Web site. Because you're not dealing with customers face-to-face, your service policies must instill a sense of trust in your shoppers.

Many current e-commerce companies on the Net today don't understand this simple fact. Consumers expect service. Your Web store must deliver it.

Good customer service includes

- E-mail confirmations
- Multiple means of contact
- Support outside business hours
- Guarantees and return policies

E-mail Confirmations

After a customer clicks the **Place My Order** button, he or she immediately wonders what will become of his or her order. It's only natural that sending an order into the vastness of cyberspace can cause a certain amount of consternation. You can relieve much of your customer's worries—and avoid frustrations—by sending a series of e-mail confirmations that informs the customer of the status of his or her order right through the sales and shipping process.

As soon as the order is placed, an e-mail confirming that the order was received should be sent to the customer. The e-mail message should include a complete record of the transaction, including the following information:

- An order number
- What was ordered

- Who ordered it
- Where it will be shipped
- Total amount of the sale including all shipping and handling costs
- Customer service contact information in case the customer has a question about the order

Don't Include the Customer's Credit Card Number

Remember that when you send any e-mail confirmation to your customer do *not* send his or her credit card number in the e-mail. E-mail is *not* secure and should never be used to send sensitive information over the Net.

Another e-mail message should be sent confirming that the product ordered is in stock and when it will be shipped. A third e-mail message should be sent after the product is actually shipped containing the name and tracking number of the shipping company that was used.

Finally, send an e-mail to your customers after they have received their orders asking them for feedback and even offer them a discount on their next purchase if they buy within the next few weeks.

Provide Multiple Means of Contact

Always provide a number of different ways that a customer can contact your customer service department. There are several ways to do this.

List your customer service e-mail address on your Web site and include in it all e-mail correspondence with your customer. In addition, tell people where you are located. Include your company's address, telephone number, and fax number on your Web site. DVD Empire at `www.dvdempire.com` does this very well on its site (see Figure 13.4).

List a telephone number for customer service. Let customers know when a live person will answer the telephone. If you use an answering machine, be sure you leave a message that tells the caller when they can expect their call to be returned.

Invest in a toll-free telephone number and list it on your site. Not only is a toll-free number relatively inexpensive, it goes a long way toward building a level of consumer confidence in your business. If you'd rather not deal with the hassles and expense of staffing a toll-free customer service line, then out-source it. There are many service companies that will staff a customer service line for you on a fee-per-call basis. Finally, think about offering live chat on your site and use it for customer service.

Provide Support Outside of Business Hours

Although your Web store is available to customers 24 hours a day, 7 days a week, 365 days a year, you are not. So, to support customers outside of normal business hours, be sure your Web store has a FAQ section. Even though a FAQ cannot tell a customer if his product is in stock or when it was shipped, it is useful for providing clear instructions about how to use your product or service and troubleshooting tips in case customers run into trouble after hours.

Remember that it pays to keep all line of communications open with your customers and to provide a quick response to customer e-mails.

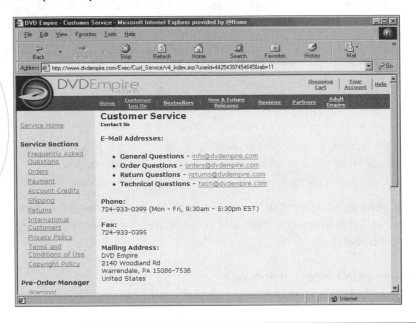

Figure 13.4

DVD Empire lists its complete contact information, giving the shopper multiple ways to reach them.

Guarantee the Sale and Provide Clear Return Policies

One of the best ways to gain customer confidence is to offer them a money-back satisfaction guarantee. As an e-business, you should offer a money back guarantee with your products and clearly state your guarantee policy on your Web site.

Offer a Satisfaction Guarantee

There's no excuse not to offer your shoppers a 100% satisfaction guarantee. This will build up trust in you and your e-business.

If you prefer not to offer any kind of money back guarantee, then list your terms of sale and your return policy and procedures on your site. Remember that shoppers don't like surprises. Be sure they understand the terms of their purchase before they push the **Buy Now** button.

Tell the shopper under what conditions he or she can return a product. How many days or weeks do they have to decide to return it? Will they get a refund or a credit? Who pays the shipping back to you? You or them? If the product is defective, who is responsible for replacing it? You or the manufacturer?

Be clear and specific and list all details about your return policy on your Web site.

Convenience—Are You Easy to Do Business With?

When a shopper comes to your Web store, he's got his credit card in hand and he is ready to buy. So don't let your Web site get in his way.

A Web store with a poorly designed navigation structure will frustrate a shopper. Even though you have a great offer, if the shopper can't easily find it and buy it he'll click off to your competitor and probably will not come back.

A lot of thought must be given to how a shopper can search for products on your site. If you offer a shopper multiple navigation options it will help her find what she is looking for fast. Have the capability on your site for shoppers to search by

- Product name
- Price
- Product category
- Manufacturer

The more site tools shoppers have to search with the faster they can get to the products they're looking for, and the faster you'll make a sale.

> **Offer Live Customer Support—Without the Expense**
>
> Want to give live customer support on your site to shoppers? Don't want to spend the money for programming? Then use ICQ (www.icq.com/download/), Yahoo! Instant Messaging (messenger.yahoo.com), or AOL's Instant Messenger service (www.aol.com/aim/). Shoppers can download the free desktop application and communicate with you in real-time if they have a question.

But finding a product to buy is only the beginning. Just as important as price selection and service is convenience. How easy is it to navigate through your site? Getting lost in a site is discouraging and will send the shopper away fast if they can't easily find their way through your Web store. Good site navigation entails telling your visitor where they are, how they got there, how they can get back, and where they can go next.

If your site navigation is done properly, your shoppers should be able to get to where they want to go in just three or four mouse clicks. Be careful when designing the navigation bar on your site. Graphic links to the different sections of your site are nice and give a professional look to you Web store. But also include text links that duplicate your graphic navigation at the bottom of your pages in case your site loads too slowly through a shopper's browser.

Remember, your Web site should be intuitive to navigate. Your site pages should provide a visual map of how to get from one place to another that says, "Here's where I am; this is what I clicked on to get here. If I click on that, I'll go there next."

Security—How Trustworthy Is Your Site?

Good Web sites establish trust. Online shoppers can be a very skeptical bunch. They've been trained by the media to expect all kinds of online scams that are waiting to pick their pockets. If up to now you've given them a reason to buy from you, now they have to trust you enough to plunk down their money.

Build Trust in Your Site with Shoppers

Shoppers are looking for proof that your site is trustworthy to deal with. A good way to do this is join *eTrust* or the *Better Business Bureau (BBB)*. eTrust certifies that the personal information you give a site is protected and the BBB shows that you abide by the BBB way of doing business. You can join these organizations online at `etrust.com` and `bbbonline.org/reliability/index.asp`.

You build trust in your Web site in two ways:

- The customer knows his or her credit card number is secure when placing an order on your site.
- The customer knows that the private personal information he or she gives you is kept personal and private.

Credit Card Ordering

Shoppers are very concerned about using their credit cards to make purchases online. There are two things you can do to help your customers feel secure enough to place an order on your Web site.

First, be sure that your Web store is running on an SSL secure server. Check with your ISP or Web hosting service and be sure your store is either running on an SSL secure server or that they can make it available to you. If your transactions are not being placed through an SSL secure server, then find an ISP or hosting service that will provide it.

Shoppers can see right away if your server is secure by looking in the bottom left corner of their browsers. If they see a broken key or an unlocked lock, they know that their order will not be placed securely.

Make Shoppers Comfortable Using Their Credit Card on Your Site

Credit card companies state that you are responsible for the first $50 of fraudulent charges if your card is stolen. Offer to cover the $50 credit card company charge if the shopper is a victim of credit card fraud while shopping at your store.

Second, after an order is taken at the secure server, many times the order information must be e-mailed to you for processing. If so, be sure that the e-mail method is using some kind of encryption key. You can avoid all this if your SSL secure server sends the information encrypted to your credit card company for process and charges the customer's credit card.

Some shoppers just will not place an order online with their credit card no matter how secure it is. For these types of customers, provide a toll-free telephone number to call in their order to you. Also provide an order form on your site that they can print, fill out, and fax to you.

Privacy Policies

The Internet is a great medium of commerce. With it, you can create new marketing methods, tap new markets, and target potential customers with electronic ease. And it also can get you sued by millions of consumers for violating their privacy!

If you thought spamming consumers with unwanted e-mail was a blight on your company's reputation, consumers are even more upset over the incessant abuse of their personal privacy—not to mention the government investigating the business practices of e-businesses. But the need to gather a certain amount of information is needed by companies to personalize and better serve their customers. After all, how can you connect with a customer if you know little or nothing about them?

There has to be some kind of balance between protecting a consumer's privacy and the need for your business to target and personalize your offers to your customers.

Have Shoppers Rate Your Site

BizRate (`bizrate.com`) has exclusive real-time access to more than 60% of all customers making online retail transactions. To participate, you simply allow BizRate to solicit feedback from all your customers who make a purchase at your site. BizRate solicits feedback twice, once at the point-of-sale, and again after the expected date of fulfillment. Feedback covers 10 service attributes, from ease of ordering to product shipping and handling.

Consumers are sensitive to what's done with their personal information but it doesn't mean they're against giving it if the circumstances change—including getting something back for the information.

Still, e-businesses need to know what the privacy equation is in order to get the cooperation of consumers and customers to give up their personal information. And the principles of that privacy equation include what the FTC calls the "fair information practices." They are *notice, choice, access,* and *security.*

First, give your site visitor notice that you are collecting information and/or tracking their behavior and then gives them a choice to avoid such tracking. Second, and this is more difficult, give consumers access to the data collected on them and provide them with the security that their data is kept private. And the best to give your shoppers that warm & fuzzy feeling of security is to provide a third party *privacy seal of approval* on your site.

A number of privacy protection organizations have appeared to help soothe the concerns of online consumers. And they do this by offering third party privacy seals to e-businesses. This is a good way to gain the trust of consumers since these third party consumer privacy protection organizations certify your privacy policy.

There are two types of privacy seals programs. One has strict guidelines that prohibit sites from sharing consumer information they collect with other business partners or using it for direct marketing programs. Other privacy seal programs award their stamps of approval to sites that simply stick to whatever privacy promises they made. That could include passing on personal information to advertising networks or other businesses as long as they spelled it out in their posted privacy statement.

In Privacy We Trust

The oldest and most well known of privacy seal programs is TRUSTe at www.truste.org, which was started in 1997 by the Electronic Frontier Foundation. To display the TRUSTe seal on your site requires a TRUSTe audit and an annual fee of $299 to $6,999 depending upon your e-business revenue.

Self-regulation was the preferred approach that the e-commerce industry is using today— until COPPA came along.

The Children's Online Privacy Protection Act (COPPA) was enacted in late 1998, and became effective in April of 2000. COPPA bars the online collection and use of personally identifiable information from children under the age of 13 unless verifiable parental consent is provided.

You must be aware of this law!

There have been reports that the FTC might seek up to $11,000 per COPPA violation. It does not take a mathematician to figure out that penalties can really add up. So if your e-business caters to children under the age of 13, be forewarned! Make sure you understand the COPPA regulations. They can be found at www.ftc.gov/opa/1999/9910/childfinal.htm.

DMA Can Help You Build a Privacy Policy

The Direct Marketing Association (DMA) can help you build a privacy statement for your site. Simply fill out the questions on its Privacy Policy Creation Tool Web page, submit it, and the Direct Marketing Association will send you a Web page to post to your site. Find the form at www.the-dma.org/library/privacy/creating.shtml (see Figure 13.5).

Consumer privacy issues and concerns can have a drastic effect on your ability to market to, connect, and create an ongoing relationship with your customers, all of which are critical to the success of your e-businesses in the future. A lot of thought should be given to your privacy policy and how you communicate it to visitors and customers to your site.

So be sure that your Privacy Policy clearly states the following:

- What information is collected when shoppers buy from you
- How you use this information
- What you intend to do with it

Finally, make your Privacy Policy accessible right from your home page.

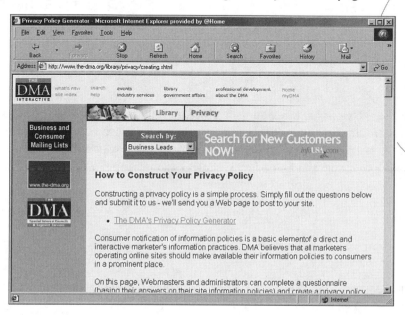

Figure 13.5

Have the DMA build a Privacy Policy page for your Web site for free.

SELLING TO THE WORLD! SPRECHEN SIE DEUTCH? FRENCH? SPANISH? JAPANESE? OR...?

Did you know that when in Japan, you should always present a gift with two hands? This is also true with presenting business cards. And that you should avoid giving gifts in sets of four? The word "four" in Japanese is "shi," which is also associated with the word for death. White symbolizes death too, so packages should never be wrapped in white paper.

I bring these up as examples of how easy it is to make mistakes when dealing with another culture. The Web is global—the *World* in the *World Wide Web*! If you're going to sell into the global marketplace and you don't understanding the culture of the customer you're selling to, you're setting your company up for costly mistakes. Building an international marketing strategy is more than just translating your site into another language. Your company faces not only the challenges of language but also the regulatory challenges of import and export rules, taxation, social and political issues, and fulfillment and customer services problems. Any one of these items, if mishandled, can quickly torpedo your global sales efforts.

Use a Free Translation Service

Need a quick and simple translation of your offer? How does free sound? At the FreeTranslation.com site at www.freetranslation.com, you can do it for free, libre, libero, frei, and livre! Keep in mind that the simple translation of words does not always provide a clear meaning of what was originally meant. For that, you need to use a professional translation company.

If you're going to target consumers overseas, there are a number of important elements to keep in mind.

First are the language and cultural challenges. Mere word-for-word translation of your product or service offer is not enough. There are cultural nuances that must be considered. Certain products may be offensive in certain cultures. Are you selling leather products? Don't try selling leather products made of pigskin to a Muslim audience. Pigskin comes from pork and pork is a no-no in the Muslin religion. Another cultural problem to avoid is the incorrect tone of product instructions. In Japan, for example, you wouldn't say, "Don't press the right button." You should say, "It would be much better if you pushed the left button."

Every element of your visual offer, including language and navigation, needs to be designed with this kind of cultural sensitivity.

In addition to the language and cultural challenges, there are the local customs and legal issues for individual countries. Customs, tax, or tariffs charges must be easily figured into the final sale to an international customer. Finding the right software that can calculate international shipping charges, value-added taxes, duty, and other international charges is of prime importance if you're going to sell into the global market.

Once the order is taken, your company must start thinking about fulfillment. Do you ship from one country to another or do you set up a local warehouse and shipping center in the countries you do business in? And what about customer service and merchandise returns?

Will That Be Cash, Check, or Charge?

Most of the world does not use credit cards. So when you market to your global customer make sure you let them know you can and will take other forms of payment. Checks, debit cards, and/or electronic forms of cash.

Building a global fulfillment system is one of the biggest challenges your e-business will face. One of the best solutions to these problems is to outsource your fulfillment and customer service operations to companies that actually reside in your customer's country.

And don't think that selling services is any easier and has fewer problems selling products internationally. Take Charles Schwab as an example. Selling financial services in Europe should be a breeze—right? That's what Schwab thought, too. Europeans know all about buying stocks, bonds, and mutual funds. So, when the online broker Schwab at www.schwab.com opened a site for clients in Britain in 1998, many of the Brits balked at online trading. They were accustomed to trading paper stock certificates—not electronic trades. Because Schwab refused to issue paper certificates to its online customers, the site generated only 15,000 new accounts in 12 months.

Even if your e-business does not have the resources of a large company to plan and execute a global business, there are companies that can help. *bCrossing* is one such company (see Figure 13.6).

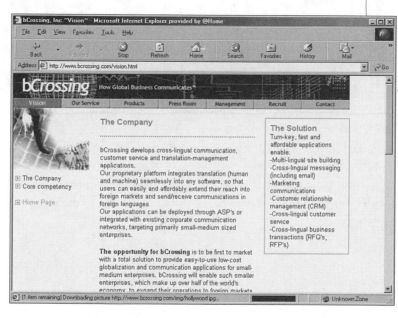

Figure 13.6

Planning on selling your wares overseas? Then check out bCrossing.

bCrossing at www.bcrossing.com/vision.html will handle the front-end of your e-business if you are marketing to a customer overseas.

A company on the Net that can help your e-business on the fulfillment side is From2.com. From2.com at www.from2.com is an international logistics company that provides an all-inclusive solution for e-commerce merchants to deliver goods to international customers.

As for the offer itself, your e-business can use any one of several translation companies on the Net to translate your offer from English to other languages. One such service is Wholetree.com at www.wholetree.com (see Figure 13.7). It offers technology for your eBusiness that handles multiple currency purchases and multilingual technical support, and recognizes input and provides output in multiple languages.

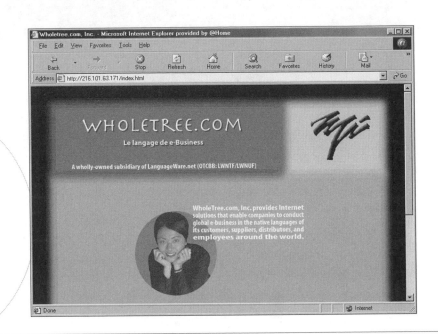

Figure 13.7

Wholetree.com will help you set up your product or service offer to sell into the international marketplace.

Remember, the World Wide Web is no longer an English-speaking, U.S.-centric marketplace. Your e-business has to be prepared to sell anywhere in the electronic bazaar that's called the Internet.

CHAPTER 14

THE SEVEN CARDINAL SINS OF E-COMMERCE

In This Chapter

- Learn the seven cardinal sins of e-commerce and how to avoid them
- Discover examples of good and bad Web site designs.

I was raised in the Roman Catholic tradition and have fond memories of the Catholic grammar school I attended while I was a kid. I recall Sister Mary Theresa, one of my instructors. She was quick with her wit and with her knuckle-rapping ruler. She also taught us to avoid the seven cardinal sins of Vanity, Greed, Lust, Envy, Gluttony, Wrath, and Sloth.

Now that I'm an Internet professional, I can see a strong parallel between the seven cardinal sins taught to me as a child and the seven cardinal sins of e-commerce.

This chapter discusses those e-commerce sins and how to avoid them.

VANITY—GOING IT ALONE

There's a saying that goes "You can do anything on the Internet—but you can't do it alone." In the world of e-commerce, outsourcing is not an evil word. Many new Web stores fail to succeed due to a lack of professional design and programming know-how. The biggest challenge to a new e-business is not so much the technical aspects—although they are important—but how best to execute your business plan.

JARGON

What Is Outsourcing?

Outsourcing is the use of companies outside your business to meet the needs of or add value to your Web site. Examples are partnering with Web companies that supply informational content, message boards, credit card acceptance, and fulfillment services for your e-business.

Too few businesses on the Net use the resources available to them for order taking, credit card clearing, site hosting, store building, and so on. You can spend valuable time and resources building a site, hiring professionals to do the necessary programming, buying software and hardware, and paying advertising agencies. Instead, partner with companies on the Net that supply free or nearly free resources to set up and run your business.

Sure, having a store on Yahoo! or selling other merchant's products through an affiliate program is not as glamorous as having your own custom online business. But if you're just starting out in the world of e-commerce or have limited funds, partnering with other sites on the Web is a smart thing to do.

Even if you have the wherewithal to build a custom one-of-a-kind Web store, you can still partner with other sites to save your time and money. In Chapter 11, "Building Your Web Store," you saw how you could set up a Web store for free. In Chapter 12, "The 3 Cs of e-Commerce," you found ways to include information content and community elements on your site by partnering with content and community providers that syndicate their programs to sites free of charge.

In the chapters to follow, you will see where on the Net you can accept credit cards without the hassle of setting up a credit card merchant account by partnering with Web companies like iBill (ibill.com) and ccBill (ccbill.com) (see Figure 14.1). You will also see dozens of ways you can promote your site for free.

But you can't do it alone. There is a lot of help out there in cyberspace. Learn to use it by partnering with other Web companies.

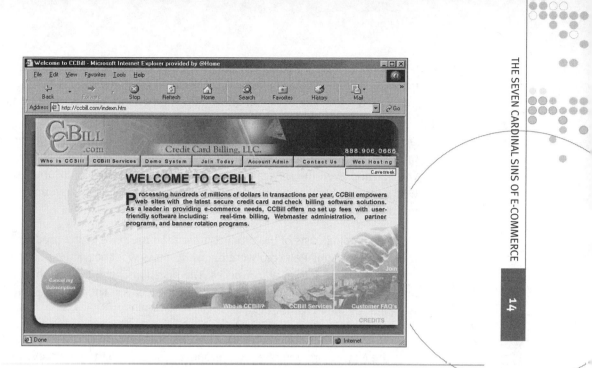

Figure 14.1

At ccBill you can accept credit cards on your site without going through the expense and time of getting a merchant account.

GREED—FORCING A SQUARE PEG INTO A ROUND HOLE

Your product sells well in the real world. Why shouldn't it sell just as well online? Right? Wrong! Just because a particular product sells well in retail stores, it's easy to think that it will, by necessity, sell well online. Take a hard look at what you're trying to sell.

Look at the product—even the service—you are going to sell over the Net and ask yourself these questions.

- Can my product or service be pictured and clearly understood through electronic means only? Even when *virtual reality* becomes a reality, viewing a product through cyberspace will never replace the hands-on experience of the real world. Yes, there are attempts at adding 3D to an e-commerce site such as Boo.com (boo.com). But such a site is programming intensive and visitors need to have a fast connection to view the product offerings properly. So, pick a product to sell that does not require the shopper to physically handle before he or she can purchase it. If your product or service requires a personal sales touch, you might have problems selling it online.

JARGON

What's Virtual Reality?

Virtual reality is a method for creating 3D environments on the Web. On a virtual reality page, it is possible to move around through a virtual room, pick up things, open a door, and do other acts that you can perform in the real world.

- Is your product heavy or bulky? Will it cost an exorbitant amount to ship the product to a customer? Selling refrigerators, washing machines, and wide-screen TVs might be a good idea but think of the shipping costs to the customer and actually handling these items in your warehouse.

- Do your products carry a high product liability? Some products, if not handled properly, can cause physical harm or property damage. Be sure that the products you sell and even the service you offer are covered by liability insurance. Find out who's responsible if someone is injured using your product or if your service does not deliver as promised.

- Are the shipping costs of the product more than the price of the product itself? One of the reasons Pets.com went out of business was their attempt to sell 25 pound bags of dog food at low prices. The price was right, but the shipping costs killed them. Make sure the benefits of the products you choose to sell are not "out weighed" by their cost to ship.

Be sure you have all these questions answered before you set out to sell your product or service on the Net. Before you offer your product or service to the public, evaluate its suitability for online sales.

ENVY—KEEPING UP WITH THE NERDS

When a potential customer hits your site, is the first thing they see a straight offer to buy, or a song and dance routine of Java applets, animated icons, or other special effects that wastes the time—and delays the sale—of your visitor?

People don't care to be entertained with the equivalent of elevator music when they're looking to take action. Who cares if your competitor's Web site won "Cool Site of the Day?" What counts in business is making sales. Let customers navigate through your site at their own pace and direction, not in the way you think they should go. Don't force customers to sit through a flashy, long *splash page* before getting to the site's home page. Don't make potential customers wait for a variety of images to appear, move around, and disappear from the screen before the home page appears. You can be sure that they'll be gone before your flashy animations are through.

JARGON

What's a Splash Page?
A splash page is a first or front page of a Web site. This page usually contains a clickable logo or message, announcing that you have arrived. The real information and navigation for the site lies behind this page on the home page or welcome page.

Finally, be sensitive to customers with older systems. If your site has a lot of flashy graphics, offer a text-only option for viewing your site.

GLUTTONY—IS IT BIGGER THAN 60K?

That pretty graphic on your home page that takes several minutes to load? Get rid of it. People want simplicity over cool graphics. Faster loading is better than eye candy. If your total page size is more than 60K, put it on a diet. In fact, most designers agree that a page should not be more that 48K and that includes graphics.

If you're selling products on your Web site, there's no getting around the need for product shots. If you need to place a lot of product shots on a page, use thumbnails—smaller sized pictures—instead. If the shopper wants to see a larger version of the product, they can click it and be sent to a Web page that contains only that product, along with a detailed description and buy button.

To create a good customer experience, use graphics only when they serve the customer's goals.

SLOTH—NEGLECTING SECURITY AND CUSTOMER CONVENIENCE

You want to make visitors comfortable while they are shopping on your site. You do that by making your site easy to do business with and offering a safe and secure way for shoppers to buy with their credit cards at your site.

People are concerned about sending their credit card numbers over the Net. Sure. People are getting more comfortable with the idea, but that doesn't mean you should sit there like a bump on a log and not soothe the fears of your visitors by telling them—and I mean tell them—that your site is secure and they can safely send their card number to you over the Net.

Tell them upfront—on your home page—that their credit card purchases are secure like ThirskAuto does, (www.thirskauto.com) (see Figure 14.2). Direct them to a page on your site that explains how the customer's credit card number is protected when they use it on your site. To make them feel more secure, promise to pay the $50 liability charge that the shopper would incur from their bank if their card number were stolen when used on your site.

Keep a Running Total

Keep a view of what's in a customer's shopping cart on every page of your site. It could be a simple text box that says, "You have 3 items in your shopping cart—total amount $26.95." This is a useful service to provide for your shoppers.

Make it easy for your customers to shop around your store by adding an online shopping cart. Think about this. You just bought a product at your neighborhood store. To buy another one, you need to pay for it, leave the store, and enter it again. Sounds silly, right? Well, without a shopping cart on your site, that's exactly what you're asking your customers to do.

Figure 14.2

ThirskAuto tells the shopper right up front on their home page that the shoppers' credit card purchases are secure.

If you really want to drive customers away from your site, make it hard to navigate. According to a recent research paper by Creative Good, Inc., "Thirty-nine percent of test shoppers failed in their buying attempts because sites were too difficult to navigate." Make your site navigation simple—not cute. Use labels such as Contact Us, About Us, Our Catalog, Services We Offer, or Shop Now. Forget naming sections Joy Ride, Buzz the Bean, or Cool Stuff.

Don't be lazy with security and convenience. Place your Web store on a secure server and provide an easy-to-use shopping cart and site navigation system for your customers.

LUST—YOU GOTTA LOVE THOSE PLUG-INS

Get this. You walk into your favorite retailer and at the door you're stopped and told to go down the block and get a special pass before you can enter the store. You comply, right? In your dreams! Or, how about this? You're at the checkout counter ready to pay but you're told to go across the street and buy a special wallet to complete the purchase.

Well, that's what you ask a visitor to your site to do when you tell them that they need a plug-in to view your site or a special *eWallet* to make a purchase. People don't want to have to download anything to view your site or buy from you. Don't lust after some cool way to display the goods and content of your site or offer a convenience that's inconvenient to get.

Help Your Shoppers Fill Out Order Forms

No one likes to fill out order forms every time he goes to a new site to buy. That's why eWallets are the latest shopping trend to hit the Web. Consumers fill in all their purchasing information once and then when they go to a Web store the eWallet fills in the order form for them. There is a problem with most eWallets, though. Consumers have to download them onto their computers. By using a service like Microsoft Passport, the consumer enters his purchasing information onto Passport's secure Web site. No downloads are necessary. When they buy at a Web store that accepts the Passport eWallet, shoppers can enter their information easily into the order form. Consider making your Web store Passport enabled. Find it at `passport.com`.

Suppose you must have shoppers download a plug-in to experience your products. For example, you have an online music store selling CDs. You want to give shoppers the opportunity to hear some sample tracks from a CD before they buy. They will most certainly have to download an audio player plug-in like Real Audio at `realaudio.com`. If you say your site needs RealAudio to listen to the sample CD tracks, then make sure it links to the download page on the RealAudio Web site.

If you keep it simple you won't give your customer a reason to click his way over to a competitor.

WRATH—DO YOU HATE YOUR CUSTOMER?

Want to really drive customers from your site? Use frames, have them register, provide no site search engine, and ignore international customers.

Let's take these one at a time.

Framed sites are bad news. Most search engines can't find your site because they hide your real content from the search engine and visitors can't bookmark the page they're actually interested in—only the framed page they're on. Also, customers can get lost easily navigating your site through frames.

If you want to irritate your visitors, count their time onsite in milliseconds by forcing them to register before using your site. Or, forget that the first W in the World Wide Web stands for World. Think globally. Remember that users from other countries can easily access your site. If you want your e-business to be truly global, respect other cultures and keep in mind that they might not be familiar with American expressions or respond to American advertising.

Oh, and don't forget to throw in a lot of small pop-up windows giving a pitch after each mouse click to really drive your shoppers nuts.

How Does Your Site Measure Up?

Want to see the best of the best? Check out the best examples of e-commerce sites rated by ZDNet. Find it at www.zdnet.com/ecommerce/stories/evaluations/ 0,10524,2298732,00.html. And if you want to see the worst examples, you can find them at www.zdnet.com/ecommerce/stories/evaluations/ 0,10524,2298718,00.html.

Be considerate of your shoppers. Tell them which Web browsers to use to best view your site such as "This page is best viewed by Netscape 3.0 and above." And though techno-speak might be familiar to you, many newbies to the Net might not understand it. Don't confuse shoppers new to the Net by using techno-jargon.

If your site commits any of these seven e-commerce sins, immediately say your *mea culpas* and correct them.

PART IV

DELIVERING THE GOODS

CHAPTER **15**

TAKING THE ORDER

In This Chapter

- Learn the important elements of an online order form
- Discover the different ways you can take an order at your Web store
- Learn how to protect your sales from fraud
- Learn the different Internet Tax proposals and their effect on your business

Creating a shopper-friendly e-commerce Web site and locating it on a server is a lot of work. But that's only the beginning. Your next task is to find and implement the various services needed to quickly and safely make a transaction.

In one way or another you have to be able to take an order and accept payment for it. The customer must be notified that his or her electronic order was accepted and that your company acknowledges the order. Let's face it—without human acknowledgement, customers want to be secure in the fact that after they purchase from you, their order is not floating around somewhere in cyberspace. Your electronic process of taking an order has to give the same warm fuzzy feeling that they would get placing it with a real person.

Finally, you have to protect yourself from those who would try to steal product from you by placing bogus orders or using stolen credit cards. You might have protected your customer's credit card by using a secure server but that doesn't protect you from fraudulent credit card use.

THE ORDER FORM

The purchasing relationship that you have with a customer starts with the order form. Up until then, your shopper was sold on your Web store and decided to make a purchase from you. Is the order in the bag? Not necessarily. You still can blow it. You still can make the customer abandon his purchase if your order form is not easy, fast, and convenient to use.

Whether the customer fills out a form on your site and pays by credit card or prints the form from your Web page and mails or faxes it to you with their payment, how you design your order form and the order form process itself can make the difference between keeping the sale you made and losing it to a competitor.

So, here are the elements of a good online order form:

- Registration Request
- Customer Contact Information
- Product Information and Order Costs
- Customer Billing and Shipping Information
- Optional Services Request

Break Up Your Order Form

You have to collect a lot of information on your order form. So don't put your entire order form on one Web page. Break it up into logical steps with short pages for billing and shipping address, credit card number, contact information, shipping information, and so on.

Registration Request

Shoppers like convenience and as an online merchant, you want to provide it. One way is to have the customer sign in before starting his or her order. If a customer has ordered before, he or she might already be registered at the site. By registering with your Web store, you can populate or automatically fill many of the order form fields for your customer.

Don't Get Pushy

Asking a customer who is ready to buy to register is one thing. But never ask a shopper to register at your site just to shop. Ask them to register or sign in only when they are starting the purchasing process.

Another use for registration is that you can keep the customer's credit or debit card on file and stored on your secure server. That way, all the customer has to do is supply a password at the time of checkout and they don't have to enter their card number and send it over the Net again.

There are both positives and negatives to customer registration. Some shoppers, no matter how secure you claim your Web store to be, do not like the idea of a merchant storing their personal information. And if you store their card number, they get even more nervous! So, making registration mandatory to purchase at your site might not be a good idea. You could lose a sale that you've worked so hard to get.

Give Your Shopper a Cookie

Another way to track customers who don't want to register and populate the fields of your order form is to use a *cookie*. A cookie is a small piece of information that your Web server sends to a shopper's computer via the shopper's browser. Cookies can contain information such as login or registration information, online shopping cart information, user preferences, and so on. Keep in mind though that users can refuse cookies placed on their machine by simply turning off that option in their browser.

So, it's important to give your customers a choice. Privacy concerns are just as important as credit card concerns with online shoppers today. That is why it is very important to have a full and easy-to-understand privacy statement on your site, as mentioned in Chapter 11, "Building Your Web Store."

It's very important to let shoppers choose their comfort level. First, make registration an option. Then sell them on registering. Explain how registering their personal information makes shopping at your site faster and more convenient for them. If you have a secure server, tell them that any personal information they give you will be kept secure and private. (You did remember to place a Privacy Policy Statement on your site. Right?) Then let them choose whether to give you their shipping information and/or their card number to store on your site.

When should you ask them to register? Ask them if they'd like to register before they place their order, and if they don't, ask them again after they have ordered.

Customer Contact Information

If your customer has not registered at your Web store, then you'll need to collect his or her contact information.

Your order form should have two separate fields—or spaces—for the customer's name. It should have one field for the first name and one for the last name. After the name, provide a field for the customer's e-mail address. Always collect the e-mail address. This will be the means by which you will do almost all communication with your customer—such as order confirmation, product stock status, and shipping notification.

Finally, ask for phone numbers. And the word *numbers* is plural for a reason. Always get two phone numbers from your customer—the home phone and the day phone. Why? The first reason is obvious. If you need to contact the customer by phone you need a number to reach him both during the day and at home in the evening and on weekends.

The second reason is not so obvious and it has to do with fraud prevention.

Getting two numbers from your customer can help prevent the fraudulent use of a credit or debit card. If a customer is using a stolen card number and you suspect that it's stolen, having two numbers available for confirmation helps you decide whether the order is legit or not. If you call and both numbers don't work or the person on the other line did not place the order, then you know you might have a possible fraud on your hands. Contact the customer by e-mail and let him know of the problem. Dollars to donuts, you'll probably never hear from him.

Product Information and Order Costs

Customers need to know at every point of the ordering process what they're buying and how much it will cost. This is why your order form should supply information on the product they've ordered. Show them the name of the product, the product code number, its price, and description. And if the product they ordered comes in different colors or sizes, be sure these are listed with the product information.

In a sense, you're verifying that your site knows what the customer ordered even during the ordering process.

And don't make the mistake that some e-commerce sites make. Your order form should automatically generate the product information. Don't make the customer remember the product information and enter it into the order form (see Figure 15.1). Want to lose a sale really fast? Do that.

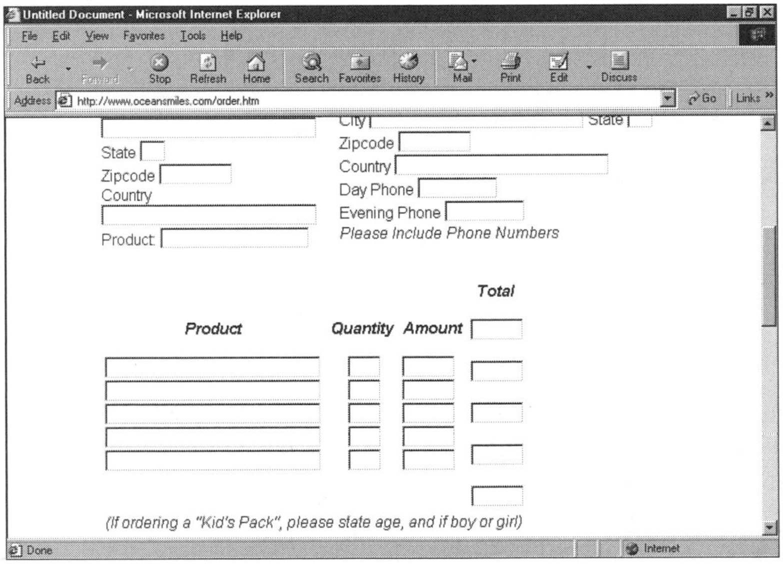

Figure 15.1

Here's a good example of a bad way to design an order form. Never ask the customer to enter the products he is going to buy.

You should also give the customers the opportunity to choose the shipping method. Allow them to choose whether they want their order shipped by ground or by air—next day or second day—and show them the difference in costs.

Finally, show all the costs before asking the customer to enter his or her credit or debit card. Provide a page before finalizing the order that details what the customer is buying, how much it costs, and the shipping and handling charges. Show the total amount the customer's credit card will be charged or account debited. If the customer is printing the order form after filling it out, show the total amount he or she should write a check for.

Customer Billing and Shipping Information

After requesting the customer contact information and confirming what he has ordered, you need to collect his billing and shipping address and his credit or debit card number. The customer's billing address is the address to which his credit card bill is sent. Your credit card processing company will compare the billing address against the customer's name and credit or debit card number to verify that the card number matches the billing address. This is the first layer of merchant fraud protection.

You also must ask for the customer shipping address. This might sound redundant but it's not. First of all, the customer might want to have the product shipped to her work and not her home. She might be buying a gift for her husband or family and doesn't want the gift to be opened at home by mistake. Second, the customer might be buying the gift for someone else and would like to have the product shipped to that person.

Ask for the Customer Credit Card Number Last

On your online order form, ask for the customer's credit card number last. This serves two purposes. First, it makes the customer comfortable that they have all the information they need up to that point to make a final purchase. Second, if the customer abandoned the order form before completing the sale, you've captured his or her contact information upfront that you can use later to send a special offer enticing them to come back to your Web store and buy.

If the billing and shipping address is the same, you can avoid having the customer type the same address twice by asking him to check a box on the order form that says, "If the billing and shipping address are the same—check this box." Your software can then fill in the shipping address automatically so the customer doesn't have to.

Finally, provide fields for the customer's credit or debit card. He will need fields to enter his card number, the expiration date of the credit or debit card, and what type of card it is— MasterCard, Visa, American Express, Discover, and so on.

Optional Services Request

Customers like special consideration and perks. So, if your Web store intends to offer special optional services or promotions, they also should be included on your order form. They should be easy to find and use. Here are some examples:

Gift Wrapping—You might want to provide a gift-wrapping service for your customers. Provide this option on your order form. If it's a free service ask your customer if they would like to have it and confirm it by checking a specific box. If you charge for the service, tell the customer what the charge is and be sure to include it on the total cost page that you present to the customer before accepting the payment.

Coupons and Discounts—If you are running a special promotion in which you distributed regular or electronic discount coupons, have a field where your customer can enter the coupon code number and have the discount be reflected on the total cost per page. The same goes for any frequent buyer discounts that you might apply.

Remember, your order form can make or break a sale. So be sure to include all the elements to make your customer's buying experience match the shopping experience he or she has had on your site.

HOW DO I PAY THEE? LET ME COUNT THE WAYS

One of the best ways to make it easy for shoppers to buy from your Web store is to provide them with a variety of ways to pay for your product or service. People are different and have different ways of managing their money. Various customers have different comfort levels and different ways they like to pay for merchandise. Your Web store should cater to this difference and plan to allow your customers a choice between several payment methods to ensure that *everyone* will be able to do business with you.

The first thing that comes to mind when shopping online is buying online. That's what the Internet is about. And the easiest way to buy online is with a credit or debit card, so you must set up your site to accept both. But accepting credit or debit cards are not the only ways the customer can pay for products or services.

Some people will not use a credit card. Not because they're concerned with online security—they'd just rather pay cash for their purchases. So you need to be able to accept checks—both electronically and mailed in—and COD. And you also should be aware of the new payment kid on the block—*eCash* and it's cousin *microCash*. Over the last few years or so these new forms of electronic payment have come of age and many Web consumers are starting to use them.

But these are all payment types. You also should consider odering methods. Your e-business should be able to take orders online from your Web site, by telephone, fax, and even mail orders. Any and all these payment types and methods should be considered when setting up a payment plan at your Web store.

So, let's take a peek at each one.

Ordering Methods

Your site should be set up to take orders through a variety of methods. When a customer arrives at your site, he or she should know that they have the flexibility to place an order with you online or otherwise. Consider offering customers as many of these payment methods as possible:

- Secure Online Ordering
- E-mail Ordering
- Ordering by Fax or Mail
- Ordering by Telephone

Secure Online Ordering

If you are going to take any kind of sensitive financial information from your customers, such as credit or debit card numbers, you must have your Web store on a secure server. All transactions between the customer and your store should be secured by using the *Secure Sockets Layer (SSL)* protocol, which prevents third parties from discovering the credit card information.

Customers can tell if they are entering their card number into a secure Web page by looking in the lower-left corner of their browser. They will see right away if the little lock is locked or if the little key is unbroken. Some later browsers also will post a security alert box within the browser, stating that the customer is entering a secure section of the Web site.

Don't risk the chance of giving your e-business a bad rep and hurt your chances of making sales in the future by having a customer claim (whether true or not) that he had his credit card number stolen when ordering from your site. There are no ifs, ands, or buts about it. If you accept credit or debit cards for payment, do it on a secure SSL server.

E-mail Ordering

E-mail is a very unsecure way to take an order and is not recommended. Still, some customers might want this option so here's how to take e-mail orders and still protect the customer's credit or debit card information.

JARGON

Is There Such a Thing as Secure E-mail?

Secure e-mail is available using encryption systems such as PGP and S/MIME that are built into most e-mail programs. But this method is not very well known and is bulky to use because of the private and public encryption keys that must be used. If you intend to accept orders via secure e-mail, remember to include your public key—the key that you publish for all to see—on your Web store. Find out more about PGP and how to use it at www.pgpi.org.

Have the customer e-mail you all the information about his order except his card number and expiration date. Be certain he does include his phone numbers. Then call the customer to get his card number and complete the transaction. Another way, yet still not advisable, is to have your customer send his card number in two pieces in two different e-mail messages.

Ordering by Fax or Mail

To help facilitate fax and mail ordering, you should make your order form printable from your Web site. You can either provide customers with a blank order form, or provide the option of printing a completed order form—without their card number—for faxing.

After they have their order form in their hands they can either fax or mail it to you. Be sure that you have a dedicated fax line at your business. This way there will be less chance that a buying customer will get a busy signal—and you won't lose an order.

TIP

Use a Fax to E-mail Gateway

If you want to use a fax to e-mail service, check out JFAX (www.j2.com).

A new use of faxing is the fax-to-e-mail gateway. This type of Internet service converts a customer's fax into an e-mail message, thus relieving you of the need for a dedicated fax number. This eliminates the chance of your customer getting a busy signal when he tries to fax you an order and also allows you to pick up orders from a remote location.

Finally, if you're going to give customers the option of ordering through the mail, be sure your customers can easily find your complete mailing address on your Web site.

Ordering by Telephone

Statistics say that many people shop the Net, choosing a store, locating a product to buy, and then calling the online merchant to place the order. You should make it easy for your customers to do just that.

But accepting phone orders does have a downside. Remember that the Net is global. Not only can you get orders from around your country, but around the world! So if you do give customers the option of phoning in their orders, you would need to man phones 24 hours a day 7 days a week. This is not feasible for a small to medium size business. You can rely on a simple answering machine or a voice-mail service or outsource your phone orders to a third party answering service. For all these options, be sure you offer a toll-free number for customers to use. Also, include a standard telephone ordering number so that international customers can place orders.

A nice solution would be to answer the phones on your time. You can do this by posting your telephone order days and times on your Web store. Another solution is to use the rapidly developing technology of Web and telephony services. A provider of this technology is Instant Call at www.globalonlinetelecom.com/instantlivetalk (see Figure 15.2). Instead of calling you, you call them.

Here's how it works.

You place an Instant Live Talk button on your site for when a customer wants to order via telephone. With one click of the button, it instantly connects you on the phone with your customer.

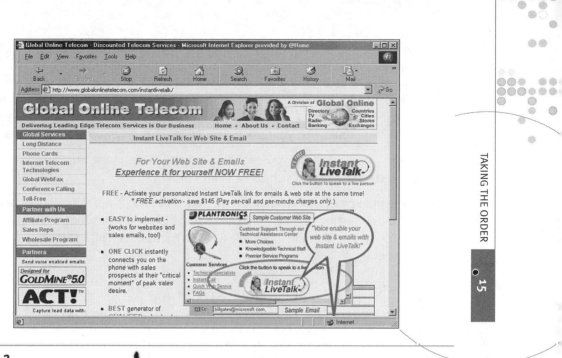

Figure 15.2

Place Instant Call's InstantCall button on your site and customers can alert you to call them when they have a question. No additional software or hardware is required.

Payment Types

After you've established the different ways customers can place and order with you, you need to consider the types of payment you'll accept. Online merchants can use all the payment types that merchants use in the real world. In addition, there are payment types that are native only to the Net.

By offering customers a variety of ways to pay for their merchandise, you increase the likelihood of making a sale. So, consider offering customers as many of these payment types as possible:

- Conventional Payment
- Credit and Debit Cards
- Digital Cash
- Telephone Billing

Conventional Payment

Believe it of not, in this world of instant gratification and freely available credit many people still prefer to pay with cash. You should make this traditional way of paying for products and services available to customers at your Web store. Accepting payment in the traditional way includes paying by check or COD.

When a customer wants to pay by check, he normally uses one of your offline payment methods. A customer sends his order through the mail or faxes it to you. When dealing with checks you run the risk of having the check bounce because of insufficient funds. With payment by check you have one of two choices to make. Either you hold the check until it clears the customer's bank, or you take the risk and ship when you receive the check. You could limit your risk further by using a check verification service.

In the matter of CODs, you can limit your risk by requiring that the customer pay for the product with a cashier's check or money order.

The whole process of sending checks back and forth is not very Net-like and is inefficient. But a new technology has emerged over the last few years that can make the act of paying by check a lot more palatable for Web merchants. This technology is called *Electronic Checks*.

Accept Checks via Fax, Phone, or the Net

Using software from Software Solutions, you can print customer checks from any printer and deposit them in your bank. Simply request their account information and print the check in seconds. Find it at `softwaresolutions.net/vcheck/`.

In its simplest form Electronic Check systems merely require the customer to fill out a form at your Web store. This data is then transferred to the merchant where it is converted into a paper check by using blank check forms in a standard office printer. Check out CheckMax (`www.chekfaxx.com/chekfaxx.htm`) for one such service. Also, check out ECCHO. ECCHO (`www.eccho.org`) is a not-for-profit national clearinghouse, and its primary objective is the development and promotion of electronic check presentment.

Credit and Debit Cards

Taking credit cards online is critical to any online merchant because credit cards are still the most popular way for paying for goods and services on the Net. Don't just accept Visa and MasterCard. Accept American Express and Discover, too. The more card types you can accept the more opportunity for a sale you'll have.

Accepting credit cards also gives you the advantage of having funds automatically and electronically deposited in your account within 2–3 days.

Also think about accepting debit cards at your Web store. Debit cards deduct the amount of the customer's purchase directly from her checking account. If you're planning on selling to European customers, accepting debit cards is a must. They are more widely used in Europe than credit cards. And they are catching on fast in the United States. CardData reports the annual growth rate of debit cards is surpassing those of credit cards.

Digital Cash

Digital cash or *eCash* is a Net-native form of payment. The main drawback to digital cash is that both the customer and the merchant need to have an account with a bank that issues it. The bank provides customers with a piece of software called a *purse*. The purse manages the transferring of digital cash. Customers take money from their checking or savings account and convert it into digital cash that is then transferred to their purse software. It's then encoded and stored on the their hard drive until it is spent.

A payment technology that is developing will allow just about anyone to sell anything on the Web. It's called *microCash*. It enables customers to make very small purchases—anywhere from a few pennies to a few dollars—without having to use a credit or debit card or writing a check. This is good for Web merchants because the costs involved in charging a credit or debit card for such a small amount surpasses the price of the sale itself.

What would a Web merchant use microCash for? How about paying for a stock quote; or a news article; or an installment of your new book. Or even for a daily joke. You could open and run a successful Web store selling bits of information for pennies a piece—something you could never do in the real world.

Ain't the Net grand!

Telephone Billing

An alternative to all these payment types is a blend of the old and the new. A company called eCharge (www.echarge.com) has created a payment system called *eCharge Phone* that allows Internet users to shop online and securely charge items to their normal phone bill (see Figure 15.3).

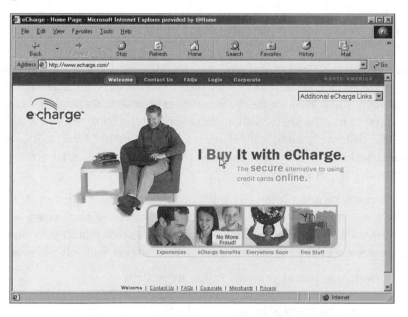

Figure 15.3

With eCharge you can bill a customer's order right to his phone bill.

Aside from convenience, one of the benefits of eCharge Phone is that it's so secure. eCharge Phone connects directly from your modem to a switch that automatically captures the billing information. There is no transfer of private data or account numbers over the Internet. The only drawback right now is that you can only charge products up to $300 a piece.

ONLINE FRAUD

Building an online business takes a lot of work. Nothing can be worse than seeing all your hard work lost through credit card fraud. Although there has been a lot of discussion in the media about credit card fraud, the fraud committed against online merchants has gone practically unnoticed.

In fact, it's the online merchant who is the true victim of Internet credit card fraud. The Internet itself makes the process of credit card fraud easier in many ways. Visit the newsgroups and you find lists of stolen credit card numbers readily available. There are even programs easily available online that generate new valid credit card numbers!

Verification Does Not Protect You from Fraud

Don't make the assumption that just verifying a credit card—getting an authorization number—is sufficient fraud protection. All this verification process does is check that the card has not been reported stolen and that it has sufficient free credit available to fund the purchase.

Why doesn't your bank protect you against fraud? Because your merchant agreement with them says it can't.

Transactions by merchants on the Net fall under the heading of MOTO—Mail Order/Telephone Order. Most credit card merchant account agreements leave you, the merchant, 100% liable for fraud committed at your Web site. And that's not all. You're also required to pay the $15–$25 chargeback fee that the bank hits you with when the charge on the customer's stolen card is reversed by his or her bank. If you accrue too many chargebacks, your merchant account can be terminated. After terminating, it's nearly impossible to get another one.

Not a pretty prospect when you think about it. Just the thought of credit card fraud can take the wind out of your e-commerce sails. So, before you dream of counting all the money you'll make with your online store, you need to protect your online business. It is guaranteed that you will experience an attempt to defraud you either sooner or later.

So, how do you protect yourself? Follow these steps.

How to Avoid Online Fraud

The first level of fraud protection is AVS. AVS stands for *Address Verification Service*. But it has its limitations.

AVS compares the billing address of the customer with the records held by the card issuer. If the card number and billing address match, AVS gives it a thumbs up. The problem is, the card could still be stolen and a thief can ask that the order be shipped to another address.

What About SET?

The credit card industry has been working on a new standard for credit card security that would protect both the consumer and the merchant. The standard is called SET. SET is the *Secure Electronic Transaction* protocol developed by Visa and MasterCard specifically for enabling secure credit card transactions on the Internet. It uses digital certificates to validate the identities of all parties involved in a purchase and encrypts credit card information before sending it across the Internet. However, it is likely to be several years before the use of SET becomes widespread.

AVS has other problems too. AVS only works for addresses in the United States. So, if you have an international order AVS will not help. If you sell software or information that can be downloaded instantly, AVS provides no protection. All a thief has to do is obtain a valid billing address that corresponds to a stolen credit card number and your instant buy becomes and instant fraud!

Warning Signs of Fraud

So how can you reduce your vulnerability to fraud? By looking for these common warning signs that an order is possibly fraudulent.

Your first red flag is noticing that the bill to and ship to addresses are different. Look out for a billing address that's in one country and a shipping address that is in another. But keep in mind that many legitimate customers will buy a product and have it shipped to an address other than their billing address. Some merchants will not accept these types of orders. The problem here is that you can lose a considerable number of orders using this policy.

A good thing to look out for in these cases is the size and amount of the order. Be wary of big orders, especially for brand-name items. If someone is ordering a high-priced item or a large number of items—like three MP3 Players at once—and the ship to and bill to addresses do not match, then investigate the order further.

Untrustworthy E-mail Addresses

You can find a list of free e-mail domains on the AntiFraud Web site that are used most frequently in fraudulent transactions, along with an very extensive list of domains that have been used for fraud at antifraud.com/redflag.htm.

Another tip off is the e-mail address. With fraudulent orders the customer's e-mail address is often one of the free e-mail services like Hotmail, MSN, or Yahoo! A thief will do all he

[handwritten margin note: Add To The policy a call verification Billing Add, 0 ding Add, Date of Birth]

can to avoid being traced, so an untraceable e-mail address from one of the free services is a great way to hide his identity. A high proportion of fraud orders come from these free e-mail services.

A red flag should be raised if an order specifies express or next day shipping. Another clue is a suspicious billing address such as 123 Main Street. You can check to see if an address is real by using Yahoo! Maps at `maps.yahoo.com`. And finally, if someone places a very valuable order and asks that it be left at the front door, be suspicious. It could be a sign that a thief is using an innocent person's house as a drop-off point. If an order is for a high-priced item, request that it be signed for.

TIP — Fraud Prevention Services

For a list of some automatic checking tools for fraud prevention, check out AntiFraud.com at `antifraud.com/benefits.htm`. AntiFraud provides a number of antifraud services like Automatic E-mail Screening and Instant Fraud Alerts, among others. Another fraud prevention service is supplied by CyberSource at `cybersource.com/services/risk`. Its Internet Fraud Screen automatically calculates your risk associated with an order.

You Suspect Fraud—What Do You Do?

You have a great order but you suspect fraud. If you do, follow these steps:

1. Call the customer. Use the phone numbers you requested and collected from him. When you contact him, don't automatically assume that you're dealing with a thief. The customer could have entered incorrect information and you don't want to offend him and lose the sale. In general though, a thief will not want to have a long conversation with you.

2. If the billing address doesn't match or is incorrect, ask him to give it to you again. If the area code doesn't match the billing address's city, ask him why.

3. Ask the customer for the name and phone number of the establishment that issued the card. Both are usually printed on the back. If the customer cannot supply it, this is a sign that he doesn't physically have the card—just the number.

4. If you still feel uncomfortable with an order even after talking to the customer, ask him for payment in advance.

Remember, it takes a lot of orders to replace just one order lost to fraud. So, it's better to pass on the ones that you're not 100% certain about.

CHAPTER 16

FULFILLMENT AND SHIPPING

In This Chapter

- Learn how to accept cred.␣␣␣ls at your Web site
- Find out whether it's better to set up your own credit card merchant account or use a third-party billing system
- Learn how to choose shopping cart software and which software is available
- Discover how to set up a credit card merchant account
- Discover how to choose a fulfillment partner to ship your orders

When I was a young lad growing up in New York, my buddy and I would trek down to our local mom-and-pop food store on the corner for groceries. The little old man who ran the small store had no cash register or receipt book—not even a shopping cart. You used a small basket that you would carry through the store filling it with your purchases. When it was time for you to check out, he would write the price of each item on the back of a brown paper bag, tally it up, and place your purchase in the same bag.

Although primitive by today's shopping standards, he provided all the elements that a Web store should provide today: a shopping basket, a checkout process, and a receipt. Even shipping was covered. You delivered the goods to your home yourself.

Over the last 40 years, the old mechanical cash registers gave way to computers with a drawer followed by laser scanners that feed information into a sophisticated database system that tracks pricing and inventory. The Net has evolved too. The few short years that e-commerce has evolved on the Net have seen three generations of the sales-enabling process. The current generation of e-commerce technology is called the shopping cart and is often referred to as *storefront* or *store-building* software. We saw this technology in Chapter 8, "Hosting Your Store for Free." Using just a Web browser, you could add and delete products, change prices, run special sales promotions on certain products, and pick up your orders.

To fully automate the buying process, every shopping cart software solution requires the use of a credit card and the ability of the merchant to accept them. But taking and processing the order is one thing—delivering to a customer is quite another. So let's look at what's involved in taking, fulfilling, and delivering an online order to your customer.

THE SHOPPING CART

The first question to ask yourself is, "Do I really need a shopping cart software program to take orders on my site?" If you're selling only a few products in your Web store, you can probably get by with a simple Web page order form. But if you sell more than a few products or offer a service, making the customer switch back and forth from the order form to the product pages will drive him from your site forever.

Free Shopping Carts

You don't have to pay for a shopping cart on your Web store. There are dozens of free shopping cart programs that you can easily add to your site. Check them out at www.onlineorders.net/links/Free/.

So, if you sell a number of products that have a number of different variables connected with them, you need to install a shopping cart on your site. If you're going to do serious e-commerce, a shopping cart is essential. With the proper shopping cart software your customers will be able to

- Place an order on the same page where it's pictured and described. A simple Add to Cart button on each product or service catalog page gives your customers the convenience of choosing a product to buy, then lets them continue to shop at your store.
- Select to buy more than one product at a time and choose different colors and sizes.
- Calculate and tally all the items in the cart at one time, giving the shopper a running total of what's in his or her cart and what the charges might be.

- View the final order, including all charges that will be made to a customer's credit card, including taxes, shipping, and handling.

When choosing a shopping cart package, be sure you answer these important questions.

Is the package easy to set up? Do you have to place it on your server (which will take some technical knowledge) or do you just "bolt it on" to your site (the credit card order is processed on the shopping cart provider's secure server)? How long does it take to set up the shopping cart? If it's through a service that bolts on to your Web store, then the process should take no more than an hour.

Can products be added and deleted easily and quickly? Does the shopping cart offer the option for different attributes for each product such as size and color? Do you have to manually retrieve your orders or are they faxed or e-mailed to you? Is the shopping cart connected directly to your credit card service and automatically processed or do you have to process the cards yourself? Will the shopping cart software compute taxes, shipping, and handling? Can it compute international shipping rates and tariffs? When the order is confirmed will it send out a confirmation e-mail to the customer?

If you're using a shopping cart service, what about fees? Are they per sale, per item stored, or a flat monthly rate? Is their server secure?

Pick a Card—Any Card!

Here's an all-in-one site to view a large selection of credit card merchant accounts that you can review for your e-business. Check it out at
`www.onlineorders.net/links/Credit_Card_Merchant_Accounts/`.

Some of the better store-building products are reviewed by Sell-It at `sellitontheweb.com`. To go directly to the shopping cart reviews, head to `sellitontheweb.com/ezine/features.shtml#carts`.

THE CASH REGISTER

The shopping cart or the shopping basket is only one of two parts of a shopping cart. The second part is the cash register. The shopping cart keeps track of and tallies the order; the cash register records, processes, and charges the customer's credit card.

The customer's credit card information is transmitted through a Secure Socket Layer (SSL) to your credit card processing agent. Any fully functioning shopping cart software must reside on a secure SSL server to protect the sensitive credit card information of your customers. If you are hosting through an e-commerce hosting service or are hosting yourself, it's essential that you take the customer's orders on an SSL server.

After your customer has entered his credit card information into your shopping cart's order form and clicks **Confirm My Order**, that information is sent from your SSL server to your credit card processing agent's server—or what's called the *Payment Gateway*. The Payment

Gateway, or credit card processing agent, performs a very important function. The agent is responsible for verifying the customer's credit card information and confirming that there are sufficient funds in the customer's account to cover a purchase.

What's a Payment Gateway?

The Payment Gateway verifies that a credit card is valid and that the card-holder has enough credit in his account to purchase the product he selected. A Payment Gateway is just an agent and does not verify that the card is stolen or being used by someone other than the cardholder.

The Payment Gateway then passes this information on to your bank, which then contacts the customer's credit card issuer that approves or denies credit. This notice is then passed back down the chain to the Payment Gateway and then to you.

For you to accept credit cards and have the customer's card charged to your account, thereby collecting your money, you must establish a merchant account at a bank. Establishing a credit card merchant account can be tricky and fraught with problems if you don't do it right. In addition, there are thousands of what are called field agents that aggressively recruit small merchants into Merchant Account programs that sound great on the surface but have hidden costs that can drive up the costs of accepting credit cards.

Setting Up a Merchant Account—The Rules

You must be very careful when choosing a merchant account. If you choose incorrectly, the costs incurred on each and every credit card sale you make could dramatically affect your bottom line.

Know the Fees

Setting up a merchant account and the processing of a customer's credit card has certain fees associated with it. It's not done for free. By not knowing what the required fees are, you can make a mistake that will cost you extra money on each and every credit card sale you make.

- Merchant Account Setup Fees
- Discount Rate
- Transaction Fee

Read the Fine Print

Many credit card field agents use fraudulent tactics to get your business by advertising a ridiculous rate like 1% to clear credit cards, and then you find out that it is 1% on top of 3% from the bank and additional percentages from the Payment Gateway. Make sure you get all the information before signing up for a merchant account.

- **Merchant account setup fee**—These can run from a few hundred to a thousand dollars. Most merchant account set up fees are in the $400–$600 range.

- **Discount rate**—Using the word discount makes it sound like you're getting a deal. You're not. This is the percentage of the sale that your merchant bank will charge you on each credit card charge. For example, if your customer has purchased $100 in merchandise from you and you're going to charge his card $100, you will have to pay your merchant bank a percentage of that sale to process the customer's credit card.

  This percentage can range between 2% and 3% for Visa, MasterCard, and Discover and 3% to 5% for American Express. So if your discount rate for a Visa card is 2%, your merchant bank will take 2%—or $2—of that $100 customer purchase and deposit the remainder in your bank account. And by the way—that percentage is on top of the total credit card charge—including shipping and handling.

- **Transaction fee**—This fee is in addition to the discount fee and is the charge that your merchant bank assesses to process the credit card sale. Expect to pay between $0.25 and $0.70 per transaction.

The fees don't stop there. Your merchant bank might require you to pay a monthly statement fee on top of all the other fees. Statement fees range between $10–$15 a month. You also might be charged a minimum processing fee of up to $25 a month. This fee is usually waived if your credit card sales meet your merchant bank's minimum monthly credit card sales. There also might be a holdback for charge-backs. Your bank might want to hold a sizable deposit against your sales to cover any charge-backs that you incur.

JARGON →

What's a Charge-Back?

A *charge-back* is what your bank does when they reverse a charge on your customer's credit card. Reasons for this include fraudulent or unauthorized use of the customer's credit card or just dissatisfaction with your product if you've refused to take back the product and issue a credit to their account.

Paying the Fees

Whether or not you really have to pay all these fees depends on the merchant bank you choose. The credit card business is very competitive and now that e-commerce is the hottest thing in business, many banks are aggressively lowering and even eliminating fees to attract e-businesses. There are hundreds of credit card programs available to e-tailers today and if you do your research, you'll find merchant banks that will not charge statement fees, minimum monthly processing fees, or even setup fees. But you have to take the time and make the effort to look around.

Get at least five price quotes. You can find a free impartial listing of merchant account providers and their primary rates and fees at MerchantWorkz at `MerchantWorkz.com` (see Figure 16.1). Another place to check is the Payment Processing links of About Electronic

Commerce Guide Gordon Whyte's site at `ecommerce.about.com/shopping/ecommerce/` `msub10.htm`. He has a very comprehensive list of credit card payment processing sites and Payment Gateways.

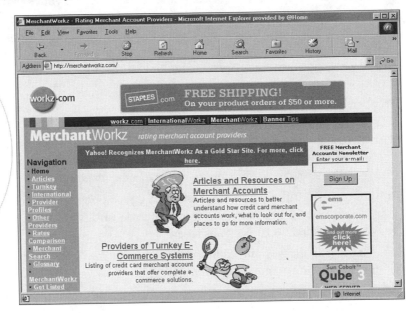

Figure 16.1

MerchantWorkz provides a free impartial listing of merchant account providers and their rates and fees.

And don't be afraid to push these providers into a bidding war. With a little research and planning, getting a merchant account can be painless and inexpensive. It also can protect you from less-reputable providers who know they can make a quick buck off a new Web merchant who's new to the game of accepting credit cards.

Finally, you might have to pay additional fees for purchasing hardware or software to send your credit card sale information through the payment gateways to your merchant bank. That's why it's important to choose a payment gateway/merchant bank package.

Choose a Payment Gateway/Merchant Bank Package

Don't try to save money by choosing a payment gateway that does not have a standing relationship with a merchant bank.

Unless you're a financial genius or someone who enjoys the pain of making separate online systems work together, choose a payment gateway and merchant bank that already work together. In reality, when you choose a payment gateway, your merchant bank is already chosen for you. You might not get the best price from the payment gateway's bank, but you will save yourself a lot of time and expense trying to integrate two systems from scratch. Know the fees to ensure that you're getting a square deal.

TIP

Directory of Payment Gateways

e-commerce Guidebook has a good list of prominent e-commerce companies that provide payment gateways for online transactions. Find it at www.online-commerce. com/directory.html.

So look for a payment gateway/merchant bank package where the payment gateway has prearranged the credit approval system and payment system of a merchant bank for you. Pick a package that works with all major credit cards and your account will be credited directly by the payment gateway's merchant bank. Also, remember to find out how funds are deposited in your account. Some merchant banks will send a monthly lump sum to your bank, and others will pay on every transaction as it happens.

Do I Need My Own Merchant Account?

If you have a small site, or are on a limited budget, or just want to dip your toe into the e-commerce waters, you might not want to go through the time, trouble, and expense of setting up your own merchant account. You can still accept credit card orders for products and services at your Web store just like the bigger sites—and do it securely.

There are a number of Web sites on the Net that offer to process credit cards for you for a flat fee. There are no setup charges, no hardware or software to install, and no monthly minimums to meet. When your customers are ready to buy, you simply direct them from your Web site to one of the service company's secure Web pages. Once there, your customer inputs his credit card information and buys your product or service.

So, what's the catch?

First of all, most of these companies accept only credit card orders for information or services. If your online business sells a service, a piece of downloadable information, or software, then this type of service is ideal. The second catch is the fees. Instead of paying merchant account fees of up to 5%, these companies charge fees as high as 10% to 15% of your credit card sale.

One such service company is ibill (ibill.com). It makes online sales of intangibles such as access to subscription sites, content, or services easy for merchants who do not qualify for, or who want to acquire, a merchant account. ibill's fees start at 15% and go down to 12% depending upon the volume of your sales.

ccBill (www.ccbill.com) is a similar service to ibill. It also processes only credit card sales for services, subscriptions, and downloadable information. ccBill fees vary depending on the volume of sales done during each accounting period. These fees are never more than 14.5% of revenues charged during a one-week period. Both of these companies handle all billing inquiries and customer service problems relating to them.

ABANX (abanx.com) is a little different from ibill and ccBill. In addition to accepting payment for services and information, ABANX accepts payment for product. ABANX provides your Web store with a centrally located shopping cart system, real-time secure SSL encrypted

FULFILLMENT AND SHIPPING

16

211

checkout servers, and handles the majority of billing inquiries including the necessary accounting. Using its Client Administration Interface, you're able to manage your account with ABANX, view any new orders, place refunds, and view your account statement.

ABANX collects 12% of the total amount charged to the customer. There are absolutely no startup costs, no monthly fees, or any other charges to utilize their service.

So, the choice is yours. Either way, you can take and process credit card orders on your site, which is essential to the success of your Web store.

NEW PAYMENT SOLUTIONS

"They're still using money, Spock—we've got to find some." That was the lament of Captain James Kirk in the movie *Star Trek: The Voyage Home* when they tried to board a bus in Twentieth Century San Francisco. The concept of money had drastically changed from our century to theirs. In fact, it's already changing for us today. That is, actual money—the paper and coins we've come to love—is fast becoming information.

When you pay your credit card bill, or the mortgage or the utility bill, the transaction is an information exchange. Once you've written that paper check, data is transmitted between your bank, your creditors, or your vendors. Money has become simply a sequence of bits and bytes of electronic information and for e-commerce, payment for goods and services through electronic means is a natural extension of the same process.

Although many of the current online payment schemes that you can use today are still rather conventional, changes are in the air. Although the consumer's credit card or bank account is where payment will come from, how the payment is made on the Net can take a variety of forms—as a pre-paid payment option, as a person-to-person (P2P) service, or in the form of an Internet escrow service. These types of alternative payment systems could be useful for your online business.

Examples of these types of payment methods are eCount at www.ecount.com and RocketCash at www.rocketcash.com. eCount let's Net consumers conduct secure online transactions at any online store through the use of prepaid personal accounts. Consumers can add as little as $5 to their ecount to open an account. When they register and are accepted they choose a unique User ID and password and are issued a 16-digit MasterCard account number and an expiration date, which together can be used to access the balance of their ecount at online merchants that accept MasterCard. eCount was developed for those consumers unable or unwilling to use their credit cards to pay for goods and services online. With eCount, consumers never have to give out their credit card online again.

RocketCash allows kids to purchase goods online without their parents' credit cards. Parents, or anyone for that matter who wants to extend a pre-paid purchasing limit to another party, can set up an account at RocketCash. A credit card number is entered into the RocketCash system, a spending limit is assigned, and a password is given to the user of the RocketCash. The user can then shop at the different authorized merchants that are on the RocketCash site.

If you decide to start an online auction business, one problem that you will have is the opportunity for fraud by users of your service. For example, scam artists on eBay promising one thing and by delivering another have cheated many eBay buyers. Up to now, the best way consumers could protect themselves was through the use of an Internet escrow service such as Tradenable at `www.iescrow.com/`. Now, Companies like PayPal at `www.paypal.com` and ProPay.com at `www.propay.com` have entered the P2P space offering secure payment services between consumers and businesses.

CHOOSING A FULFILLMENT PARTNER

You're making sales and getting tons of orders—but how do you fill them? Your e-commerce site is more than just a catalog and shopping cart that lets your customers choose products and purchase them using a credit card. True, the *e* in e-commerce means electronic, but until the day comes when *Star Trek* transporter rooms are invented, you'll still have to move those atoms from a warehouse to your customer's front door.

So the question is, "Who's going to do it?"

> **Directory of Fulfillment Services**
>
> About.com e-commerce Guide, Gordon Whyte, has a good list of fulfillments services companies on the Net that you can use to outsource your fulfillment operations. Find it at `ecommerce.about.com/shopping/ecommerce/msub26.htm`.

Will you have your own warehouse filled with inventory and a staff of shipping and receiving people? Or do you outsource this to a third-party service? My advice is not to go it alone. Alhough you might have dreams of being the next Amazon, you have to walk before you can run. Outsourcing your receiving, shipping, and handling makes fulfillment and distribution simpler and more efficient—especially for a small to medium-size eBusiness. In addition, outsourcing enables you to focus on your core business—selling product. Having to both market and fulfill product will only divide your attention.

Besides, you can always bring fulfillment in-house after your sales and staff get large enough to support a warehousing and shipping operation.

So, how do you choose a third-party fulfillment service? What are the things to consider? They are warehousing, fees, integration, and insurance.

- **Warehousing**—Find out how large their warehouse is. How many different companies can they service? Do they have an efficient way of separating your company's merchandise from others? It's a very good idea to visit a fulfillment house and check out how their warehouse is laid out and physically see where your merchandise will be stored. Will they charge you for the storage space that your products occupy? How much? Find out how many orders a day they're capable of shipping. Will your business requirements put a strain on their daily shipping capabilities? How much of their shipping capabilities will your business eat up?

- **Fees**—Ask how the third party will charge you for their service? Most fulfillment houses will charge you a setup fee, a monthly management fee, and a pick-pack-and-ship fee. Ask if receiving of your products is included in the monthly management fee or if it is an extra charge. If so, is the extra charge based on a per-box basis or a per-hour basis?

- **Integration**—Ask how they will receive orders from your Web store and send their shipping and receiving reports to you. You might ask if the fulfillment house can seamlessly integrate their system into your Web store. The ideal scenario would be this: Your Web store takes the order and sends all the shipping information to the fulfillment house electronically. The fulfillment house fulfills the order and sends a shipping report back to you electronically. Barring that, you might have to collect the order information offline and e-mail or fax the orders to the fulfillment house. The fulfillment house might have to e-mail or fax you back offline when the products are shipped. Either way, you'll need to know when the product is shipped, what shipping carrier was used (UPS, FedEx, US Post Office), and the tracking number to e-mail to your customer.

- **Insurance**—Ask about insurance. Are they fully covered for fire, theft, and flood? Make sure that your products are insured while in their care.

Using Your Suppliers for Fulfillment

You don't have to go through the process of finding and negotiating with a fulfillment house to ship your goods. You might be able to eliminate the middleman. If you're buying from distributors or directly from the manufacturers of your product, you might be able to convince them to drop-ship their products to your customers.

JARGON

Don't Ship It—Drop-Ship It!

You should ask whether your product supplier will ship your orders for you instead of warehousing them yourself. This is called *drop-shipping*. By having your suppliers ship your orders to your customer, you can save a bundle on warehousing and shipping costs for yourself and pass the savings to your customer.

This is a good solution if you don't want to invest your money in inventory and pay storage and fulfillment fees to a third-party fulfillment house. That's how many large e-tailers started their business. Take Amazon as an example. It worked directly with the major book distributors, who drop-shipped books to Amazon customers.

There's another advantage to having a drop-shipping agreement with your distributors. Because you're not actually buying and warehousing inventory, you can list on your Web store every product that your distributors sell without actually buying them. This gives shoppers the impression of a much larger store than you have. In addition, you might be able to negotiate a better deal from your distributors. Because you're a customer and it's their goods you're selling, they see you as more of a partner and might charge less for fulfillment than a third-party fulfillment house.

THE TAX MAN COMETH

Currently, Congress has declared a moratorium on taxing Net sales to study the issue. This moratorium will not last forever so you should consider how you'd be collecting taxes on sales made at your Web store. Although the task sounds daunting—collecting taxes for 30,000 existing taxing jurisdictions—there are some solutions if Internet tax legislation is passed.

Two companies are working on a Web-based tax calculation system that they plan to make available to small to medium-sized e-businesses. Both will provide e-businesses with a tax server that acts like a central data repository for small to medium-sized businesses. Taxware at `www.taxware.com` will provide a tax server that will charge by the transaction with charges as little as $25 a year. Another tax software vendor, Vertex at `vertexinc.com`, is also considering a Web-based approach.

If Internet tax legislation is passed, your Web store will have to charge city, county, and state taxes. So you should prepare for this eventuality. Stay up to date on what's developing on the Net sales tax issue at `webcom.com/software/issues/0sii-tax.html` (see Figure 16.2).

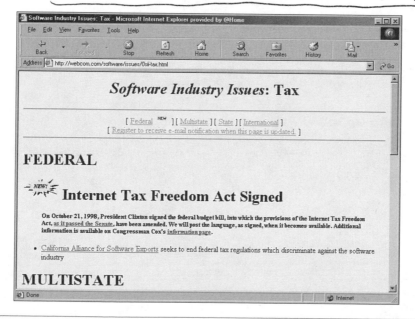

Figure 16.2

As a Web merchant, it's important to stay on top of what is happening on the Internet sales tax front. The Software Industry Issues site will keep you up to date.

CHAPTER 17

CUSTOMER SERVICE

In This Chapter

- Learn the important elements of customer service
- Learn how good service, satisfaction guarantees, and the proper handling of returns can increase your business
- Discover the ways to handle disgruntled customers

The quickest way to e-commerce failure is not delivering on what you promise. Your promise to your customers is a good product or service, at a fair price, delivered promptly. But your responsibility to the customer doesn't end there. What you do or do not do after the sale determines whether your customer returns and buys from you again.

Here's another important point. It's generally known that it's five times more expensive to get a new customer than it is to keep an existing one. So, growing your e-business includes not only attracting shoppers to your site, but also keeping the customers you have. You keep a customer by providing good customer service. Customers—even potential customers—need to know that you care enough about their business to service them when they have a problem.

In the wide world of e-commerce, customer service can spell the difference between success and failure of your e-business.

SERVICE ELEMENTS

We've talked a lot about making your Web store customer-friendly and easy to use. If your site seems difficult to buy from, a shopper will move on to your competitor. But good site design, an easy-to-use shopping cart, quality products or services, the speed of your site, and your selling price are all for naught if the quality of your customer service is below par.

An investment in good customer service is one of the best customer-retention investments you can make. And customer service strategies should be applied at every stage of the purchasing process.

Good customer service is not offered just after the sale. Good service is everything that takes place before, during, and after the sale. Wouldn't you rather influence shoppers to buy when they're considering making a purchase and not just when they're ready to buy? Then, after the sale, wouldn't you want the ability to bring them back again to your site for repeat purchases? A well planned out customer service strategy or online help desk can accomplish all of these.

So how do you build good customer service into your Web store? Easy. Walk a mile in your customer's shoes. Ask yourself what kinds of service you would expect before, during, and after a sale.

Customer Service Starts Before the Sale

Picture this. A first-time visitor comes to your Web site. He or she came with a shopping list in hand and the thought of making a purchase. What can you do to make this first-time shopper feel comfortable enough to buy from you?

Create a First Time Visitor icon and place it very visibly on your home page. It's a great way to welcome new visitors and give them a feeling that help is just a mouse click away. The icon brings them to a First Time Visitor Web page that contains a brief description of the customer service that they can expect when they buy from your Web store. RM Carspares at www.rmcarspares.co.uk/docs/first.html has a good example of a First Time Visitor page (see Figure 17.1).

For instance, provide your customer service e-mail address, toll-free customer service phone number, fax number, and your customer service hours. Include your customer satisfaction guarantees and return policies. Tell them how their order will be handled—how fast their order will ship, how you will confirm their order, when it's shipped, and how to track it after it's shipped. Also, provide a link to your FAQs (Frequently Asked Questions) about your products and services and tell the shopper that you have a secure site where they can use their credit card without fear.

Finally, direct new customers to the fastest way to place an order on your site, such as a list of specials for first time customers or the product or service directory page of your Web store. If you have a product or service search function on your site (if you have lots of offerings, you should), include this on the First Time Visitor page.

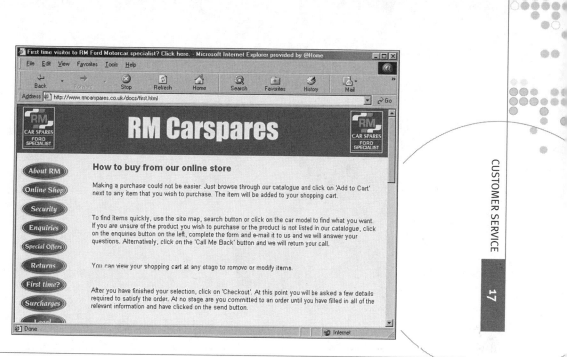

Figure 17.1

RM Carspares invites the First Time Visitor with a User's Guide to its site.

Get Your Free Search Engine

Need a search engine for your site? Don't want to pay a lot for it? How about free? Matt Wright's Simple Search Engine gives your site a search engine that can search up to 300 Web pages or so on your site. Find it at www.worldwidemart.com/scripts/search.shtml.

If executed properly, your first time visitors will get a nice warm and fuzzy feeling about your Web store and feel secure enough to make that first purchase.

Now, let's look at some other types of customer service elements that you can provide to encourage a shopper to make a purchase. They are

- Customer Care FAQs
- Dedicated e-mail
- Discussion boards
- Guarantees and warranties

Customer Care FAQs

Customer Care FAQs (Frequently Asked Questions) can be used to list the most common answers to customer service questions that a shopper might have. They not only list in an easy to understand way your customer service policies, but also list the most common customer service problems and how you will solve them.

A company with a plug-and-play help desk is Right Now Technologies at www.rightnowtech. com (see Figure 17.2). Its product is an online help desk that builds a database of questions already asked by customers.

Figure 17.2

Right Now Technologies helps you automatically build a database of questions and answers that are then made live and searchable.

Customer Care FAQs let shoppers answer questions by themselves all in one place. Ask yourself—would you like having to visit one area of your site to learn about a product, then another to buy it, and a third to see how long it will take to ship? Of course not. So place all this information in your Customer Care FAQs.

The easiest way to start building a Customer Care FAQ is to ask yourself what questions a customer would ask most often. Just frame a simple answer for each question and you have your FAQ. Not only will this benefit the shopper, it also will save hours of phone support. A way to continuously update your FAQs is to add recurring questions that are asked of your visitors and customers that you may receive via e-mail and phone calls.

Dedicated E-mail

When the FAQs are not enough, e-mail comes to the rescue. A dedicated e-mail address for customer service is a must for your Web store and is one of the easiest ways to provide online service and support for your customers. Set up at least one e-mail address for customer questions such as support@yourbusiness.com. You might even consider setting up several e-mail aliases to extend your customer care services.

What's an E-mail Alias?

E-mail aliases are additional e-mail addresses that point to another e-mail address. All messages sent to an e-mail alias are automatically forwarded to the specified real e-mail address. This way you can have more than one e-mail address on an e-mail account.

With e-mail aliases, you can forward customer e-mail to the appropriate person or department in your company. This way you can create different e-mail address for different customer concerns and problems. For example, you can create a separate e-mail address for general customer questions, product questions, order status, and product return requests.

Keep in mind that receiving the e-mails is only half the task. You must answer them, too—and answer them in a timely manner. Shoppers and customers expect to have their e-mail answered within 24 hours—at the latest! So check your e-mail regularly throughout the day.

A simpler and easier way for your shoppers and customers to ask questions of you is to provide a Web-based form for each area of concern that when filled out, e-mails the information to you. The benefit here is both to the customer and to you. With a specific Web-based form for each customer service problem, you can request the type of information that you'll need to more quickly address your customer's questions and concerns.

TIP

Automate Your E-mail

Compose a series of brief e-mail replies to common questions from shoppers to your site so you can respond quickly to e-mail inquiries.

Discussion Boards

Here's another customer care strategy. Why should you do all the work? Let your customers ask questions of each other. By offering a discussion board on your site, you can give customers and potential customers a way to discuss your product or service with other users.

In addition, you can pick up valuable market research from the comments posted there that can help you design better customer care policies, choose better products, improve your service offering, and build a loyal customer base. This will help build a strong online community (one of the 3 Cs of e-commerce, remember?) on your site. You can even solicit customer feedback and advice, giving your customers the impression that you care about their needs and are willing to make changes to your policies and improve your offering.

Reward Your Customers for Good Advice

Why not reward customers who give you good advice for improving your customer support? Their feedback is the best you can get—and worth it. Hold contests or award rebates on future purchases for the most helpful advice. Or use the customer product review approach that Amazon provides site visitors.

Guarantees and Warranties

One of the best ways to build customer confidence in your Web store is to tell the shopper of any product or service warrantees and your satisfaction guarantee.

If you have a satisfaction guarantee (and you should), let the shopper know that right up front. Put it on your First Time Visitor page and in your Customer Care FAQs. To be blunt, you should offer nothing less than a 100% customer-satisfaction guarantee on all the products and services you sell. These guarantees come in three types:

- **100% Satisfaction guarantee**—Customers must be 100% satisfied with their purchase. If not, they should be able to return the product within 30 days of receipt for either a full refund or a credit on a future purchase.
- **100% Product warranty**—If your products carry a manufacturer's warranty, say so. If not, consider replacing the product yourself.
- **100% Price guarantee**—Guarantee that your customer will not find your product or service at a lower price at another Web site. If they do, offer to refund the difference in price.

Consider using one or more of these guarantees to build customer confidence in your Web store and to make more sales.

Managing Returns for Customer Retention

The old adage goes, "A satisfied customer tells no one. A dissatisfied customer tells ten of his friends." On the Net, a dissatisfied customer can tell thousands of other consumers about a bad shopping experience. And one of the worst problems with a disgruntled customer is dealing with his or her returns.

Pay Your Customers to Complain

Even negative feedback is useful in running your business. Sometimes it's better than positive feedback. So, run a "Complaint Contest" to elicit feedback on your site and service. You can easily do this by sending an e-mail to recent customers informing them of the contest and solicit complaints. List a set of question in the e-mail message for them to answer—shipping complaints, product complaints, service complaints, and so on.

If you're selling goods on the Net, dealing with returns is one of the ugly facts of life. But it's not just the problem of handling returns. The returns process itself can cost your e-business a bundle.

This headache for you has created an opportunity for others—and a returns solution for your e-business. One that can help your e-business manage its returns easily and less expensively.

Returns are normally counted as part of the cost of doing business, but they should be viewed as a business-building opportunity. The Return Exchange, at www.TheReturnExchange.com/ (see Figure 17.3), offers a one-stop shop for a company's returns problem. It provides a plug-in that allows e-tailers to make its service the Returns button for their web site. After clicking on the Returns button a customer fills out an online form and sends the form along with the merchandise to be returned to the Return Exchange's warehouse—not the merchant.

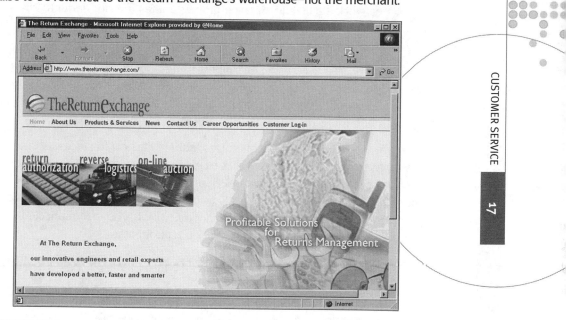

Figure 17.3

The Return Exchange supplies a complete end-to-end return process management to e-commerce retailers.

Upon receipt, the merchandise is inspected and prepared for one of three methods of disposal. The product is returned for credit to the manufacture, the product can be repackaged and put back in inventory, or the Return Exchange can use it's product liquidation process that consists of using online auction channels to sell returns directly to the consuming public.

It would pay to look into the services of these returns management companies.

Serving the Customer During the Sale

Servicing the customer during the buying process is just common sense. You want to remove as many sales objections as you can to allow the shopper to make a buying decision, so you have to think ahead. Two of the best ways to make a customer comfortable with a purchase at the point of sale is to provide real-time stock status and shipping time information.

If a customer knows the stock status of a product and when it will ship, you will eliminate many of your customer service problems. Amazon does a very good job of informing the potential customer of what books are in stock and within what time frame they will ship. Keep in mind that what you promise you must deliver. So, if you find that a product offered by a customer is not in stock or if shipping of the item will be delayed, be sure to contact the customer immediately and inform him or her when the product will be shipped.

Sometimes stock status and shipping time estimates are not enough. There are times at the point of purchase when the customer needs additional information to make the sale. This is where live customer care becomes important.

You can offer free live customer support using ICQ at `www.icq.com/download/`, Yahoo! Instant Messaging at `messenger.yahoo.com`, or AOL's Instant Messenger service at `www.aol.com/aim/`. Shoppers can download the free desktop application and communicate with you real-time if they have a question.

There are a number of new technologies that enable you to place customer support right on your Web site that customers click to get in touch with a real live human by phone or by online chat. Services such as LivePerson (see Figure 17.4) at `www.liveperson.com` offer a pop-up chat box that allows instant customer contact with a real person whereas OnCall by WebEx at `corporate.webex.com/about.shtml` lets you communicate in real-time with your customers using just your browser and a phone line.

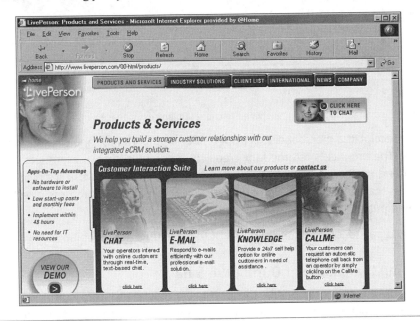

Figure 17.4

With just a click of a button, LivePerson opens a small chat window on your site where customers can chat with a customer service agent and ask questions.

Another service is Instant Call at `www.globalonlinetelecom.com/ic-d/icdhome.asp`. When a site visitor clicks the **Instant Call** button on your site, Instant Call phones you and the customer and links the calls for instant communication.

Service After the Sale—The True Test of Customer Care

You might say that service after the sale is where the rubber hits the road. You've spent a lot of time, money, and energy getting the sale—now you have to keep it.

Online customers are a skittish bunch. No matter how comfortable you've made them in buying from your Web store, after that buy button is pressed, they still want to be secure in the fact that their order has been received and that their product has been shipped.

To soothe the customer's concerns about an order and to eliminate many e-mail messages to your customer service department, be sure that you send a real-time instant order confirmation to the customer as soon as the order is placed. The order confirmation message should include an order number, what they bought, where it will be shipped, and the total amount of the order including all shipping and handling charges and applicable taxes.

After their order is shipped, another e-mail confirmation should be sent with relevant shipping information and order status. If for some reason you cannot ship within the time promised on your site, send an intermediate e-mail keeping the customer informed of the status of his order and when it might ship.

TIP

Help Your Customers Track Their Shipment

Here's a good customer service idea. Provide a link on your site to the multitracking shipment Web site at `www.fedex.com/us/tracking/`. From this site, your customers can track their shipment through more than a dozen different shipping companies, including FedEx, UPS, USPS, Airborne, DHL, and a host of smaller carriers.

After the order has been shipped and enough time has elapsed for the customer to receive it, send another e-mail asking if he did receive it and if there were any problems with the order. This proactive approach to customer service will pay off in spades. It shows that you do care about your customers and that you are willing and able to correct any problem that they might have had. In addition, if they respond to your follow-up e-mail, some customers might write you a good testimonial that—with their permission—you can print on your Web site.

Finally, despite the best efforts of your customer service strategies some customers are disappointed in the product they bought and want to return it. It's important that you have a no-hassle return policy. Remember, your prime goal is to keep the customers you have so you will have to weigh the return of a product or a refund on a service in light of how valuable your customer is to keep.

Sometimes returns are a blessing in disguise—okay, not blessings, but useful for your business. Most times customers will give you their reasons for the return and this information is good feedback on a particular product or the manner in which you sell from your sight. Collecting all the returns data and adding it to your customer service requests will help you identify merchandising problems and opportunities.

HANDLING DISGRUNTLED CUSTOMERS

Like product returns, customer complaints—if used correctly—can be a valuable resource that you can turn to your advantage. They can give you insight into problems with your selling process. Accept each complaint for what it is—a chance to learn.

First of all, answer each and every complaint promptly and politely. Before answering with a solution to a customer's complaint be sure that you understand the problem and be as specific as possible in your replies. If the customer is frustrated and complaining, expect the tone of his or her message to be angry and confrontational. That doesn't mean you should be. Respect your frustrated customers and reply to them in an empathetic tone.

But don't stop there. If you've not received a reply, follow up with the customer to make sure his or her concerns have been addressed by you. This additional e-mail will show the complaining customer that you are willing to come to a mutually agreeable solution to his or her problem. If a customer sees that you are willing to work with him or her, this will go a long way in resolving the issue.

Just remember that every complaint, no matter how illogical, should receive a reply. Your best efforts could turn a complaining customer into one of your best.

Remember that good service is essential and is a promise you make to your customer. So, don't make any promises you can't keep.

PART V

PROMOTING YOUR ONLINE BUSINESS

MARKETING YOUR E-BUSINESS

In This Chapter

- Discover how to optimize your site for search engines
- Learn the grass-root techniques of Guerrilla Marketing
- Discover how to create repeat visitors to your Web site
- Learn how to protect your Web store's online reputation

Congratulations! If you've followed this far, you have one of the best little Web stores on the Net. Unfortunately, odds are that no one has ever heard of it. In fact, too many e-tailers work on the assumption in the movie *Field of Dreams*: "If you build it, they will come."

They won't. After your Web store is built, you have to give customers a reason to come. That takes marketing—and the right kind. Your Web site is a passive form of marketing that points shoppers toward your products or services. You can't stop there. You must create a marketing plan using a set of active tools that will drive traffic to your Web store.

You've probably heard that registering your site in as many search engines as possible will result in millions of visitors streaming to your new Web store.

It won't.

Start Your Marketing with a Free Sample Marketing Plan

At Bplans.com you can find sample marketing plans that match your business. It takes only five minutes answering a few questions and, voilà—you have a marketing plan that you can build on. Find it at bplans.com/marketingplans/.

Yes, search engines are important, but that's where you start your marketing efforts, not where you end them. There are literally millions of Web sites on the Web all vying for the Web surfer's attention. You have to go beyond them if you are to have a successful marketing plan. To paraphrase Thomas Edison, "Success is 99% perspiration and 1% inspiration." To succeed, persevere and be prepared to sweat!

Now, there are many books written on how to market on the Internet and any large bookstore will carry dozens of them at any point in time. But all the marketing advice from all the authors in these books boils down to two marketing objectives.

- Make your site visible to consumers on the Web.
- Give them a reason to come—and then come back.

Let's take a look at each one.

LETTING THE WEB SHOPPER KNOW YOU EXIST

Making your site visible to the consumer is your first challenge. So the first question you need to ask yourself is, "How will I get consumers to visit my site?" Let's face it; rising above the din of the Web is a daunting task. But like solving any problem, breaking the tasks down into small pieces greatly increases the odds for success.

Using each of the following marketing strategies one at a time will greatly increase the exposure of your Web store and its ultimate success.

- Search Engine Optimization
  - Placing your store properly in search engines
- Grass-Roots Marketing
  - Exchanging links and banners with other sites
  - Registering your Web store with online promotion services
  - Using the Internet newsgroups and discussion lists
  - Using viral marketing

We'll start with the major search engines and discuss optimizing your Web site for them.

Search Engine Optimization

Registering your site at the major search engines is your first and most important step in marketing your Web store. Although there are hundreds and hundreds of search engines, directories, and yellow pages that you can register your site with, you should register your site first with these major search engines.

Be Careful with Free Site Submission Services

Although free site submission services such as SubmitIt! (submit-it.com) provide a way to submit your site to approximately 15 of the most important indexes, be aware that this is a cookie-cutter approach. Because just one submission must be basic enough to fit within the guidelines of all the search engines, you're not able to take full advantage of the differences each have to offer. For example, one engine might allow 75-word descriptions, but you'll have supplied only 25 words to the free submission service.

- altavista.com
- excite.com
- goto.com
- search.aol.com
- go.com
- lycos.com
- webcrawler.com
- yahoo.com

All these sites search the Web in one of two ways. Either they're a directory such as Yahoo! that searches its own database, or they search actual Web pages looking for keywords residing in the page itself.

Optimize Your Site for Search Engines

Virtual Stampede will help you build and then e-mail to you meta-keyword, description, and title tags that you can cut and paste into your Web pages. It doesn't promise that you'll appear in the top of the search results, but the code it does send you is generic enough for the top search engines. Find it at virtual-stampede.com/tools.htm.

There are two recent additions to the search engine world that search the Web a little differently, and you should also register with these new search engines. Google! at google.com (see Figure 18.1) uses text-matching techniques to find pages that are both important and relevant to a search. Google! keeps track of which pages actually get chosen when presented in a search result. The next time that keyword is searched on, it remembers which pages were selected by the user before and presents those pages high on the search results list. Direct Hit at directhit.com is a similar site that ranks search results according to what other people have selected as the most relevant and popular sites for their search request.

Also consider the list of search engines and directories at Search Engine Watch. Search Engine Watch at searchenginewatch.internet.com/links/Major_Search_Engines/ The_Major_Search_Engines/index.html lists additional important search engines that you should submit your site to.

Registering your Web site at the major search engines is relatively simple. The challenge is making your site appear at the top of the search results list when a shopper searches for an e-tailer that sells your products or services. To accomplish this feat, you have to optimize your site for the major search engines.

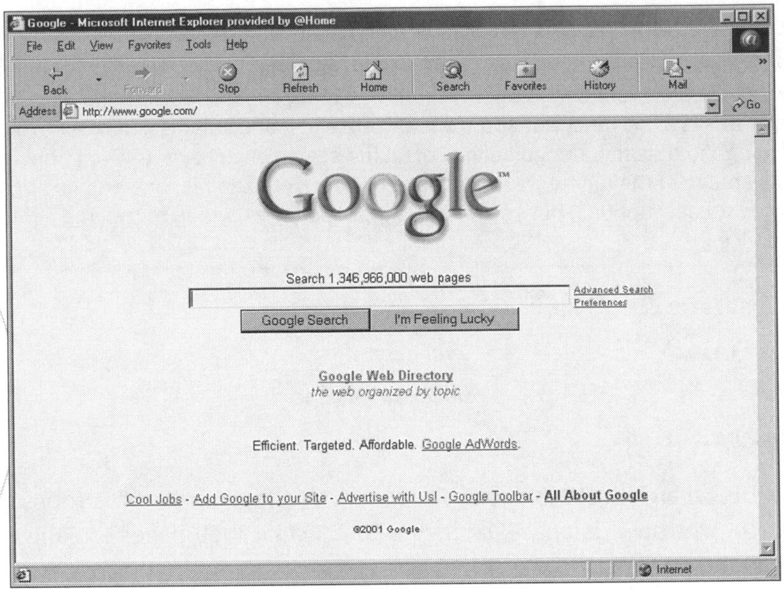

Figure 18.1

Google has become one of the most popular search engines on the Web. Make sure you register your site with it.

Optimization is more art than science because each search engine uses different search rules. But there are some key things you can do to ensure that your Web store does not come up as site number 1,000 in a search results list. Now there are many books and online services that claim to guarantee top placement in the major search engines if you use their tricks and services. But the search engines regularly change the ways they search the Web, so many of these tricks do not hold true for long.

> **TIP**
>
> **Optimize Your Site for Search Engines**
> If you really want to learn the current tricks of the search engine trade, then visit Search Engine Watch at searchenginewatch.com.

Whatever your choice, you need to know the general basics of how search engines search the Web. As I said before, search engines fall into two basic groups. Some search their own database, such as Yahoo!, and some search actual Web pages looking for keywords residing in the page itself, such as AltaVista. This means you have to know how to register with a search engine directory, such as Yahoo!, and what search engines, such as AltaVista, look for.

> **TIP**
>
> **Are You Listed in the Search Engines?**
> Some search engines make it easy to confirm that your Web page is in their catalogs. With others, it can be more difficult. Here's a way to find out whether your Web pages are listed in the major search engines. Check out the URL checking information along

with many other useful tools at Search Engine Watch, `www.searchenginewatch.com/webmasters/checkurl.html`.

To optimize for both, you have to keep the following in mind.

Page Titles, Keywords, and Your Web Pages

It's very important that you take care when creating the title, description, keywords, alt tags, and the first paragraph of your Web pages. The search engines in one way or another will read this text and use it to return a list of search results to the Web surfer making a search.

Don't make the mistake of creating a page title that's good for people but bad for the search engines. Don't use a title for your page such as "mySoftware Store—We Sell Computer Software." With a title like that, you're asking to be overlooked by the search engines. Keep this rule in mind: All your most important keywords must be in the title tag. Make a list of all the keywords that describe your Web store and create a title tag that uses them with the most important words first.

A good title tag for your page would read:

> `<TITLE>`Productivity software for business and home office use—selling word processing, spreadsheet, database, and presentation software including utilities and accessories—mySoftware Store, your store for business productivity`</TITLE>`

Notice that your company name is near the end of the title tag. Why? Your page description will probably be truncated by the search engine, so you want your most important information on what you offer upfront.

Another reason for all this verbiage is that the three most important places to have keywords and phrases are your title tag, your metatags, and your first paragraph. You want them to all contain the same important words because this will improve your ranking in a search result. Why? Because all these keywords in all your tags increase your keyword density and improve your rankings.

Now let's look at your metatags.

TIP

Don't Forget Your Alt Tags

When placing graphics on your Web page, include a text alt tag for each graphic. An *alt tag* is a small text description of the graphic included in the HTML code with the graphic that the search engines can read when searching your Web page. Search engines can't read a graphic so an alt tag is important. Another advantage of alt tags is that they increase the keyword density on a page.

The metatags are important to getting a good ranking in the search results. Metatags come in two flavors—the description metatag and the keyword metatag. The description metatag is a brief description (about 100–200 characters) of what's on a Web page.

The description metatag looks something like this:

<META name="description" content="Productivity software for business and home office use—selling word processing, spreadsheet, database, and presentation software including utilities and accessories">

The other metatag is the keywords tag. Create a set of keyword phrases that explain your page or site and list them in the metatag separated by commas.

After you have your keywords, turn them into key phrases. Don't repeat a key phrase, and don't repeat any individual keyword more than five times or so. The reason for this is that many of the search engines will penalize you for doing this.

Here's an example of a keywords metatag:

<META name="keywords" content="productivity software, word processing, accounting software, spreadsheet software, productivity tools for business, home office computer software, virus protection, modems, surge surpressors">

Where Do You Rank in the Major Search Engines?

To find out how well your site is positioned with the major search engines, use a service called Position Agent, which will show where you're coming up in the various search engines. Get a free trial at positionagent.com/free.htm.

Finally, pay attention to the first paragraph of the Web page you are registering with the search engines. The first paragraph of your Web page should duplicate and expand upon everything in your title and metatags. Make sure the first paragraph has all your key phrases in it. Turn those keywords, key phrases, and title into a welcoming message that will make a good first impression on the consumer visiting your site.

Grass-Roots Marketing

After you've prepared your Web site for the search engines and carefully registered with them, your thoughts now should turn to promotion. Your first question is probably "How can I make a big impact on the Net—fast?" The Web is filled with sites such as ZenithMedia at www.zenithmedia.com/mapuse00.htm that can point you to useful sites to market your Web store (see Figure 18.2).

Keep in mind that unless you have substantial resources (or happen to be a relative of Bill Gates), promoting your new e-business takes a lot of hard work and time to see results. Make the most of your time with these basic grass-roots marketing strategies to launch your e-business.

Promotion does not mean advertising. So, before you go out and spend a bundle of money advertising, start your marketing first on a grass-roots level. This gives you a chance to find out what works best for your e-business and what doesn't before you put your limited resources toward a full-fledged marketing plan.

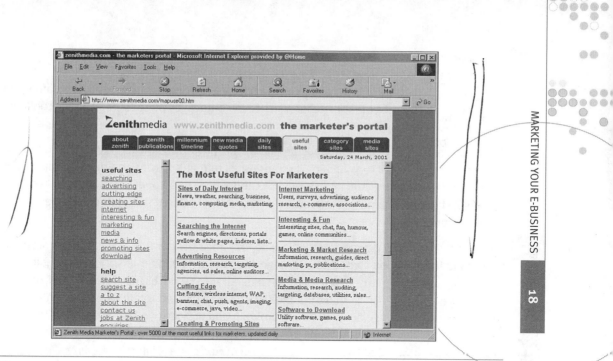

Figure 18.2

ZenithMedia will direct you to the most useful sites for marketers on the Net.

Swapping Links and Banners

After registering your site with the search engines, the first grass-roots marketing initiative should be to search for sites that will link to you and vice versa. Swapping links can come in two ways:

- **Reciprocal linking** Placing links on your page to complementary product sites that, in turn, place links to your site on their page.

- **Banner exchanges** Swapping banners that advertise your site with the banners of other sites.

First go to the top search engines that you've registered with and—using the keywords and key phrases you're using for your Web store—search for content and community sites that would match the products or services that you are selling.

Who's Linking to Your Web Store?

A quick and easy way to find out who's linking to you and to see if your link-swapping activities are bearing fruit is to use the link-checking tool at Virtual Stampede. Find it at `virtual-stampede.com/tools.htm`. Another way is to use the link-checking feature at AltaVista. It can show you every page it has on file that has a link to your Web site. Just go to the main page and type in the search window your URL like this: `link:www.yourstore.com`.

It will then bring up the results of the sites that are linked to you.

For example, suppose your site sells cigars and another site sells humidors. A relationship made in Web heaven! Look for sites that sell products or services complementary to your own, then contact them and offer a reciprocal linking arrangement. The same goes for cooking sites. If you sell kitchenware, then contact recipe sites or gourmet cooking communities and ask to exchange links.

Although time consuming, reciprocal linking pays off handsomely in the long run with increasing traffic to your site. The more sites that link to you, the more shoppers you will draw to your site. And even though it can take up to a couple of months to begin getting substantial amounts of reciprocal links from other related sites, this should be one of your top priorities.

Another way to get reciprocal links is to exchange banner ads. You can either work directly with the sites you contact to exchange one another's banner ads, or you can join a banner exchange program such as LinkExchange at `adnetwork.bcentral.com`. LinkExchange will place your banner on more than 400,000 Web sites and rotate its banner on your site for free. LinkExchange administers the program and provides you with reports as to how many times your banner was shown around the network and how many times it was clicked on. Check out bCentral (see Figure 18.3) at `bcentral.com` for other promotion services.

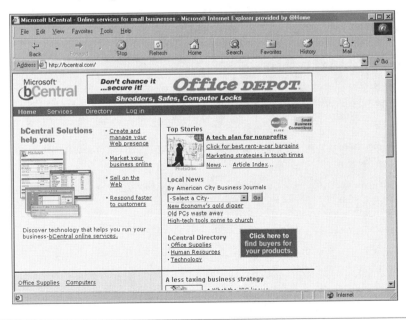

Figure 18.3

Microsoft's bCentral offers a good selection of promotion services for your e-business.

After you have submitted your site to the search engines and started to communicate with other sites to get reciprocal links and/or joined a banner exchange network, you want to focus your time on e-mail discussion lists and newsgroups.

Sow Your Participation and Reap Site Visitors

One of the best ways to get the word out about your company and what it offers is to join in the community gabfest that's on the Internet. By monitoring and participating in newsgroups and discussion lists, you have the opportunity to respond to potential customers and promote your product or service. And because you will be communicating with others with similar interests, you might find that there are other e-tailers on the list or in the newsgroup that you might want to form a strategic relationship with to increase sales for one another.

For example, if you sell camping gear, you might find that an e-tailer who sells freeze-dried food is also a participant on your discussion list or in the newsgroup you monitor. You might strike up a relationship where you would promote his product on your camping gear site and he would do the same in turn. You might even decide to work together offering bundled products to each other's customers—thus both increasing sales. Or perhaps you might sell travel packages and form a relationship with a luggage site.

The possibilities are endless. Participating in the newsgroups and on discussion lists is an easy way to find and form these strategic relationships. Where do you find these lists and newsgroups? Liszt (`liszt.oom`) has a searchable directory of more than 90,000 mailing lists that you can participate in. The List of Lists (`catalog.com/vivian/ interest-group-search.html`) is another site packed with discussion lists to join and TileNet (`www.tile.net/lists/`) will point you to newsgroups in just about any subject area.

Don't Get Flamed!

It's very important to remember that the newsgroups and discussion boards are *not* advertising vehicles. You cannot post blatant ads on the boards. If you do, you will get flamed—that is, others will respond with negative comments about you and your e-business. So don't risk it.

Finally, although you can't blatantly advertise your Web store on the lists and groups, you can still get your Web store some visibility by creating a good sig file.

A *sig* file—or a signature file—is a text tag that you can place at the bottom of the e-mails that you send out. When you participate in an e-mail discussion group or post to a newsgroup, your sig file can be attached to your message. Created properly, a good sig file can attract shoppers to your Web store. In reality a sig file can act as a small promotional message at the end of each and every posting that you do.

The trick, of course, is to create a compelling sig file. Do this by creating a brief 4–5-line statement that describes a specific benefit your product or service provides, why that benefit is important to your target customers, and why they should respond to you now. It's cheap, fast, and it works.

Here's an example:

```
************************************************************
```

Shop at FlowerFresh.com for the freshest flowers on the Net

This month's Mothers Day Special

One Dozen Roses for $19.95

http://www.flowerfresh.com

```
************************************************************
```

Viral Marketing—Spread a Cold: Catch a Customer

Let's face it. The best kind of marketing is the kind you don't have to do yourself—especially if you're a small business on the Web with a limited advertising budget. Viral Marketing is like it sounds: it's word-of-mouth and self-propagating.

Viral marketing has been around forever. Spreading the word through word-of-mouth was the world's first form of marketing. The Internet has taken this organic form of marketing to new heights by making communications better and communities of people tighter—thus making word-of-mouth even more effective.

Viral marketing can be either *frictionless* or *active*. When an audience spreads the word about your product or service by just using it—like the free e-mailservice Hotmail or electronic greeting cards—then viral marketing is frictionless. If the viral marketing campaign requires that your audience actively recruit new customers—as with AOL or ICQ Instant Messaging—then its active viral marketing.

So how do you spread the word of your Web store virally on the Net? Motivate your customers and visitors to do it. Here's how:

- **Tell 'em Sam sent you**—Reward your steady visitors for bringing new visitors to your site. Create a special referral program that your steady visitors can sign up for. Have them invite their friends to visit and if they do, have them mention the referrer's e-mail address and the referrer earns something free from your site.

Get Your Visitors to Market You

Here's a good idea to spread the word about your Web store. Ask visitors who like what you offer to e-mail your URL to a friend along with his comments. Place a form on your Web site that can be filled out by visitors and e-mailed to any address they enter. If you want a free service that does this and is easy to place on your site, check out Recommend It! (recommend-it.com).

- **Got any good jokes lately?**—I don't know how many times I've forwarded jokes or scam and virus alerts I received in my e-mail to friends and associates. So, create a funny newsletter or an e-mail alert that someone would pass on to friends.

- **Take my site, please!**—This is similar to "Got any good jokes lately," but in this case you give away your best assets. Don't just send out a notice about new content on your site—send out summaries by e-mail and ask people to forward them on (with copyright and URL attached, of course). A variation on this is to let other sites reprint your content on their site, with appropriate credits and links to yours.

MARKETING YOUR E-BUSINESS

18

CAUTION

The Downside of Viral Marketing

A downside to Viral Marketing is that you're letting others do your marketing for you. Although this will save you money, your message and your brand are in the hands of someone else. There's a fine line here between spreading the word and diluting your brand. A good example of negative branding as a result of viral marketing is the spam mail that you receive from friends and family. If you've been on the Web any length of time, you could have received e-mails promising that if you send an e-mail to everyone you know, you will receive a free case of Coke or a trip to DisneyWorld.

The challenge is to exercise some control over how your message is delivered and how others perceive it. But when you master this technique, your message and your site can spread as quickly as the common cold. The bottom line is this: For a viral marketing program to work, you have to create something people want to use and make it easy for them to share it.

Finally, don't expect a Viral Marketing program to pay off immediately. Like a real virus, viruses don't become epidemics until they reach critical mass. Your virus must propagate through the host population until it reaches a certain threshold of visibility and scale.

Think of it this way. Suppose a real-world virus doubles every year. In the first few years it's scarcely detectable. But within a few years after that it suddenly becomes an epidemic. You should understand that you're playing the same game. Viral Marketing takes time. So be patient, be fruitful—and go out and multiply!

TARGETING SHOPPER TYPES

All shoppers are not created equal. Different things motivate them in different ways. Knowing what grabs a particular type of shopper's *attention* will help you market your product or service better.

So before you can get a consumer's attention, you have to know who they are. According to a study from Media Metrix and consulting firm McKinsey at www.mckinsey.com, every online consumer falls into one of six eShopping types. They are

- Simplifiers
- Surfers
- Connectors
- Bargain Shoppers
- Routine Followers
- Sportsters

Knowing what kind of customer you want to target will help win them over by giving them more of what they really want. Let's look at them one by one.

Simplifiers—These types of shoppers are impatient but lucrative. Though they spend just seven hours a month online, they account for half of all Internet transactions. They like things simple and direct and the convenience of Internet shopping. You can grab their attention by showing them end-to-end convenience and proving that they will save time by buying at your e-business.

Surfers—These shopper types are consummate browsers and love to window shop. They spend 32% of all their time online and look at four times more pages than other Net users. They're drawn to new features and content. You can grab their attention by constantly updating your offering and your site.

Connectors—These shoppers are new to the Internet and less likely to shop online. But they can be reached. They are very brand conscious and are drawn to brick-and-mortar brands they know. Win them over by emphasizing affiliations with strong offline brands. They also enjoy connecting with others online. Community is big with them so offer them a chance to chat with others of their like on your site or provide a service where they can send free e-mail greeting cards to their friends and family.

Bargain shoppers—Their name says it all. They enjoy ferreting out bargains and have an unerring instinct for what's a good deal. Grab their attention with low prices. Be prepared to compete actively on price, offer auctions and classified ads, provide price comparisons and get them involved in a community on your site where they can exchange shopping tips and stories with other bargain shoppers.

Routine followers—These types of shoppers are information addicts who use the Net mainly for the information it provides. They're attracted to news and financial sites. Get their attention by emphasizing news. Be first with new information and offer real-time data and they will return again and again to your site.

Fans—This type of shopper is a sports and celebrity enthusiast, who live for the next score or the next tid-bit of gossip. They're attracted to sports and entertainment sites. Grab their attention with updated sports and celebrity information and help them connect with other fans through chat rooms, discussion boards and e-mail discussion lists.

In addition to the previous attention grabbing strategies, there's another very powerful incentive that cuts across all customer types that you could use to attract the attention of your target audience.

It's the word **FREE**.

Customers Can't Pass Up a Sweet Deal

Chocolate has a strong pull on people—especially if it's free. So SmartCasual sent out an e-mail to its prospect list with "mmmmm...c h o c o l a t e!" in the subject line telling the recipient that they could give free chocolates to friend if they registered at SmartCasual's site. More than 20% of those who visited the site converted to opt-in registrants.

The word **FREE** to consumers is music to their ears. It definitely gets their attention. In fact, according to a study by Jupiter Communications and NFO Interactive in 1999, 45% of online purchasers claimed that they made their first purchase or transaction at a site because of a promotion.

The most popular promotions mentioned in the survey were

1. Free Shipping—58%
2. Limited Time Discount—35%
3. Free Gift with Purchase—33%
4. Free Coupons—32%
5. Free Sweepstakes—24%

Notice the word **FREE** appears in four of the five popular promotions. What first time buyers are looking for is free shipping, free products, cash and rebates. Make the power of the word **FREE** work for you.

PERMISSION E-MAIL MARKETING

What could be better than a marketing piece that's easy to use, costs no money to produce, next to nothing to send, and reaches millions of prospects in a matter of minutes. That's e-mail marketing—one the most cost effective ways for an online business to market and get people to purchase goods and services. There simply isn't an easier, cheaper, more direct way to talk to someone online.

Although it sounds easy, e-mail marketing does take a lot of work to do properly. You must start from a clean e-mail list of people who have confirmed their willingness to receive your e-mail offer (have opted-in), then target and personalize that offer for the best response. And that's the most important part of e-mail marketing—send only to those who have asked to receive your offers.

JARGON

What's Opt-In E-mail?

Opt-in e-mail is the direct opposite of spam. People who opt-in to an e-mail list have said in advance that they are willing to receive unsolicited e-mail from companies on the Net that meet the list criteria. For example, someone who would like to be kept informed of newly released software might opt-in to an e-mail list that announces new software products.

The opposite of responsible, or opt-in, e-mail marketing is spam. And spam is the bane of any good e-mail marketing program. Although sales are made from spamming e-mail addresses, your online business reputation can be harmed in the process.

So, before you plan your grandiose e-mail marketing scheme, be aware that opt-in e-mail marketing is really Permission Marketing. So it's a good idea to find out how to get that permission and what are the ways to get the best results.

Best Practices of Permission Marketing

So just what is meant by permission marketing? Permission marketing means getting the consumer's permission to e-mail them an offer before it shows up in the e-mail box.

It works like this. When a consumer visits a permission marketing-enabled e-business, registers at it, or buys something from it, the consumer is asked, "Would you like to receive information from us periodically about new sales, or receive our newsletter?" The consumer then responds with either a "yes" or "no" by clicking in a box. If the answer is "yes," then the consumer has given permission. If it's "no," he hasn't.

Don't Pre-Check Permission

When collecting information from the consumer as a way to build your customer database, make sure you ask their permission to send them e-mails. Just because they bought from you, or answered a survey for a free gift, or have given you information for whatever reason, doesn't mean they are interested in further e-mails. Provide a check box on the form asking if they would like to receive further e-maile-mails from you. DO NOT automatically pre-check the box. Have them check it manually.

This may sound very simple, but there is more involved. If at any time the consumer wants to opt-out of your e-mail marketing pieces, then he or she needs to be able to easily do so by visiting your Web site. Either set up an automated listserve that automatically removes an e-mail address from your database when a recipient e-mails it, or list an opt-out URL in your e-mail that directs the recipient to a separate URL on your site that they can go to easily remove their e-mail address from your list.

This next is a very important point—the consumer gave YOU permission to e-mail him or her, not anyone else. So DON'T give or sell the customer's e-mail address, that is, his or her permission to be e-mailed, to any other company or person.

So, in what ways can you get the permission of consumers? As stated before, you can ask if they want to be informed of future sales, or get insights into the products you sell, or news they are interested in. But there are other ways.

You can offer consumers a chance to win a prize in exchange for their e-mail address. You can offer them points that they can exchange for products after they've accumulated enough of them.

With permission marketing, you *GET* by *GIVING*. Although spammers are currently getting good response rates on their e-mail blasts, that's changing fast. Consumers are wising up and are demanding that the spammers be curbed.

What's SPAM?

Spam is unsolicited e-mail. It's the junk mail of the late twentieth century. It clogs e-mail servers around the world and sucks up needed bandwidth on the Net and it's the quickest way to create a bad reputation for you, your company, and your product.

If you're thinking about spamming, think about this first.

Anti-spammers rarely complain just to their Internet Service Provider (ISP). They complain to *your* ISP, your ISP's backbone provider, and just about everyone else, is in between you and the electronic path to the recipient. And these providers will often terminate your Net connection, if just to stop the complaints.

If losing your Internet connection is not scary enough, then listen to this. The Mail Abuse Prevention System at `mail.abuse.org` runs the Realtime Blackhole List (RBL). They have compiled a list of IP addresses of known spammers and offer this list to their subscribers. And who are these subscribers? E-mail administrators. Using the RBL list, these administrators reject any e-mail that originates from those IP addresses. That's right—*any e-mail*—not just *bulk*!

JARGON

What's an IP Address?

An IP address is a unique 32-bit Internet address consisting of four numbers, separated by dots (209.12.152.88). Every server connected to the Internet has an IP number.

You're probably thinking that the RBL list only includes pornography sites and get-rich-quick spammers. It doesn't. It also included what the anti-spam community call mainsleaze— a combination of mainstream and sleaze. These are legitimate companies that use questionable e-mail practices. That is to say, they don't use opt-in e-mail lists, or, in other words, *permission marketing*.

Getting permission is extremely important for your e-mail marketing strategy and the reputation of your e-business. So plan to do it right.

ATTRACTING SHOPPERS TO YOUR SITE

After you have the consumers' attention, you have to bring them to your site. So, your next challenge is to give shoppers a reason to come to your store in the first place— then give them a reason to return. To attract visitors to your site, you have to promote not only your products or services and your unique selling position, but also give the consumer a reason to visit your Web store right now! Here's one way to get repeat visitors to your web site. Auto-HomePage (`auto-homepage.com`) is a software package that you install on your server that creates an auto home page for customers that gives them news feeds, a reminder service, an address book, calendar, notepad and a ToDo List with their choice of links and information that return them to you Web site (see Figure 18.4).

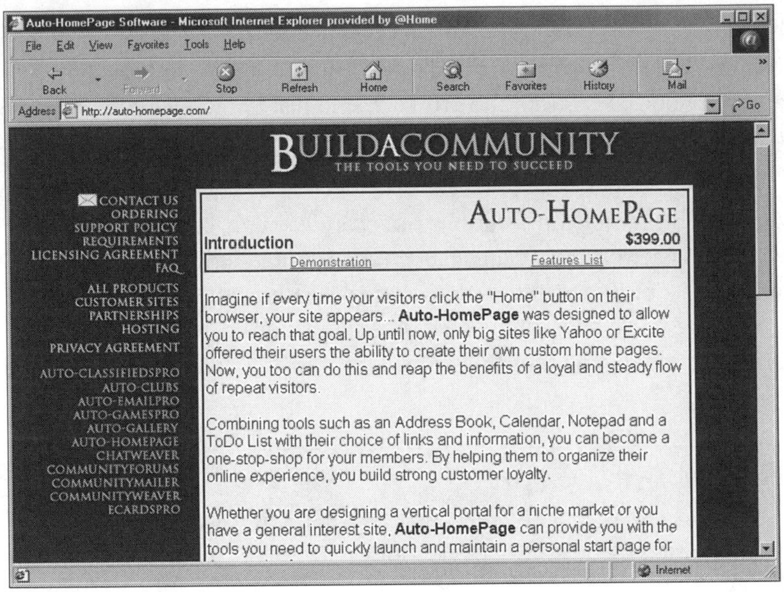

Figure 18.4

Auto-HomePage offers software that creates an auto home page for customers that gives them news feeds, a reminder service, and much more.

The marketing strategies to attract consumers to your site fall under two groups. These are the ways to attract Web consumers to your site and keep them coming back.

- Promotional Announcements
  - Continually announce special seasonal, event, and limited-time promotions.
- Loyalty Programs
  - Build loyalty programs to keep shoppers coming back.
  - Conduct surveys to find out what your customers want and need.
  - Attract visitors to your site by giving away something free.
  - Establish a free e-mail newsletter.

Armed with this list of simple but powerful marketing strategies, you can give your Web store the success it deserves.

Promotional Announcements

A great way to get shoppers to your Web store is to offer them a timely product or service. Better yet, have them tell you when they would be willing to shop.

First, design your product or service offering around seasonal promotions. Use the major holidays such as Christmas, Hanukah, Easter, Valentine's Day, and Father's and Mother's Day to design special sales and promotions to draw shoppers to your site. Then give the shopper who visits your site a chance to tell you when he or she would like to be contacted with offers from your Web store.

Offer shoppers a reminder service. Allow shoppers to enter the details of any event they want to be reminded off, such as a birthday or anniversary. Send this reminder to them via e-mail along with a link to your Web store with products that are made to order for the event they are reminded of. Another idea is to send shoppers at your site an e-mail when a selected product or service they are interested in changes in your store—such as perhaps a price drop or a special limited time sale. This service is covered in further detail in Chapter 21, "Contests, Give-Aways, and Promotions."

In all your promotions, try and give away something a shopper might value. It could be something as simple as a free piece of information that a shopper might find useful. With your promotion, inform him that he can find this free information on your site and send him to that page on your Web store. You might even offer a trial size of a product or a small piece of the service you offer.

If you sell software, offer a shopper a free demo to download from your Web site. If you offer a cooking course, give him the first lesson free.

You could tie these free offers to a customer survey asking the shopper a series of questions that lists his interests and helps you market to him in the future. But surveys can be tricky. It's a well-known fact that the more information you ask people to fill out, the fewer people will complete the form. But there is a way to collect as much information as possible without having the shopper bolt for the mouse button and abandon your survey.

Ask for the information in stages.

First, ask for his e-mail address to receive the free offer. After he enters his e-mail address and hits **submit** and your server has recorded it, direct the shopper to a second page that has a form that asks for a little more information. After the shopper hits **submit** on that page, direct the shopper to another page and another form to gather further information. Thank him for his help and offer another form on another page.

At each step you'll lose people who won't complete the additional information, but you'll get many who will fill out more information than they would have if you had asked for it all at once. And besides, you will at least have their e-mail address to send them promotional material in the future.

Kibitz with Other e-Business Owners Like Yourself

The Net can be a lonely place and business owners often talk to other business owners to exchange ideas and get advice. So check out the message boards at BizWeb2oo. They provide a free forum to discuss issues directly related to Internet marketing. Find it at bizweb2000.com/wwwboard/.

It goes without saying that you will tell the shopper that his or her information will be kept in the strictest confidence—right? Remember your privacy guarantee?

You can program your own surveys, but that takes some programming skills. An alternative to that is to use one of the survey services on the Net. Zoomerang (`zoomerang.com`) is a free Internet service that enables businesses to easily conduct surveys using simple to use templates. Another service is ClickToSurvey (`clicktomarket.com`). ClickToSurvey's service is not free—costs start at $200 per survey and 50 cents a response—and you can set up a survey form right on your site in few minutes.

Loyalty Programs

Getting good responses on your promotional activities is great. But a response is not a relationship. And you get that with loyalty programs. Loyalty programs also are known as incentives, membership clubs, frequent buyer programs, and rewards programs.

How important can a loyalty program be to your eBuinsess?

Jupiter Communications wrote that 56% of online consumers would buy more often if awarded loyalty points. The Harvard Business Review stated that companies could boost profits by nearly 100% by retaining just 5% more of their customers and that cutting defections in half can more than double a company's growth rate.

As you can see from these estimates, a well-run loyalty program can be of great value to a new e-tailer.

A loyalty program can help you identify loyal customers, and a good loyalty program at your Web store can accomplish a number of marketing objectives. First, giving incentives to new shoppers can get them to purchase from your Web store. Second, a loyalty program encourages repeat business. Finally, with a loyalty program, you can track and build customer profiles with every customer transaction associated with your rewards program.

A loyalty program entices shoppers to become customers and then encourages them to purchase more often by offering rewards. Customers are encouraged to buy more by earning points, which they can redeem for special promotions and free products. You can set up a loyalty program yourself—but why bother? There are several good ones already available on the Net that you can join and will perform all the administration tasks necessary to run the program.

TIP

Get a Plan, Man!

To stay on top of your marketing, you need to have a marketing maintenance plan. Sell-it-on-the-Web provides you with an Online Marketing Maintenance Plan that's easy to follow and important for you to do. It outlines the marketing tasks you need to do on a daily, weekly, monthly, and quarterly basis. Find it at `sellitontheweb.com/ezine/opinion034.shtml`.

Beenz

www.beenz.com

Beenz is a new form of Web currency. Your e-business can reward shoppers with Beenz for filling out a survey, registering to receive your newsletter, or even each time they buy a product or service from you. Shoppers can spend their Beenz on movies, gift certificates, travel discounts, music, and more.

MyPoints

www.mypoints.com

myPoints has more than 200 direct marketing partners, including 1-800-Flowers, Barnes & Noble, Target, Olive Garden, General Cinema, Blockbuster, and CBS Sportsline. It has created a bevy of practical and easy-to-redeem rewards, such as gift certificates. Their Web-based interface enables you to control your own Point awards on your site. Shoppers earn Points from all participating merchants across their network.

NetCentives

clickrewards.com

NetCentives offers its ClickRewards, where shoppers at your site can earn ClickPoints redeemable for frequent flyer miles on 10 major airlines, hotel stays, car rentals—even merchandise.

CyberGold

www.cybergold.com

CyberGold differs from the other loyalty programs by actually rewarding shoppers with cold, hard cash that is conveniently deposited into their checking account.

LEARNING WHAT'S SPREAD ABOUT YOUR COMPANY

Customers and potential customers are comparing your business to the competition and telling stories about you according to their experiences. In the offline world it's hard to track what individuals say about a company, but on the Web you can monitor these comments and participate in these interactions.

Prior to the Internet, consumers had a hard time searching for others who had purchased products that they were considering. Not so on the Net.

One thing that the Net is very good at is its ability for people to spread the word about what concerns them. Every time someone interacts with your company, he or she is forming an opinion of you, your company, its products, and its people. For good or bad, newsgroups, discussion lists, newsletters, chat rooms—even personal Web sites—have given consumers and competitors the chance to talk about your company and the goods and services you offer.

The oldest form of Internet consumer interaction is Usenet, which has several thousand newsgroups where people post opinions on practically everything. Over the years, consumers have exchanged experiences and opinions about merchants—both online and off—in groups like misc.consumers and alt.consumers.experiences.

But these conversations are not invisible to you. With sites like Deja.com at `www.deja.com`, e-marketers can locate and read comments made about their company. Deja.com has organized the USENET discussions and categorized for easy searching on a particular subject or issue. In addition, services that combine Web postings with e-mail discussion lists, such as Topica at `www.topica.com` and eGroups at `groups.yahoo.com/`, make it easier to monitor such discussions.

Discussions in these communities could touch on a particular product or company like yours and occasionally there is so much discussion—both positive and negative—that it becomes easy for prospective customers to develop a profile of your company that you would not like. Monitoring these discussions and responding to negative comments will help protect your company and brand reputation in the marketplace.

Over the last few years, a whole new set of sites have sprung up to fulfill a customer-service need that had long been felt by consumers. Sites like ePinions.com at `www.epinions.com`, and ConsumerReview.com at `www.consumerreview.com` both enable consumers to post raves and rants about their experiences at stores, both on and offline. These sites should be monitored as well for these are places where consumers can get frank opinions about products, services, and vendors from consumers that are either disappointed or delighted. When you see a negative comment posted, respond to it. If someone posts a negative comment about your product or service, reply with a message thanking them for their feedback and state you'll consider improving your service or changing the product. If someone is dissatisfied with an order, offer right then and there to settle their complaint. Show that your company is customer-focused and open to change, and you can deal with negative comments to the benefit of your online business.

Using these Web sites you can monitor what consumers are saying about your and your online business and be prepared to either answer them if incorrect or use the feedback to improve your product offering and customer service.

CHAPTER **19**

SPEAKING THE LANGUAGE OF NET ADVERTISING

In This Chapter

- Learn the alphabet zoo of Net advertising
- Discover the different ways you can advertise your Web store on the Net
- Learn how to place banner ads on banner networks
- Learn the difference between direct e-mail advertising, newsletter advertising, and eZine advertising
- Learn how to measure your ad strategy

If a marketing plan provides your business with a strategy to find and attract customers, how and where you advertise your business is one of the ways to make your buisness visible to potential customers. It costs money to advertise, so it's important to know how and where to spend your limited online advertising budget. For that, you have to understand what Net advertising is and how to do it properlyon the Net.

Paid advertising is a necessary evil and is used to maintain and increase awareness of your e-business, introduce new products, generate new customers, offer special programs, grow market share, and penetrate new markets. The following are the advertising vehicles available to you to promote your site:

- **Banner Ad**—An electronic billboard or ad in the form of a graphic image that resides on a Web page.
- **Newsletter Advertising**—Placing your promotional ads in electronic newsletters that are e-mailed to a base of subscribers.
- **Direct E-mail Advertising**—Sending your promotional message directly to individuals via e-mail.
- **eZine Advertising** An eZine is an electronic magazine that is distributed to you via e-mail. You subscribe to it like any real-world magazine.

Most marketing experts agree that you should devote 3% to 8% of your annual sales to your total advertising and promotional budget. But before you pull out your wallet and get ready to spend ad dollars to advertise, you should first know how to speak the lingo of Net advertising.

THE LANGUAGE OF NET ADVERTISING

Like a bunch of eager bunnies, Internet advertising has split, combined, and multiplied into a bewildering array of approaches to advertising on the Web. Using abbreviations such as CPM, CPC, CPA, CPT, and CPS makes the novice Net advertiser's eyes glaze. If this is you, don't feel bad. You're not alone.

So, let's go through this seemingly incomprehensible zoo of letters. Let's define them and see how using each of them can make the best use of your Internet advertising dollar. There's a new world out there for advertisers on the Net. Accountability is the word and today's Net delivers it in spades—not just audience estimates like in the real world. When you advertise on the Net, you know exactly how well your ad campaign is doing by the number of impressions, click-throughs, and responses (read sales) that you get from your advertising.

Everything You Wanted to Know About Banner Advertising

For a good series of articles on banner ads and banner ad networks, check out Wilson Web at wilsonweb.com/webmarket/ad.htm.

Impressions are correlated with awareness or brand advertising. You count impressions by how many times your ad is presented to a viewer. If the intent of your advertising campaign is to raise awareness of your product, service, or brand, then the number of impressions per dollar is of prime importance—that is, you want the most impressions you can get for the lowest ad dollar.

Click-through, in response to an ad by a consumer, simply indicates interest or intent. After a consumer clicks your ad or goes to a URL that you've advertised in an e-mail message or newsletter, click-through provides you with an opportunity to offer something for sale or even complete a sale. Other uses include filling out a survey or asking the viewer to take some other kind of action. Look at a click-through like a potential buyer opening a direct mail envelope to read the offer inside. The better the ad, the more potential it has to be acted on. If your intention is to have the viewer click your ad or go to your site, then the number of clicks—or visitors to your site—per ad dollar is of prime importance.

A *response* is indicated by either providing leads for future sales or the sales themselves. A response also could include the downloading of a piece of software. If your objective is to actually make a sale or have the viewer complete an action, then the number of responses per ad dollar is of prime importance.

Now let's see how impressions, click-throughs, and responses play out in the alphabet soup of Net advertising.

CPM or Cost Per Thousand Impressions

You want to get the best bang for your ad buck, right? So knowing about CPM—or cost per thousand impressions—is important.

CPM is the number of times your ad is viewed. Another way to think of it is the number of eyeballs that see your ad. When you buy based on CPM, you're paying each time a consumer views your ad. Click-throughs to your site and sales are not your prime objective here. Brand or image awareness is. Compare it to the FedEx or UPS commercials on TV. They don't want you to take action right then and there, but to have you remember them when you're ready to ship something.

Use Banners As Lead Generators

Banners can be used not only for advertising your product or service but also as a draw to pages where you can get sign-ups for your store's newsletter. Create a separate Web page for sign-ups or even surveys and link to it from your banner ad.

You calculate CPM in this way. CPM is the total ad cost divided by the total possible impressions—or eyeballs that see your ad—in thousands. The lower the CPM, the lower the cost to reach your audience. For example, an ad that costs $5,000 and is seen by 100,000 people will have a CPM of $50 (5,000 divided by 100). The ad is costing you $50 to reach 1,000 viewers of a Web site or receivers of an e-mail message or newsletter. Today, CPMs can run as low as $3 or as high as $75. Run of site ads have a lower CPM than ads that reside on targeted pages of a Web site. For example, if you sell sporting goods and buy a banner ad on Yahoo! that appears every time someone does a search on sports, that will carry a higher CPM than if your ad appeared randomly across the whole Web site.

CPC or Cost Per Click

Impressions are good for branding or making shoppers aware of your e-business. But if you want to pay only for consumers who actually open your ad and view it, then you want to buy advertising based on CPC—or cost per click.

CPC is the number of times your ad is clicked or how many people actually go to the URL you are advertising. Your objective is to have them "open your direct mail envelope" and view your offer. Currently, you can expect anywhere from about a half of a percent to a 3% click-through rate on a CPC ad. The rate depends on how strong your offer is to the consumer.

Keep in mind that consumers on the Web are bombarded by literally thousands of ad messages every day in the form of banner ads, e-mail promotions, and ads in newsletters that they subscribe to. Like you and I, consumers have developed a subconscious filtering system to filter out most of these ads. So you have quite a difficult time rising above this din of advertising.

> **TIP**
>
> **Banner Ads Can Take Orders, Too**
>
> You can actually use banner ads to take orders directly in the banner by using rich media. Rich media banners have a built-in order area, expandable order forms, and even secure server technology to protect credit card transactions. Check out an example at Enliven at www.enliven.com/campaigns/amex_ftd.htm.

How do you get through to your customers? Take a look at the following factors:

- **Consistency**—First of all, you must run your ads enough times to break through the consumer's awareness level. Most advertising experts claim that you must run the same ad at least three times in the same place before it begins to register with your audience.

- **Visibility**—There are a number of factors that can influence the impact of your ad and get the consumer to open it. First is the size of your ad. If you're using a banner ad, then obviously larger ads have more impact. Where the banner ad is placed on a Web page also affects an ad's impact. Having your ad appear above the fold—being seen as soon as the page loads without scrolling down to see it—is important for visibility.

CPA, CPT, and CPS

The last group of abbreviations in this advertising alphabet soup is CPA, CPT, and CPS. All three of these fall, more or less, under the same umbrella. Using these schemes you are paying only for an actual response to an offer, not just a view or click-through.

> **TIP**
>
> **Create Your Own Promotion Campaign**
>
> You can easily create your own promotions—such as mini storefronts, surveys, lead generation, and sweepstakes—and run them on your site on just a cost per action (CPA) basis. Check it out at IQ (iq.com).

- **CPA (Cost per action)**—This is the number of times the desired action takes place on your site, such as a sale, a registration, or a download. Here you want to pay only for those people who actually take action. They've viewed your ad, clicked it, and responded by actually buying something or downloading a piece of software. You can expect normal direct mail response rates from 1% to 3% of those who respond to your ad. If your offer is targeted and on a targeted site, the response could go as high as 5%, 10%, or even higher.

- **CPT (Cost per transaction)**—This is the cost per lead. This type of banner ad is similar to CPA but you are paying only for those people who click your banner ad and either fill out a registration form or are sent to a page on your site where they can view the full offer.

- **CPS (Cost per sale)**—Like CPA, you are paying only for leads that generate a sale.

Not every one of these approaches is perfect for everyone. You need to decide what type of action you are willing to pay for, and then negotiate your best deal. Just as there is room on the Web for more than one successful business model, what might suit one content site might not suit another, and what might suit one advertiser might not suit another.

It's good to keep in mind that the number of sites are accelerating on the Web and there are now an overabundance of sites and ad serving companies that are selling ad space. There is literally a glut of ad space on the Web. So be patient. Check out each opportunity against the objectives of your ad campaign. And remember that what might work on one site—impressions or responses—might not work on another.

ADVERTISING STRATEGIES AND PLACEMENT

The first step in designing your ad campaign is to define your customer. You need to be very specific about the age, gender, marital status, geographic location, religion, political affiliation, occupation, educational level, and so on so that you can buy the proper ad placement.

Pay Only for Visitors to Your Web Store

Using the search engine at www.goto.com you pay only for shoppers who go to your site. GoTo gets paid only when a visitor actually clicks the listing. They are very open about this as the cost charged to the advertisers is listed with each entry. Most are only a few pennies a hit.

If you're selling games for children, you don't want to advertise on a site or in a newsletter that sells apparel. So, knowing your customer is of prime importance. The more accurate you can be in defining your most likely customer, the easier it is to refine your message and select the appropriate media to reach that customer.

Speaking of refining your message, identifying your customer's specific wants and needs is necessary to write the proper copy to get the customer to act on your message. Sure, you sell computers. But different people use computers in different ways. Do you craft your advertising message to consumers who need a computer for the home, their business, or just to surf the Web? Your customers' different wants and needs will dictate the message you send them.

Finally, be sure that your ad message includes who you are, what you do, and why the consumer should buy from you. Then tell the customer what he should do next—the call to action—if he is interested in what you are selling.

Now you're ready to buy those ads. Here's how:

Banner Ads and Ad Networks

The first advertising tool to consider in promoting your Web store is the banner ad. A banner ad is like a small billboard that resides on a Web page. The standard full-size banner ad is 250×80 pixels. But even though almost every ad-supported site sells the full-size banner ad, less than 20% of them rely on that alone. At least half of these offer several smaller sizes—usually 120×60 and 88×31. Because of their size and the limited room for your message, it is no surprise that the smaller banner ads are 1/2 to 1/3 lower in cost than the full-size banner ad.

There has been a recent addition to the family of banner sizes, formats that are larger than the traditional banners detailed above. The click-through rates of banner ads have dropped, in some cases, below a half of a percent. This has prompted some companies to use larger and different banner ad formats.

In the past, banner ads were traditionally placed at the top, bottom, or sides of the Web page. The new enlarged banners—in most cases—are more or less square in design and placed within the copy of the Web page itself with the text wrapping around the ad similar to a printed magazine. Sizes for these ads range from 180×150 to 336×280 and 240×400.

The other new ad size is called a skyscraper ad, and runs vertically down the side of a Web page. It is much longer than the standard side banner ad you've seen before. Sizes for these banner ads range from 120×600 to 160×600.

The standards for these new sizes and those of the traditional banner ads can be found at `http://www.iab.net/iab_banner_standards/bannersizes.html`.

It's a Banner Debate

The debate of the effectiveness of banner ads continues to this day. For the latest on the debate, check out AdAge, the authority in advertising, at `adage.com`; AdWeek, the other authority on advertising, at `adweek.com`; and Fast Info, a newly formed association of advertisers, advertising agencies, and others to determine a standard on Internet advertising measurements at `fastinfo.org`.

Currently, there is a glut of banner ad space on the Web. In fact, most available banner ad impressions on the Web go unsold. And this situation is unlikely to change for many years, as page views are being created at a much faster rate than new ad spending. So you should be able to buy ad space on most second-tier Web sites for much less than the standard $25 CPM that is asked for today. A small number of large, prominent, and/or special types of sites like Yahoo! and others in the Top 100 Media Metrics traffic report continue to charge high CPMs.

> ### Reduce Your Cost of Advertising
>
> Another way to reduce your cost is to buy ads as ROS (run of site). If you're not looking for specific locations or targeting within a Web site, you can run your banners ROS. With ROS buys, your banners can appear anywhere on the site wherever there is available space.

Computing and Technology and Reference and Education sites charge between $50 and $60 CPM. Business and Finance and Shopping and Auctions charge $40–$50 CPM. Automotive, Comics and Humor, General News, Home and Garden, Society, Politics, and Sports and Recreation sites charge $30–$40 CPM. Games, Kids and Family, Movies and Television, Music Portals, Search Engine, Travel, and Regional/Local sites can charge $20–$30 CPM. Community sites and Yellow/White Pages sites charge $10–$20 CPM.

If you buy in volume or offer a larger time commitment, you can reduce these charges significantly. Or, Instead of trying to lower your overall cost, ask whether the site would be willing to offer you bonus impressions or a free sponsorship of their e-mail newsletter. If you can get some of these add-ons, they might provide you with an opportunity to test that ad vehicle without an additional outlay of ad dollars.

Buying banner ads from individual sites is one way to get your message out. Another is to buy ads on a Banner Network. About.com Guide for Advertising Online at `adsonline.about.com/business/adsonline/msub6.htm` has a good list of interactive ad networks that you can place your banner ad on (see Figure 19.1).

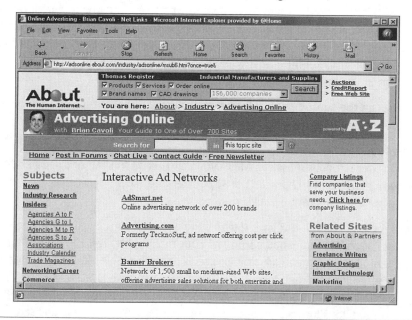

Figure 19.1

If you're looking for a list of advertising networks, check out the NetLinks from Brian Cavoli's About.com Guide for Online Advertising.

Opt-In E-mail Advertising

Crafting your own message and e-mailing it to a list of prospects is one of the most cost-efficient ways to advertise. But if you're not careful and don't do your homework, it could be one of the most costly advertising mistakes you can make. Direct e-mail can be very effective if you know your target market and can find an opt-in e-mailing list that closely matches your customer profile.

First, be sure that any e-mail list that you rent is an opt-in list. People hate unsolicited e-mail. This is spam, and your offer and your business will leave a bad taste in their mouth. By renting opt-in lists only, you know that the people on those lists have asked to receive e-mail offers in a particular category. This also is helpful to you because you can target your offer and send it directly to those prospects who would be willing to open your offer when they receive it.

Direct E-mail Should Catch the Eye

When sending out a direct e-mail piece, do not use the words FREE or BUY NOW in your message. This is a sure way to get your e-mail message sent to the trash bin. Take the time to explain your offer without the hype. And remember to play up benefits—what's in it for the customer—and not features.

Next, consider the format of your e-mail.

Use ASCII text only. The majority of people who use e-mail have e-mail readers that can read only text. So sending out e-mails with hyperlinks and graphics embedded in the message could make it unreadable. Keep your message simple and short. Deliver your most important information up-front. People don't have a lot of time, so you have to grab their attention in the first few lines of your message.

People scan the subject lines of their e-mails first. So, make the subject line your headline. If it's compelling, they'll open your message.

Remember to include a lot of white space in your messages. Be careful with CAPS. Don't overuse them in your message. Make your pitch easy to scan and read and remember to use wide margins—64 characters or fewer per line. This helps make your message readable with many different e-mail programs.

Finally, before you roll out your e-mail campaign with a full list, test one element of your message at a time to a small portion of your mailing list. Test the subject line or headline in the e-mail message you are going to send to the list. Select a test set of names from the list you're going to e-mail to and see what the response is from your test sample. Next, pick another sample from your list and using the subject line that got the best response form you previous test, test the body of the message. You can use this same technique to test the layout of your e-mail message—even the P.S. at the end of it.

After you've determined what works, then send your message to the full list.

Both PostMaster Direct at `postmasterdirect.com` (see Figure 19.2) and CopyWriter at `copywriter.com/lists` provide opt-in e-mail names to use in your direct e-mail advertising campaign.

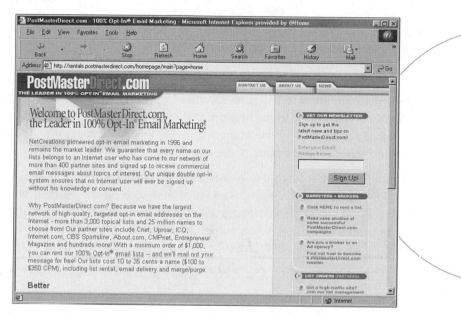

Figure 19.2

PostMasterDirect offers thousands of opt-in e-mail lists that you can use to send your promotional message to.

Advertising in Newsletters and eZines

The cyberworld has its equivalent of the printed media of the real world. They are the e-mail newsletters and eZines (electronic magazines). These two media are great places to target your advertising message. There are thousands upon thousands of newsletters you can advertise in and hundreds of eZines, each focusing on a particular market niche.

Why advertise in an e-mail newsletter or eZine? Why not just stick with advertising on Web sites? Studies show that the average Internet user returns to only 5 to 10 Web sites. To get a better mind share of the consumer, you need to send your message to where the customer lives—his or her e-mail box. People who subscribe to newsletters and eZines have specifically asked to receive them. Because of this, your advertising message will be better received.

The most common form of advertising in a newsletter or eZine is the *text flag*. Text flags are featured bits of copy, about five lines or so, which rest amidst the larger content of a newsletter or eZine. They are usually set off from the rest of the text message by lines (=) or stars (*) like this.

****

THE PERFECT GIFT FOR EVERY GRADUATE!

Give the gift that will be used again and again --
Webster's New World College Dictionary, 4th Edition.
http://www.amazon.com/dictionary/websters.htm

****

A good place to find newsletters to advertise in is PennMedia (`pennmedia.com`). Penn Media offers newsletters in the network that get read, such as daily jokes, daily quotes, daily golf tips, and many more. You get up to 50 words for your ad and all advertisements are included in the body of the newsletter.

Advertising in eZines targeted to your types of customers is another way to reach your specific audience. List City has the Book of eZines (see Figure 19.3) at `www.list-city.com/ezines.htm`, which is a database of advertising contact information and rates for hundreds of eZines on the Net. If you publish an eZine, you can join its Advertising Exchange Directory, which consists of listings of eZines interested in advertising exchanges.

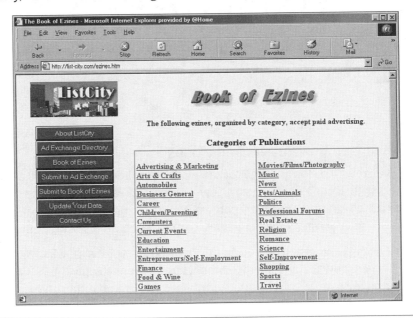

Figure 19.3

The Book of Ezines has contact information and advertising rates on hundreds of eZines.

LifeStyles Publishing at `lifestylespub.com` offers an eZine Broadcast Promotional Package that broadcasts your message thousands of times across targeted eZines for one special pricing. And for a list of all eZines around the world, visit E-Zine-List at `www.meer.net/johnl/e-zine-list`. Although not recently updated, it currently lists more than 4,000 eZines that you can review.

MEASURING YOUR AD STRATEGY

There's a story about a businessman lamenting about his advertising campaign. He said, "50% of my advertising doesn't work. I just don't know which 50%." The bad news is that an advertising campaign does cost money. The good news is that advertising on the Net is easy to track. With the proper tools and strategies, you can see right away if the dollars you're spending are paying off in traffic and sales.

But before you can start measuring the results of your advertising strategy, you need to know what to measure. And what you measure are hits, visitors, and page views.

First, you need to understand the difference between *hits* and *visitors*. When someone claims that they get 100,000 hits on a site each day, that does not mean that the site gets 100,000 visitors. A hit on a page consists of two things—text and graphics. A Web page is most often made up of two elements—the copy on the page and any graphics pictures or images. A hit counts each individual graphic, picture, or image on a page plus all the text on that page.

So when a visitor opens a Web page that has text and three images, it counts as four hits. One for all the text on the page and one for each image.

Use Doorways to Track Ad Campaigns

If you're running more than one ad on the Net, a good way to track the results of each one is to create separate Web pages—or doorway pages—on your Web site. Each doorway page has a unique URL that is not accessed through your normal site navigation. You can then create a doorway page for each ad that you are running on the Net—one for each different banner ad, one for each direct e-mail campaign, and one for each newsletter or eZine ad you place.

The entire page, regardless of how many hits it represents, is counted as one *page view*. A shopper can view any number of pages when he or she visits your store. So one visitor could view several pages in one visit. If you have 100,000 hits a day, and those hits equal 10,000 page views, and if each visitor views an average of 10 pages per visit, you would have approximately 1,000 visitors a day to your Web site. Pretty good numbers if you can get them.

But approximate numbers of visitors is not good enough. If you really want to measure your advertising efforts, you need to know the exact number of visitors to your Web store that your advertising has generated. In addition, you want to know not just the number of visitors that visited your site but the number of *unique visitors* who came to you site.

A unique visitor is a person who comes to your site only once during a particular span of time. For example, a shopper might visit your Web store, and return two or three times during the day. The shopper made two or three visits to your store, but counts as only one unique visitor. You could set the time between visits to any period you want—per day, per week, or per month. So 50,000 visits to your Web store per month might represent only 10,000 visitors.

Obviously, when evaluating your advertising, you want to know how many unique visitors are driven to your Web store and if they buy. The more unique visitors who are sent to your site through advertising and the more sales that are made from these visitors, the better spent was your advertising dollar.

Tracking the visitors to your site involves a number of factors, depending on how much you want to pay for tracking software for your site and what you want to track. A quick and easy way to track the number of visits to your site is to place a counter on your home page or the page that your advertising has directed the shopper to. Yahoo! lists a number of sites where you can get a counter for your Web site. Go to Yahoo! at `search.yahoo.com/bin/search?p=access+counters` and you will find a directory of access counter sites (see Figure 19.4).

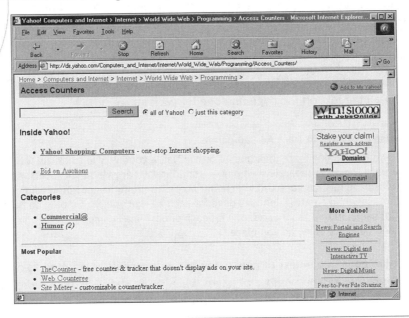

Figure 19.4

At Yahoo! you can find a list of Access Counters that track and analyze your site traffic.

Keep in mind that these counters record only the number of visitors to your page—not the number of unique visitors.

To do some serious analysis of your site traffic and to see how well your advertising dollars are being spent, you need a professional site traffic-tracking program like WebTrends (`www.webtrends.com/`). Many of these can be found again at Yahoo! under Business_and_Economy/Business_to_Business/Communications_and_Networking/Internet_and_World_Wide_Web/Software/World_Wide_Web/Log_Analysis_Tools.

CHAPTER **20**

PROMOTING YOUR SITE FOR FREE!— FROM MEATSPACE TO CYBERSPACE

In This Chapter

- Learn the free ways to promote your Web store offline
- Discover the online ways to list your site on multiple search engines and indexes for free
- Discover how free classified ads can promote your Web store online
- Learn how participating in communities on the Net can help promote your Web store
- Learn how to get others to market your Web store for free

Advertising costs money. There's no way around that. But there are a lot of ways—and I mean a lot of ways—that you can promote your site for free.

Sure, the Big Dogs who inhabit the Web with their bloated advertising and marketing budgets pose a real problem for your company's visibility. But your bark can be heard above those of the Big Dogs, and you can do it without stretching your limited financial resources to the breaking point.

Before spending money on marketing, use the Internet marketing vehicles that are free. Free is good. And unless you're a small business owner who has a spare million or two lying around, or your brother-in-law is

Bill Gates, making use of the free marketing opportunities on the Net can help stretch your marketing and advertising dollar.

Spending your time and not your money will help you maximize your Web visibility and traffic and stay within your marketing budget. If you spend your time wisely and follow these strategies, you can go a long way in giving your site the visibility it needs.

So, let's get started.

START IN THE REAL WORLD

Before you venture into the online world of free promotion, you should start with what can be done offline to assist the promotion of your business Web site. Most times these promotional vehicles can be done with little or no additional expense.

First of all, spread that URL of yours around. You burned the midnight oil thinking up a cool URL that tells the world who you are and what you do. Good. Now it's time to tell the world!

TIP

Attract More Traffic to Your Site—from Traffic!

Okay, so it's not free. But for $29.95 added to your advertising budget, you can get your URL viewed by hundreds of people a day. Osworth Consulting and Marketing sells a custom URL plate for your car or truck that complements the chrome detailing on any vehicle. The letters are bold and stand out. They are easy to read, even at highway speeds!

Find it at `freetips.com/url_plates/`.

Before you reach for your mouse, make sure you sprinkle your URL on every stitch of printed material that leaves your office. And this includes your company's e-mail address, too. Place both your URL and your company e-mail address on all literature, business cards, letterheads, invoices, and the like. This is a great source of free publicity. Get into the habit of putting your URL and your main e-mail address on all these materials after your Web site is up.

Next, let the world know that you exist. This means using both the Yellow Pages and Business White Pages. If the NBA, CBS, and Disney can do it, so can you. Also, if your business uses a POS (Point of Sale) packaging and/or display (such as at trade shows) you need to incorporate your URL and main e-mail address on them, too.

And remember. There are no additional costs to these free marketing strategies if they occur in the normal process of advertising, reprinting, or maintenance. So use them!

LISTING YOUR SITE—GETTING THE WORD OUT

In Chapter 18, "Marketing Your e-Business," we talked about registering your Web site at the major search engines and how to prepare your Web pages for it. We also talked about swapping links and banner ads with other Web sites.

But there are other places to get your site listed that should not be ignored. And most importantly—they are free! The major search engines aren't the only places to list your Web store. There are many listing services that cater to your particular business niche. There are also promotional opportunities that you should take advantage of that could give your Web site a quick shot in the marketing arm.

(CAUTION) A Problem to Look Out for with Multiple Submission Services

Some search engines and directories need to be manually submitted to. Be careful using multiple submission services that require you to fill out one form for all search engines and directories. Some major directories like Yahoo! have very detailed information fields that need to be filled out. Submission services that provide just one general form to complete do not meet their directory listing requirements.

And finally, spreading the word far and wide that your site exists using free multiple listing services won't hurt either. So make sure you list your Web site on

- Multiple Submissions sites
- What's New sites
- What's Hot and Cool sites
- Business listings

Start here with these free services and spread the word that your site exists. Be sure you let it be known what you offer the online consumer.

Multiple Submission Sites

Submitting your Web site to the top search engines takes work and should be done separately for each one. There are many second-tier indexes that are worth submitting to, using one of the free multiple submission services such as the one at `ecki.com` (see Figure 20.1), which claims to be the Grandfather of All Links FREE Advertising Directories.

SelfPromotion.com at `selfpromotion.com` leads you through the process of submitting your site to more than 700 different search engines, directories, and indexes. Be aware that using this site will take a fair amount of work. Although site self-promotion is not difficult, it will take some effort, a bit of thought, and a fair amount of patience.

In addition, some search engines and directories need to be manually submitted to. Certain information that must be entered cannot be automated. SelfPromotion.com alerts you to these engines and indexes so you can manually submit to them and auto-submit to others. When manual submission is required, it's because the site is crucially important and structured so that manual submission is the best way to go, or the site administrator wants you to submit in person.

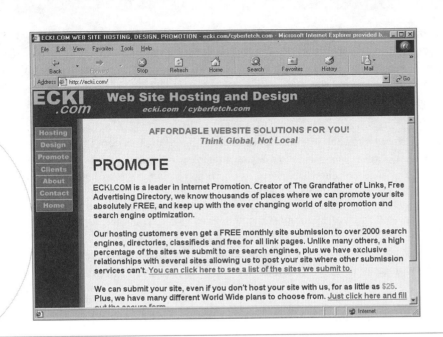

Figure 20.1

Multiple site listing services like Ecki.com can help spread your URL around second-tier indexes.

Avoid FFA Sites

Stay away from listing with the Free For All (FFA) sites. Most of them are there for one reason—to collect e-mail addresses so that they can e-mail you advertising messages. Additionally, any click-throughs you do get are of very poor quality.

At JimTools (www.jimtools.com) you can use his Search Engine Submitter to submit your Web site URL to the 46 largest engines. Then use his Directory Submitter, which will submit your site to more than 400 of the most important directories.

What's Hot and Cool Sites

Here are some other free sites to use when promoting your Web store. Although you're not guaranteed to get chosen as a "Hot" or "Cool" site, it's worth submitting your URL. These sites regularly review submitted sites and promote special sites for a brief time before moving on. Sites are generally selected on good Web design or high-quality content. If you are chosen as a Hot or Cool site, you can expect a lot of hits on your site after it is announced.

Too Cool (www.toocool.com) awards sites that are well-designed with great content. You cannot submit a link more than once or submit links of a similar nature. Cool Site of the Day (see Figure 20.2) at www.cool.infi.net is the Web's original Awards site and is very popular. But because of its popularity, it now charges $14.95 for submitting your site. In exchange for the submission fee, you receive a Cool Site freebie package valued at $45.

So, to some extent it is free. Keep in mind that paying the submission fee does not guarantee your selection as a Cool Site of the Day.

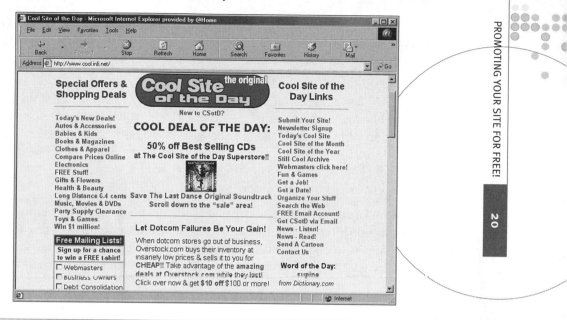

Figure 20.2

Cool Site of the Day is the oldest and largest What's Cool site on the Web. Be sure to register your site there.

Business Listings and Classified Ads

Sometimes the World Wide Web seems like the World Wide Wait. But the operative word here is world, and just because you have a local business doesn't mean you can't attract a global market. Here are some free promotional ideas that can give your business a global presence.

Spend Your Time, Not Your Money

Taking the time to learn how to promote your site will save you a bundle. Visit sites like Jim World's VirtualPromote at www.VirtualPromote.com/. It lists free promotional, advertising, and marketing resources that can offer excellent promotional information that can increase traffic to your site. It also has links to other helpful sites.

There are hundreds of business directories—as opposed to general search engines—on the Web where you can list your business by category for free. They range from excellent to so-so, so you will have to determine which ones best fit your business.

Start with e-commerce1 at ecommerce1.com/submit_a_site.htm. Its simple submission form just asks for your business name, URL, and a short description. The WWW Yellow Pages at www.yellow-pg.com also let you submit your Web store for free. Its Basic Listing lets you give customer information about your business, including your type of business, address, and phone number. Then register your Web store at ComFind at `comfind.com/intro.html`.

If you want a more extensive listing of your business, go to BizWeb at `bizweb.com/InfoForm`. BizWeb allows you to give a more detailed description of your business, including what kinds of payment you accept and a very long list of business types to choose from.

And don't overlook the guides on the Web. There are guide sites such as About.com at `about.com`, and Suite 101 at `suite101.com` that might have one or more guide sections that could relate to your business. Send the individual who is responsible for the respective section information about your site with an invitation to visit. If your work impresses the guide, your site stands a good chance of being mentioned on the Guide's site—with a permanent link! Another good reason to approach the guides is that many issue awards to sites that are considered "Best of the Web."

Finally, make use of the free classified ad sites that you can use to promote your particular product offering or service. You can use them to advertise special promotions or sales, alert shoppers to one-of-a-kind deals, give away free or sample products, or do seasonal promotions. Write a compelling enough ad and you'll generate new traffic to your Web store.

Yahoo! Classifieds at `classifieds.yahoo.com` lets you place free business classified ads in both product and service categories.

Banner Ads

Banner ads can be expensive, but you can get them for free by joining a link exchange service. Free banner link services such as Microsoft's bCentral (see Figure 20.3) at `adnetwork.bcentral.com`, BannerSwap at `www.BannerSwap.com`, and SmartClicks at `smartage.com/promote/smartclicks/index2.html` can be very useful after you have established traffic to your site.

If you decide to use reciprocal linking—banner ad or otherwise—as a promotional strategy, remember to keep the following in mind.

Every link you add to your site is a doorway to another location. After visitors click that link, they might not return to your site. So although you might gain traffic with reciprocal linking, you don't want to show them an exit to your site before you have a chance to show them your offer. Therefor, don't put any kind of reciprocal link on your home page.

Give shoppers a chance to see what you're offering before showing them an exit to other sites.

If you offer links or banners, put them on pages that are at least one level below the home page in your Web site. On your home page, you can get the chance to sell a shopper on your offering (you are selling them as soon as they hit your home page with a product or service offer, right?) before they leave to go to another site.

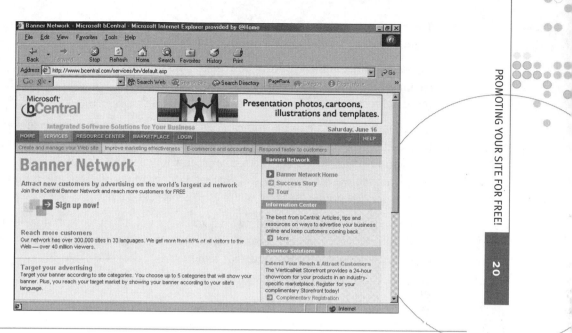

Figure 20.3

Microsoft's bCentral—formerly LinkExchange—is the oldest and most popular of the banner exchange networks.

Web Rings

Another form of reciprocal linking is the Web ring.

Web rings have been around as long as search engines and can give your Web store a traffic boost at the start. A Web Ring provides a fast and easy way for people to navigate the Web within a topic they are interested in. Web sites in a Web ring band together to form their sites into linked circles in a specific subject area. The circle—or ring—leads the visitor to each site through the ring of sites that allows visitors to the ring to reach the sites they are looking for quickly and easily.

The granddaddy of all Web rings is Yahoo! Webring at `dir.webring.yahoo.com/rw`. Member sites in the rings total more than 1,300,000, with the number of different rings totaling more than 80,000. If you are interested in placing your Web store in a ring, join one of the rings listed. Yahoo! Webring, of course, is free to join.

COMMUNITY PARTICIPATION—NEWSGROUPS AND DISCUSSION BOARDS

No man is an island, and neither is a Web site. Participation in newsgroups, discussion boards, and chat rooms on the Net is a great way to gain visibility for your e-business—and it's free!

The trick is to choose the right community participation vehicles and make a contribution to the discussion. Let's take newsgroups and discussion boards for example.

Before the birth of the World Wide Web, online marketers relied heavily on newsgroups. Although they have waned as a marketing vehicle, they still are an important free promotional resource.

With a little time and energy, you can find newsgroups where your product and expertise can lead to visitors and sales. But, remember—you *cannot* post an advertisement stating that you are open for business. That's not how it works, and if you do you will be flamed for spamming the list. To avoid this, first read the postings of the group for a few weeks to get the general nature and feel of the list. This is called *lurking*.

Next, read the FAQs for the list. It will tell you what you can and cannot post to the boards. You might find that some boards do allow you to post a message that reads like an ad. Some newsgroups are formed just for that purpose. They are

- alt.business
- alt.business.home
- alt.business.home.pc
- alt.business.import-export
- alt.business.misc

Remember, what you're looking for is an opportunity to respond to individual posts for help or enter into an ongoing discussion where your product or service might add to the discussion. If done right, when it's time for those on the newsgroup to buy, they'll remember you first.

For example, suppose you sell toys on your site and are participating on a toy or children's discussion board. Be prepared to offer advice and news about the toy industry in general and perhaps child safety—not just the toys you sell. If you have an accounting service, offer to answer specific questions on taxes.

Don't Forget to Tell Them Who You Are

Remember to add your signature or *sig* file to each message you post so people can contact you or visit your Web store off the board or list. Keep your sig file to no more than 4–5 lines.

Here's a list of the most popular newsgroups among online marketers:

- alt.biz.misc
- alt.business
- alt.business.home
- alt.business.misc
- alt.internet.commerce

- biz.general
- biz.newgroup
- misc.business
- misc.entrepreneurs

 Read Newsgroups the Easy Way

You don't need a newsgroup reader to read newsgroups on the Net. Visit Deja.com (recently acquired by Google.com) at `deja.com` for easy access to the newsgroups via the Web.

In addition to newsgroups, there are good discussion board sites that have numerous discussion boards on just about any topic that you can monitor and participate in. The best of the lot is Delphi Forums. Delphi Forums at `delphi.com` (see Figure 20.4) is one of the largest discussion boards on the Net and has more than 500,000 individual discussion forums to participate in. Forum One is almost as large with more than 300,000 forums covering thousands of topics.

Figure 20.4

You can access and post to more than 500,000 individual discussion forums at Delphi Forums.

COMMUNITY PARTICIPATION—DISCUSSION LISTS, LIVE CHAT, AND NEWSLETTERS

Besides newsgroups and discussion boards on the Net, there are discussion lists. A discussion list is an e-mail version of the discussion board or newsgroup. But instead of posting your message on a Web site, you send an e-mail to the list. By and large, interactive discussion lists usually offer better quality discussions than newsgroups and discussion boards. These discussions are in the form of e-mails and show up in your mailbox every day. When you want to post to a list you have subscribed to, you send an e-mail to the list and the list sends your message out to everyone who has subscribed to the discussion list.

TIP **You've Got a Promotion!**

In addition to mailing lists and newsgroups, don't overlook America Online. If your site or product is aimed at the average consumer, AOL's communities can be a great place to promote your Web store.

There are business-related lists that offer excellent avenues to expose members of your target audience to your business site, such as TalkBiz.com at `talkbiz.com/bizlist/index.html` (see Figure 20.5). It's hard to gauge how strong a candidate a list is for promoting your e-business before subscribing to it and watching it for several days or weeks. So, like in the newsgroups, lurk for a while to learn the rules and see who is participating. Then, join in the discussions after you're comfortable with the format and process.

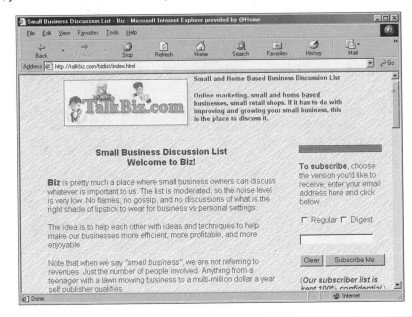

Figure 20.5

At TalkBiz there is a moderated e-mail discussion list where you can talk with other small business owners about issues concerning your business.

To find a discussion list that addresses your business product or service, go to these Web sites.

First, go to Lsoft at `www.lsoft.com/lists/listref.html`. It has the CataList, the official catalog of LISTSERV lists on the Net. CataList has more than 33,000 public discussion lists that you can subscribe to. At Lsoft you can search lists by interest, host country, view lists with 10,000 subscribers or more, or lists with 1,000 subscribers or more. Liszt at www.liszt.com has more than 90,000 e-mail discussion lists in dozens of topic categories to choose from.

NeoSoft at paml.net/ has a smaller database of discussion lists—only about 7,500—but they're worth a look-see because their lists are organized by subject. You are able to find a list easier here that pertains to your e-business.

Subscribe and Unsubscribe with Ease

ListTool.com is a free tool that makes the process of subscribing, unsubscribing, and sending commands to 816 mailing and discussion lists easy. You don't have to remember which commands to send to some obscure e-mail address to subscribe or unsubscribe. Find this tool at listtool.com.

Finally, don't forget the live chat rooms on the Net. They can be a great free source of promotion for your new Web store. And besides, you'll be talking directly—and live—to potential customers. Some of the best chat rooms for online businesses can be found at Delphi Forums Chat at delphi.com/ and at About.com at http://talk.about.com/chatcentral/index.htm

CHAPTER **21**

CONTESTS, GIVE-AWAYS, AND PROMOTIONS

In This Chapter

- Learn how to run a sweepstakes and contest from your Web site
- Discover how to give something free to attract shoppers to your Web store
- Learn how to offer coupons and spot discounts on your Web store
- Learn the importance of offering gift certificates, reminder services, and gift registries for your e-business

Your marketing bag of tricks needs to include more than just an advertising campaign. There are other ways to promote your e-business and spend your marketing dollars. The key to your e-business success is being able to generate a steady flow of new qualified prospects to whom you can promote your product or service. Contests, give-aways, and shopper services are some of the best ways to do this.

There are basically two things you can accomplish with these types of promotions. You can draw attention to your product or service offer, and you can generate a database of prospects that you can market to later.

Either way, these promotional elements should be seriously considered when creating a marketing plan for your e-business.

So, let's start with contests.

SWEEPSTAKES AND CONTESTS

Sweepstakes and contests are one of the most popular promotion gimmicks on the Net today. Do a search on Yahoo! for "sweepstakes" and you'll come up with hundreds of sites listing tens of thousands of sweepstakes where consumers can participate. Sweepstakes and contests can increase awareness of your product or service offer and drive traffic to your Web store. In addition, sweepstakes are a great marketing tool.

You can announce your sweepstakes to newsgroups, online sweepstakes groups, and search engines. You could add a feedback form on the sweepstakes page asking for comments on your Web store, product, or service. If you have a new product, consider making that your sweepstakes prize. By using your own products or services as a prize, this will target people who are interested in them. Another marketing trick is to build a list of potential customers by asking them to check a box if they would be interested in receiving e-mails, newsletters, updates, or possibly receiving catalogs of your products. And don't forget to contact all participants via e-mail when you announce a winner of your ongoing sweepstakes.

Create Your Own Sweepstakes

Dynoform lets you create personalized sweepstakes and—here's the good part—their service is entirely Web-based. There's no software installation, and set up takes only a few minutes from their site. Find it at dynoform.com/dynoInfo.asp.

Ongoing? Right! You can run a sweepstakes monthly, weekly—even daily. Announcing winners to all participants is a great way to keep your Web store and its offerings in front of potential customers.

Great promotion tool, right? So what's the downside? How about hefty fines and even jail time. Keep in mind that although sweepstakes and contests can be an effective marketing tool, you must structure them properly to ensure compliance with federal and state laws. But we'll discuss this a little later.

For now, how do you begin? As with any good marketing promotion, you need to plan the event carefully. To have a successful sweepstakes promotion, you need to

- Consider your promotion goals
- Know your target audience
- Design the structure
- Promote your sweepstakes

First step—determine your goals. That's easy. You want to drive traffic to your site. But after potential customers are there you can use your sweepstakes for any number of things, such as gathering feedback on your Web site and product offering or building a mailing list of prospects (always ask if they want to be included in future mailings).

Have a Pro Manage Your Sweepstakes

Sweepstakes Online is one of the largest sweepstakes sites in the world. They will build, maintain, and promote your sweepstakes for you. Find it at `sweepstakesbuilder.com/packages.htm`.

Next, you want to target your sweepstakes to make the most of your promotion. Match your promotion to the goals you are trying to achieve and the audience you are trying to attract. Are you after a general audience? Then offer a general prize such as cash, a CD player, VCR, or TV. Provide something almost everyone can use. If you want to target your offer to those consumers that use your particular product or service, then make the prize either your product or service, or a similar one. The prize in this case qualifies the player for you. Although you'll attract fewer entrants, the ones who do enter will be more likely to purchase your product or service in the future.

Finally, give some thought to your prize. You don't have to offer a large expensive prize, such as a trip around the world or a new Porsche, to get a good response. But don't skimp on your prize, either. If you offer prizes such as coffee mugs, mouse pads, or T-shirts, your sweepstakes will get lost in the thousands of contests on the Net today.

Run Your Own Incentive Program Without the Programming

IQ Commerce Corp at `www.iq.com` bundles services and technology required to run incentive marketing promotions online from your site or others. It aims to bring the costs within range of smaller e-commerce operators.

Structuring Your Sweepstakes

After you've determined your target market, prize, and goals, it's time to actually structure the sweepstakes.

First up are the rules. Listing the rules on your site is very important in conducting a sweepstakes. At the bare minimum you should

- Include the number of entries allowed (one per entrant or as many times as they like).
- Mention whether the sweepstakes is run daily, weekly, monthly, or just one time.
- Mention any restrictions or limits, such as age limits, if open to U.S. residents only or international.
- Tell entrants when the sweepstakes ends and when the prize will be awarded.
- Detail any and all information required for entry such as name, address, zip, phone, e-mail address, and so on.

Next, give some thought to the entry method. Will they -e-mail their entry to you in response to your advertisement or posting or are they required to go to your Web site and fill out a form? The latter is preferred if you want to ask some questions or get some feedback from the entrants or find whether they want to receive more information, a free e-mail newsletter, or a free catalog.

> **TIP**
>
> **Announce Your Sweepstakes to the Web**
>
> A good place to announce your sweepstakes is to post a message on the Usenet news-group called `alt.consumers.sweepstakes`.

In addition, make sure the following information is on your sweepstakes page:

- Provide information about your company or at least a link to your "About Us" page on your site.

- Give entrants a full description of the prize you're offering. Let them know exactly what they might win. For example, if they win a cruise or a weeklong stay in Disney World, is the airfare included?

- Make sure you provide a way to contact you in case an entrant has questions about your sweepstakes.

- Display a set of the official rules that address in detail the elements that make up the structure of your sweepstakes. Every legitimate sweepstakes must have a set of official rules. The official rules should state exactly how the sweepstakes Is structured as well as any restrictions or limitations about your promotion.

The last thing to consider is how to promote your sweepstakes across the Net. There are a number of Web sites where you can post your sweepstakes and announce it to the world. You add your sweepstakes to sites such as Sweepstakes Online at `www.sweepstakesonline.com` (see Figure 21.1) and Games & Giveaways at `www.freestuff2000.com/giveaways`.

Keeping It Legal

Adhering to the law is extremely important with sweepstakes and contests. And it goes without saying that before you run an online sweepstakes to promote your e-business, you should seek good legal council first. The key point to remember is that a sweepstakes is *not* a lottery. If your online sweepstakes is considered by law officials to be a lottery— you're breaking the law!

So what's the difference between a sweepstakes and a lottery? A sweepstakes invites eligible participants to register for a chance to win a prize. A drawing at the conclusion of the sweepstakes usually awards prizes. A lottery consists of a prize, chance, and consideration. It's the consideration part that makes lotteries illegal in most states. Although the definition of a consideration differs from state to state (you need that lawyer again), generally, *consideration* means that a willing participant is required to purchase something or pay for access to be eligible to enter the contest. Another example of consideration might be the requirement of the participant providing detailed consumer information to be eligible.

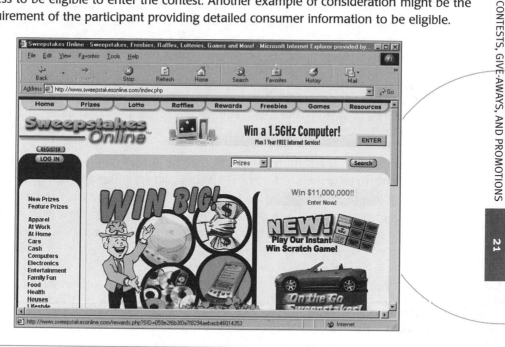

Figure 21.1

At Sweepstakes Online you can list your company's sweepstakes promotion on its site.

Keep It Legal

Keeping your sweepstakes and contest legal is very important. A mistake in the execution of your contest could cost you a lot of money in fines—even jail time! So, keep up on what's happening in sweepstakes and contest law at Arent Fox at
www.arentfox.com.

Finally, you must offer an *Alternative Method of Entry* (AMOE). Allowing participants to enter offline via mail or fax is a form of AMOE. Why should you do this? Including an AMOE for your online sweepstakes might decrease the risk that a regulator will view a sweepstakes promotion as an illegal lottery.

Besides the risk of legal action, if you run your sweepstakes improperly, or if the participants feel that it was run unfairly, you risk a public relations nightmare that will be hard to overcome. Just because you are a small business, don't think that you're safe by flying below the radar screen of state and federal regulators. Don't be lulled into a false sense of safety in numbers. Seek legal advice and run your sweepstakes properly.

GIVE-AWAYS

Stuart Brand, creator of the Whole Earth Catalog, once said, "Information wants to be free." Online merchants have been using a variation of this idea for years—give something free, then sell something. This also is known on the Net as the Yoda Principle—"Give then Take." Although this idea is not new to commerce (businesses have been using loss leaders for decades—selling products below cost to get shoppers into a store) it's the right formula for the Internet.

TIP

List Your Freebie at FreeShop

A great place to list your incentive offer, free products, services, coupons, and other incentives, is at FreeShop.com. Find it at `freeshop.com/Advertising/advertise.htm`.

A good example of this strategy is the free virtual bouquet that many flower sites offer visitors. Come to their site, send a free virtual bouquet via e-mail and perhaps become a paying customer of real flowers in the future. In a similar vein, you can send a virtual greeting card to anyone on the Net by using many of the greeting card sites. Their hope is to have you buy their real greeting cards at some later date. Another example is the search engine optimization services. They will give you a free report on where your site appears in different search engine search results in hopes of selling you their search engine optimization service after you see how badly your site ranks against your competitors.

Give-aways also provide an opportunity to cross-promote with other noncompeting Web stores. You can offer one of your products or a compatible service free to other Web stores. For example, if a site sells auto accessories, and you sell insurance products, you might offer a free comparison insurance quote. Or if a site sells running shoes, you might offer a free pair of athletic socks with each purchase. The trick here is to get the customer from the other site to visit your site to get the free product or service. The partner Web store gets the sale and you get additional visitors.

Besides giving away a product, information, or service, offering discount coupons is another strategy to attract shoppers to your Web store. At first you think of coupons as used only in the real world. And, yes, you can offer coupons on your site that can be printed off and used in your real-world store. But if you're a pure Net-based e-commerce company, how can you make effective use of online coupons?

You can offer them directly on your site.

Iq.com (refer to Figure 21.2) has a product called iQCoupons that is the digital equivalent of offline coupons. Using iQCoupons, you can create any size teaser graphic that when clicked, pops up an electronic coupon describing your offer. It might be an immediate discount on one of your products or an offer of free shipping for a limited time. The consumer views your message in a small pop-up window, and when ready to take action, clicks a print button. You can place your electronic coupon on your own site or on the banner ads you place on other sites. Research by Forrester at `www.forrester.com` has shown that the average click-through rates for online banner ads with coupons are 20%, compared to .065% for standard banner ads.

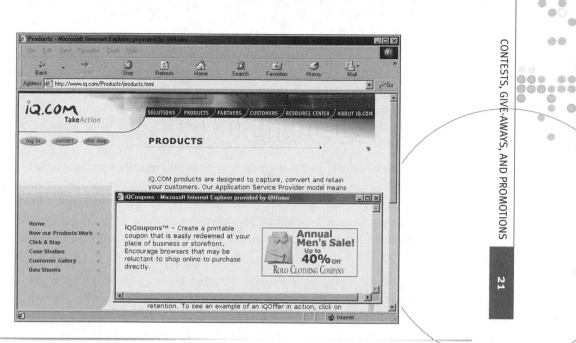

Figure 21.2

Using Iq.com's iQCoupons service, you can create the digital equivalent to an offline coupon.

SHOPPER SERVICES

Stickiness is all the rage these days with e-commerce, and for good reason. Constant advertising can get expensive, and as a small to medium-sized e-business, you need to continuously find ways to keep shoppers returning to your site—that's called *stickiness*. The following are three of the best kinds of stickiness:

- Reminder services
- Gift registries
- Gift certificates

Web consumers are a busy lot. They have a lot to think about and more to remember. That's why Web-based reminder services are so popular. Your Web store can share in this popularity if you place a reminder service on your site.

The most popular kinds of reminder services are those that send out e-mail messages alerting a consumer about an upcoming event such as family birthdays, anniversaries, seasonal gift-giving reminders, and special one-time events such as baby showers and weddings. The best way to offer a reminder service is via e-mail. Set up a page on your site where consumers can fill out a form listing the different days, times, and events that they would like to be reminded of. Capture this information in a database and send out e-mail reminders a week ahead of time. In the e-mail, inform them of the event they wanted to be reminded of and—if you can—suggest a product or service you offer on your Web store that fills their need.

But a reminder service need not be limited to these events. If you sell automobile accessories, you can attract consumers to your site offering an oil change reminder service. If you sell jazz CDs, alert subscribers to your service when new Jazz CDs are released. If you sell movies, offer a service to alert shoppers when new releases are due. And if you sell outdoor supplies to hunters, remind them of when certain hunting seasons begin. If you think a little, you can find a reason for a reminder service for any product or service that you offer.

Gift registries are another fast-growing segment on the Net. You can invest in creating your own gift registry for special occasions, or you can join one of the universal gift-registry sites on the Net to offer your products. A good example is WishClick at www.wishclick.com. In addition to increasing sales, a gift registry can help you make future inventory predictions based on how many people add your products to their wish list.

Finally, why not print your own private-labeled currency? That's what gift certificates are because they can be spent only at your store. Gift certificates can be offered directly from your site or can be sent by your visitors to anyone they want via e-mail. And here's an idea. Many times shoppers cannot spend the full amount of the gift certificate. In that case, offer to donate the remainder after the sale to charity. That makes your customer feel good.

CHAPTER 22

PR—GETTING THE WORD OUT

In This Chapter

- Learn what Public Relations is and how to create a Buzz
- Learn how to write an effective press release
- Discover where to send your press releases online
- Learn the do's and don'ts of news releases

Online publicity is an important element of your marketing plan if you're to rise above the noise level on the Net. But getting that publicity is not easy—it takes a lot of work, and can be fraught with dangers. It takes a lot of planning and preparation and is definitely *not* a one-shot effort. A well-thought-out publicity plan gives your e-business the kind of you want in the media and your community. Over the long haul, a good generates good credibility for your e-business.

The goal is to generate important coverage of your e-business at exactly the right time and in exactly the right place.

Although Public Relations (PR) is a part of marketing, it's really not marketing. Marketing manages demand whereas PR manages your company's image and its awareness on the Net. Online PR is not the process of submitting your Web store to search engines. Good PR appeals to people, not machines. Good PR builds awareness and visibility with minimal cash.

The history of the Web—short that it is—is filled with stories of how an e-commerce Web site was mentioned in *USA Today* or on *Good Morning America* and received instant awareness—and tons of shoppers! You can do that, too.

CREATING THE BUZZ

The Buzz is one of the most important and most elusive forces in all of marketing. If you've got something to sell and are either short on cash or rolling in dough to promote it, creating a Buzz about it will get you millions of dollars in free publicity. Buzz is extremely influential and after it spreads, can boost your Web store's awareness considerably.

Get a Free PR Consultation

Spread the News offers an online ten-question survey to help determine the best way to generate publicity for your venture. After the survey is completed, Spread the News will provide a free mini-PR consultation based on your answers.

Find it at `capital-connection.com/prsurvey.html`.

When you create a Buzz, it means that people are talking about you. You're mentioned in news articles, compared in features, talked about in chat rooms, and mentioned in newsgroups. It's the Holy Grail of marketing and is the marketing goal of every business today.

So how do you create the Buzz? By putting out timely press releases, interviews, and stories that showcase your e-business. And that means getting the attention of journalists.

Now, journalists are a fussy bunch. They're harassed daily by companies and individuals asking them to write about their latest "can't-live-without" product or service. But much too often, the news releases they do get are dry, boring, and have no connection to what interests them. Journalists respond to clever writing and news releases that describe how a new product or service is a solution to a business or consumer trend or problem. They respond to releases that piggyback on late-breaking stories that show how a company's product or service relates to current news.

What do you need to know to create a Buzz? First, learn how to write a compelling and timely press release. Second, know where to send it and how. Before you start, check out PR Resource at `www.prweb.com` (see Figure 22.1). It can provide you with information on what you need to know for effective PR.

The key elements of a good publicly plan include a number of elements.

- **State your key message advantages**—In any release you send out, you need to make sure that the main advantages of your product or service are clearly defined and stated. It's your Unique Selling Position again! If you did a good job defining it way back in Chapter 4, "Creating a Unique Selling Position," you should have no problem pulling your key messages out of it for your news releases. Your goal is to have these key messages reported or implied in any news story about your e-business.

- **Target your publicity**—Make a list of all magazines, newspapers, radio stations, and TV stations that would most likely carry your company story. You want to target these news outlets and make sure that what you do and the news you release match their audience interests. And remember to not just target a new source—target a particular department or individual within it.

- **Create a media calendar**—Good PR is not a one-shot deal. A good public relations plan is designed to map out a strategy for several months to a year. For PR to be effective, you need a steady stream of it. You need to craft your news releases not only for publication, but to get interviewed for a timely story as well. So look at your product or service, and then look at a calendar. Prepare to send out news releases that show how your product or service relates to holidays—such as Christmas, Easter, Valentine's Day, or Halloween—and seasonal times—such as swim and vacation season in the Summer, back to school in the Fall, winter activities in the Winter, and fashions in the Spring. Design both your marketing campaign and your public relations campaign to coincide with these events. Alert the media at each one of these points with news releases. The object here is to get the press coverage—or better yet—get an interview.

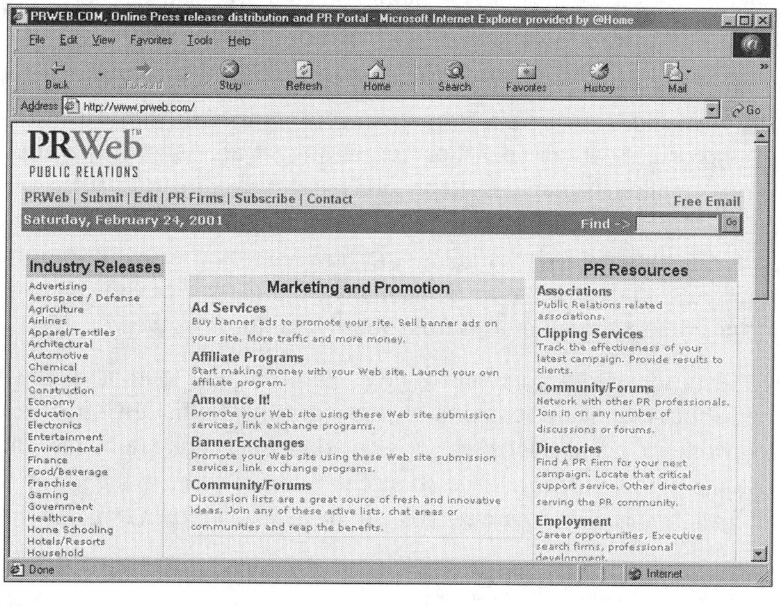

Figure 22.1

PR Resources is loaded with information on what you need to know for effective PR.

Knowing what is considered news and what's not is key in getting your news releases read. Simply stating that your Web site is open for business, or if you have redesigned your site, or have added new staff, is not in itself newsworthy. What is newsworthy is focusing on something that's already prominent in the news or is about to become so. Issue a report related to your site's main theme, or conduct a survey and issue a report on the findings, buck a trend in the marketplace, announce an award you've won, or announce when you reach a company milestone, such as celebrating your one millionth customer.

Place a Press Room on Your Site

A must for your Web store is an online Press Room. If a media outlet picks up your news release, it might want to know more about you than what's contained in your release. This is where an online Press Room on your site becomes invaluable.

Reporters have quotas to meet every day, or week, or month. They have little time to search throughout your entire site looking for the contact information they need for a story. When reporters find no contact information for background materials for the press, they can only assume that the company has little to say to the media.

So, what to do? Create a set of materials for the press at your Web site that describes who you are, what your company does, how it sells its products, and the key personnel in your e-business. Make sure to include all contact information—your Web site URL, e-mail addresses of key personnel, physical address, phone numbers, and fax numbers. This information needs to be in your Press Room on your Web site. If reporters can't reach you, they might write about your competitors rather than about you.

Online Press Rooms not only provide useful information to journalists, but they can save you time answering routine questions about your company, such as the CEO's professional background or the date of your most recent merger agreement with Amazon or Yahoo! Put that information in your Press Room and make it easy for journalists to find it. But don't stop there. Why not publish articles on your site giving the world your vision of where your particular e-commerce niche is going and how you plan to meet the needs of its consumers? If your e-business has been mentioned in an article or if the press has interviewed you, include links to those articles from your Press Room as well.

Finally, have a place in your online Press Room where journalists can request to be informed about future developments of your company. Gather their names, the media outlets they work for, e-mail addresses, physical addresses, phone numbers, and fax numbers. Also, ask them how they would like to receive news releases in the future—via e-mail, fax, or snail-mail. In this way, over time you can develop your own targeted media list.

WRITING THE PRESS RELEASE

Writing a press release is more art than science. And to be read, it must be done right.

The biggest challenge is to know what journalists consider genuine news and what they consider fluff. Being so close to your e-business, you can easily lose perspective and what you see as earthshaking news to you will get the automatic delete from journalists. Issuing too much company fluff as news will eventually result in your future news releases being ignored—sort of like what happened to the boy who cried wolf too often. So, remember to make your release newsworthy by solving a problem or filling a need. Pinpoint what that need or problem is and write the release from that perspective.

Along with making your press release newsworthy, you need to keep the following in mind when writing it:

- **Create an unmistakable opening**—The first line of your press release should read

    FOR IMMEDIATE RELEASE

    in all caps. This lets the reporters know the news is authorized for publication on the date they receive it.

- **Write a headline that gets straight to the point**—Write a headline using a combination of lowercase and capital letters, keeping your headline to ten words or less. Remember, what you say here determines whether the reader will read the rest of the release.

- **Create a strong leading paragraph**—The first part of your lead paragraph should include the City it was released from or where the event took place, the newswire it was released over, and the date of the release. It would look like this: DENVER—(BUSINESS WIRE)—Jan. 31, 2000. All releases must include a date because reporters do not always use releases immediately. Your lead paragraph should then answer the who, what, where, when, why, and how of the event. The lead paragraph is really an abstract or summary of the whole release. This is important. Journalists get lots of releases in their email and don't have time to read every release in its entirety. So you have to grab them in the first paragraph and answer their question—"Why should I care?"

- **Give the journalist reading the release the reason why it's important to his/her readers**—Here's where you give a detailed explanation from the reader's perspective. Add all background information, quotes from objective or third-party sources, comparisons with competitors, and so on. If you're sending your release inside the text of an e-mail message, format it in the style of the most common e-mail reader. Stay away from HTML tags, tabs, or columns. These are not read well by text-based e-mail programs.

(CAUTION) **Check Everything Thoroughly**

Don't trust your word processing program to catch errors in grammar and spelling. Have a few people read the release before sending it to a reporter or news agency.

- **Include a brief company summary**—Mention your company expertise in your niche, your location, years in business, and so on. Keep it short. Don't include your annual report.

- **Include complete contact information**—Give a contact name, e-mail address, and your URL. The contact name you supply should be someone who's available and capable of answering questions from the press.

- **Close the release**—Close with the characters -30- or ###, which are style conventions that let the reporter know they have reached the end of the release.

Finally, keep it short, no longer than one page in length—about 500 words maximum. And when writing your release, keep in mind the 3-30-3 rule. You have 3 seconds to catch a reader's eye, 30 seconds to convince him that he wants to find out more, then 3 minutes to tell him everything he wants to know.

An example of a well-formatted press release can be found at `www.rmadgroup.com/pr4.shtml`.

WHERE TO SEND THE RELEASE

You've done a good job of writing your release and it's ready to go. So, how do you get it out?

You can send it out yourself if you use one of the wire services. In addition, there are several PR companies on the Web that will send out your release to particular targeted media outlets. Obviously, the biggest advantage to sending out your own release is that it's free. Also, you might be able to target your releases a bit more than you can by using a commercial service. On the other hand, there are some advantages to using a service to distribute your releases. Journalists might be more receptive when a press release comes from a known source. A release from an unknown company might be immediately discarded.

One place where you can post your press release free is at PR Web at `www.prweb.com/` (see Figure 22.2).

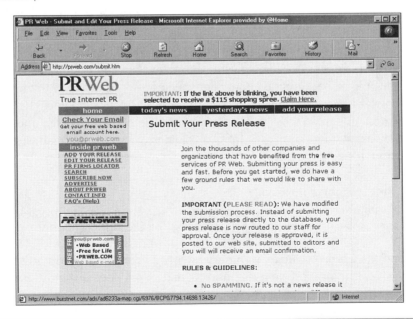

Figure 22.2

Post your press release for free at PR Web.

If you want your release to be sent out over a well-known and credible newswire you have to spend the dollars and send your release through the PR Newswire at `prnewswire.com` and the Business Wire at `Businesswire.com`.

PR Newswire is one of the longtime leaders in paid news release distribution. PR Newswire requires an annual fee and reaches 300 Web sites, online services, and leading databases where content might be published or archived. Along with leading journalist's e-mail boxes, Business Wire, the other industry giant, offers a wide range of services parallel to those of PR Newswire. It too requires an annual fee.

Media Outlets for Your Release

At Gebbie you can find links to all types of media outlets including radio, TV, daily newspapers, weekly newspapers, and magazines on the Internet. Find it at `www.gebbieinc.com/index1.htm`.

If you don't want to pay PR Newswire or Business Wire's annual retainer fee, there are publicity companies on the Net that send out press releases on demand without any retainer fees. Unless you plan on sending out news releases on a very frequent basis, these types of companies are your best bet.

URLwire

`www.urlwire.com`

URLwire (see Figure 22.3) pulls from a collection of more than 3,000 contacts across 100+ subject interest areas (and in 30+ countries). It will personalize between 200–300 separate e-mail news releases, each with content specific for the recipient. It also will build a Web-based version of your news, so that the many online news pointer services, such as Newslinx, Internet-Watch, NewsHub, and others can point to it in their daily headlines if they so choose. Costs range from $795–$2,000. The average campaign is about $900.

Internet Wire

`internetwire.com/release/index.htx`

Internet Wire sends releases worldwide to 9,000+ technology media via e-mail, top daily and national newspapers, premier technology and business periodicals, major television, radio outlets, and industry user groups. There are no word-count restrictions or membership fees. You also have automatic posting and linking for 90 days on the Internet Wire site. Cost is $225 per release.

Internet News Bureau

`www.newsbureau.com/services`

Internet News Bureau distributes to the INB Aggregate List (A-List) that includes 2,600+ journalists who subscribe to receive Web-related material (see Figure 22.4). To better serve the journalists who subscribe to INB's service, INB consolidates its material into the daily INB Press Release Digest. In addition to the A-List, INB offers Target Modules that enable a company to reach journalists who cover other topics and industries, and custom media relations services for expanding media exposure beyond INB subscribers. Cost is $250 per release. Price goes down for prepaid multiple releases. Targeted releases start at $80.

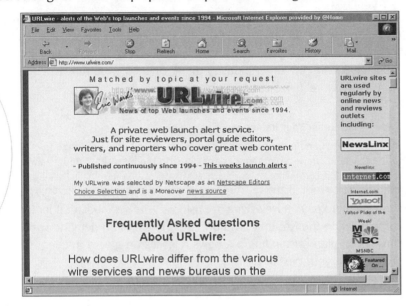

Figure 22.3

URLwire will send your release to more than 3,000 contacts across 100+ subject areas.

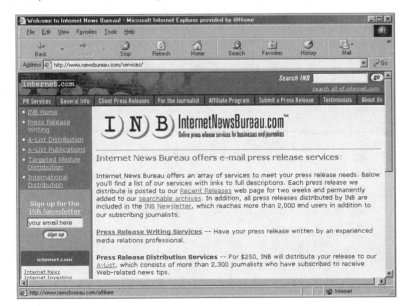

Figure 22.4

The Internet News Bureau will distribute your release to 2,600+ journalists who subscribe to receive Web-related material.

Xpress Press

www.xpresspress.com

Xpress Press is an e-mail information service personalizing news delivery to journalists based on their exact areas of coverage. All news releases are sent in separate messages to reporters who can quickly evaluate the content of the news, follow-up immediately by phone, or incorporate the content into working print articles, broadcasts, or Web pages.

More than 9,000 reporters covering more than 400 news beats in 36+ countries currently subscribe to its feed. These subscribers include Xpress Press National and regional U.S. and Canadian-based daily and weekly newspapers; UPI and AP wire; International Wires and Daily Newspapers; business, trade, and consumer magazines; and online industry-specific Web sites and publications. Also included are electronic business and industry-specific newsletters, radio and television stations, including the top 25 U.S. markets according to Arbitron rankings, and freelance and nationally syndicated writers, editors, and columnists. Cost is $225 per release.

WebPromote

www.webpromote.com/products/prelease.asp

WebPromote distributes press releases to 7,000 individual writers, tech reporters, editors, broadcasters, freelancers, and press professionals. This includes local, regional, national, and international coverage. Media includes top daily and national newspapers, premier technology and business periodicals, major television, radio, and industry user groups. Cost is $395 per release.

PR DO'S AND DON'TS

Mounting and administrating a good publicity camping takes a lot of work. So mind these Do's and Don'ts of news releases and your publicity efforts will pay off where it counts—bringing qualified shoppers to your Web store for minimal expense.

- DO make your press releases short and to the point.
- DO include all necessary contact information.
- DO spell check your release. And do it twice just to make sure!
- DO keep typefaces large and legible and readable both for e-mail and for faxes.
- DO write a clear and meaningful subject line. The subject line should reflect the contents of your release.
- DON'T write unclear press releases. If it doesn't make sense to the reader, it will not be used.
- DON'T send a release to a publication without knowing the audience or what the publication is all about.

- DON'T send attached files. Don't send a word processing document or a zipped file that the contact needs to download, unzip, read into his word processor, determine the compatibility, print, review, and so on. Most journalists will NOT open attachments. Not only is it time consuming, but they know that opening an attachment runs the risk of catching a computer virus. So even if you've written the best press release ever, if it's delivered as an attachment, it won't get read.

Keep these Do's and Don'ts in mind, and your publicity efforts can pay off big time for your Web store.

CHAPTER 23

AFFILIATE MARKETING

In This Chapter

- Discover why you should consider using affiliate marketing
- Learn the different affiliate program models and which one is best for you
- Learn how to compensate your affiliates and how to choose the right affiliates for your business
- Learn the affiliate marketing mistakes and how to avoid them

How would you like other Web sites to market and sell your company's products and services? And how would you like to pay the Web site only when their users buy your product or service or perform a task? Sounds like an online business dream, right? Well you can make these dreams reality if you use a form of distributed selling called *affiliate marketing*.

Affiliate marketing is a broad term applied to any form of pay-for-performance marketing. It's been known to have many names: cost-per-action advertising, revenue-sharing, referral programs, partnership programs, associate programs, and syndicated selling—all of which come under the umbrella term of affiliate marketing. It's hard to find an online merchant these days that does not have a link on his home page that reads "*Join Our Affiliate Program*," or "*Become a Partner*." Companies are flocking to this new kind of marketing for good reason.

WHY IS AFFILIATE MARKETING POPULAR?

Look at it this way. You have a business and need to generate sales. One way—and one of the most popular ways—is to buy ads on other Web sites. Your banner ad placed on another Web site is viewed by thousands of potential customers. But there's no guarantee that the ad will generate an action. So you pay for the ad whether someone clicks on it or not. Wouldn't it be better if you paid only if the ad performed? That's the beauty of an affiliate program—you buy guaranteed performance. That is, you pay only when an action is performed.

The benefits to you as a merchant are obvious. Your business can use an affiliate program to increase sales, drive traffic, generate qualified leads, and extend the reach of your brand through your affiliate partner Web sites.

This sounds good for the merchant. But just how popular are affiliate programs with Web site owners? Today, there are over one million Web sites on the Net that are participating in an affiliate program—and that number is growing every day. Affiliates who join a merchant's affiliate program not only earn revenue but also have the advantage of attracting additional visitors to their site who would be interested in the products or services offered.

You can look at affiliate programs as a way to get free advertising space on an affiliate's site, but that would be very short sighted and would result in a less than effective affiliate program. In fact that's one of the reasons why so many affiliate programs fail. Affiliates should be seen as true marketing partners and an asset to your company—and should be treated that way. It's important to realize that affiliates, in many ways, represent your company and their care and feeding—including educating them on your product or service and how to sell it—are important factors in a successful affiliate program. Their success will dictate the success of your program.

Affiliates cash in. You as an online merchant cash in, too. It's a strategy that you should have in your bag of marketing tricks.

A Long and Distinguished History

Affiliate marketing has been around for quite a while. But it's been getting quite a bit of attention over the last couple of years. Back in 1996, Amazon.com launched the first popular affiliate program on the Internet. The story goes like this. Jeff Bezos, the CEO and founder of Amazon.com, was attending a cocktail party when a woman he was chatting with expressed interest in selling books about divorce on her Web site. Bezos thought about it for a while, the came up with the idea of having Web sites sell Amazon's books for a commission. It gave the Web site a way to make a little money at the same time provided both additional visibility and revenue for Amazon.

It seemed like a win-win situation so Amazon introduced the Amazon Associates Program at www.amazon.com (see Figure 23.1). It was an immediate success and now claims to have over 300,000 Web sites linking to Amazon's Web site and selling its books. The idea was simple. A Web site would place a small banner on its site telling its visitors that they can buy books on a particular subject right from the site. The visitor clicked on the Amazon banner and was whisked off to Amazon's Web site where the site user bought the book that gave the Web site a small commission on the sale.

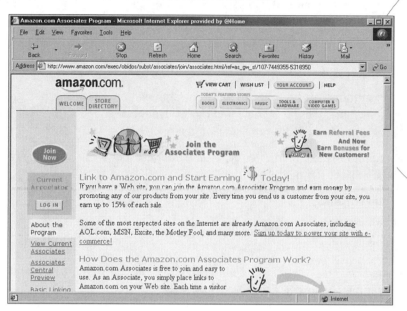

Figure 23.1

Amazon's Associate Program is the granddaddy of all affiliate programs.

Since then, affiliate marketing has caught on like wild fire.

JARGON

Affiliate Solution Providers

Affiliate Solution Providers provide a combination of the network, software, and services needed to create and track an affiliate program. Here are three of the biggest on the Net. Be Free at www.befree.com, Commission Junction at www.cj.com, and LinkShare at www.linkshare.com.

At first sight, affiliate marketing seems like an easy and inexpensive way to market your e-business. But don't let the simplicity of the concept fool you. Launching and running an affiliate program is far from easy. First of all, the percentage of affiliates that sign up for your program then become active is quite low. After you sign up affiliates, you'll find that only 10%–20% of the affiliate sites actually participate in the program meaning that they place your affiliate icon or banner on their sites. And of those 10%–20% of active affiliates only 20% of those are super-affiliates–those that produce the majority of the revenue for your program.

To run a successful affiliate program your company has to continually recruit new affiliates and reach out to existing ones to motivate them to become active in the program. Running a successful affiliate program is not easy, but when done right, affiliate marketing is a great way to market to potential buyers wherever they spend their time. Whether your potential buyers spend time on their favorite Web site or reading their e-mail, there is an affiliate marketing strategy for both.

PROGRAM MODELS

Since its introduction in 1996 by Amazon.com, affiliate marketing has grown and flourished, spawning a variety of new and innovative models, and works well as a marketing tool for individuals and for both small and large e-tailers.

Affiliate programs come in three types and your company can offer any or all of them to potential affiliate partners. They are

- Banner Links
- Storefronts
- E-mail

Combined, they represent the different ways Web sites can generate revenue from the program and merchants can acquire prospects and customers.

Using Banner Links

Web sites that join your banner links of programs agree to place a small banner or icon on their Web pages. The banner has the name of your company promoting what the merchant is selling. CDNow at www.cdnow.com (see Figure 23.2) is a good example. A Web site might place a banner for CDNow on its Web pages promoting the fact that music CDs can be bought from CDNow. There would be some promotional copy on the banner to get the Web site visitor to click on it, perhaps, a 10% discount if you buy now. When the user clicks on the banner, it sends the user to the CDNow site where she might buy a CD. If the shopper buys a CD, the affiliate sites gets a commission.

Banners are not limited to products. Some financial institutions promote their different credit cards using affiliate marketing. NextCard at www.nextcard.com is a good example. Affiliate Web sites place a banner persuading visitors to apply for a NextCard Visa card at a very low percentage rate. When the user clicks on the banner, it sends the user to the NextCard site where he or she would fill out an application. If the user is approved for a Visa card, the affiliate site gets a commission.

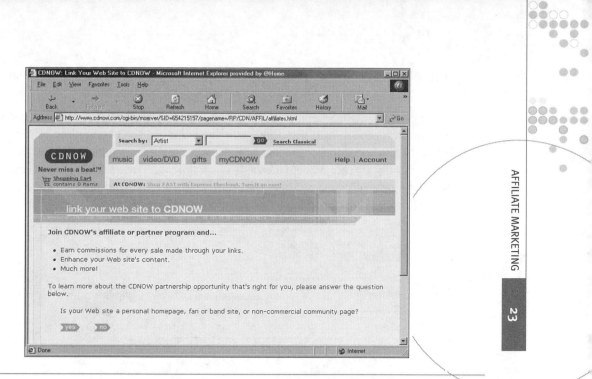

Figure 23.2

CDNow offers a very successful affiliate program to its partner sites.

Use Affiliate Program Directories to Recruit New Affiliates

To gain exposure for your affiliate program, you should be sure to submit your program to the affiliate program directories such as Associate-It at www.associate-it.com, AssociatePrograms.com at www.associateprograms.com and Refer-it at www.refer-it.com.

There are other revenue models using banners that don't depend upon commissions. Instead of paying a commission on products or services sold, you can offer Web sites a click-through affiliate program. With this method, Web sites earn revenue every time one of their visitors clicks through to your Web site (pay-per-click) or performs a task such as filling out a survey form or entering a contest (pay-per-lead). No sales are made, but your company can build up an e-mail list of prospects that you can market to later on. Examples of pay-per-lead networks include WebSponsors at www.websponsors.com and DirectLeads at www.directleads.com.

Using Storefronts

Although the banner links programs have been successful for online merchants over the years, they haven't been that great for affiliate Web site partners. The banner links approach has its drawbacks for affiliates. Primarily, when a Web site's visitor clicks on an affiliate program banner, the visitor leaves the affiliate site to complete the transaction. The affiliate then loses the traffic that he has worked hard to acquire with the small chance that the visitor would actually complete a transaction at your online store.

This is why pay-per-click programs are better liked by affiliate Web sites. If the Web site loses its traffic, at least it has the guarantee of being paid for it.

But a new affiliate marketing model has entered the picture and it has revitalized the sales commission model. With the storefront model, visitors don't leave your affiliate partner's Web sites. In the storefront model, you actually create a complete online store that looks like it resides on your affiliate partner's site. Vstore (see Figure 23.3) at www.vstore.com is a good example of this affiliate marketing approach. At Vstore, an affiliate partner can open a store that's imbedded in his site that can sell products in a variety of categories.

Figure 23.3

Vstore offers its affiliate partners a way to seamlessly integrate a complete online store on their sites. They can build a store right from Vstore's Web site in a variety of product categories.

> **Check Out the Experts**
>
> Declan Dunn, the renowned affiliate guru, sells a great training system for affiliates called "Winning the Affiliate Game." Another book/program that can really assist your affiliates is *Make Your Site Sell* by Ken Evoy. *Nothing But 'Net* by Michael Campbell is also a very useful title that will help your affiliates optimize their sites and convert shoppers into buyers.

Using E-mail

Web sites aren't the only places to conduct an affiliate marketing program. Over the last year or so, a new ripple to affiliate marketing has appeared—e-mail affiliate programs. Barnes & Noble at www.bn.com offered the first e-mail affiliate program through an affiliate solutions company called BeFree at www.befree.com.

With Barnes & Noble as its first client, BeFree launched B-Intouch, an e-mail marketing service designed to expand affiliate e-commerce capabilities to anyone with an e-mail address. B-Intouch gives merchants an opportunity to commerce-enable Internet users who don't have their own Web sites. That means anyone with an e-mail address can participate in an affiliate program. With a service like B-Intouch, you can make anyone with an e-mail address an e-marketer for your online business.

This is done by enabling the affiliates to earn money by selling products or services through a text link placed in the signature option of their e-mail message. When a person signs up to become a Barnes & Noble affiliate, he or she places a small snippet of code in the signature of his or her e-mail. This small piece of code calls a program from BeFree that automatically inserts a promotion for Barnes & Noble at the bottom of an e-mail message.

Build Versus Buy?

Should you use one of the existing Affiliate Solution Providers such as BeFree at www.befree.com or Linkshare at www.linkshare.com to track your affiliate program—or build your own? If you decide to build your own, then check out either the Affiliate Program at www.theaffiliateprogram.com/ or Pro-Track at www.affiliatesoftware.net/main2.html for their affiliate program management software.

Here's how the B-Intouch program could work for you.

A person visits your company's Web site that is part of the B-Intouch network. On your site the person clicks on a link and registers to become an electronic marketer for your e-business. Each time that person sends an e-mail, your message is then embedded into the bottom of the e-mail that provides a link to your Web site. If the recipient of the e-mail clicks through to your Web site and buys a product or service, the sender of the e-mail gets a commission.

This is quick, simple, and easy. Your company gets the sale and the e-mail sender gets a commission.

But why stop at text links in the signature field. With the growth of HTML-enabled e-mail, complete images can be tagged at the end of mail messages, imploring the recipient to click on the image offer for discounts or special deals on a product or service. Signatures can also be used to direct the recipient to surveys and free offers where his or her e-mail address can be captured and then marketed to at some later date.

Affiliate marketing is one way to be there whenever a potential buyer is in the mood to shop. Once you have settled on the type of affiliate model, your company will have to decide on a compensation plan for your affiliates.

Compensation Models

Your affiliate program can pay out commissions on the basis of clicks, leads, or sales. Which payment plan is appropriate for you depends upon the marketing strategies of your e-business. Are you looking to make an immediate sale from a click-through to your site?

Or perhaps you're interested in building a database of prospects that you hope to convert to customers later on. Once you've determined the objective of your affiliate marketing plan, then you can design a compensation plan for your affiliates.

Basically there are three types of plans:

- **Pay-per-sale**—The affiliate is paid either a flat fee or a percentage of each sale referred from the affiliate site to the merchant.

- **Pay-per-lead**—The affiliate is paid a commission for each lead (membership registration or a click to the merchant Web site) referred from the affiliate site.

- **Pay-per-click**—The affiliate is paid on a CPC (cost per click) basis for each time somebody clicks on a link to you site.

Nothing Succeeds Like Success

One of the first things to do when creating a successful affiliate program is to find out what works for others. Affiliateselling.com at www.affiliate-selling.com/ has a list of the top 50 affiliate programs on the Net.

Another aspect of compensation to keep in mind is the payment threshold. That is, how much will your affiliates have to earn before you issue a check. You might consider holding back payment until an affiliate earns at least $25, $50, or $100. Then there's payment frequency to consider. Do you pay your affiliates weekly, monthly, every other month, or once a quarter? These decisions must be designed into your affiliate marketing program.

DON'T MAKE THESE AFFILIATE MARKETING MISTAKES

On the surface, affiliate marketing looks simple. A Web site joins your program, a visitor to the affiliate's site clicks on your offer, you make a sale, and the web site makes a commission. Under the surface, it's not so simple. There's a lot involved in creating and running an affiliate marketing program and if not done right, could undermine all the objectives of your plan.

So don't make these affiliate marketing mistakes.

MISTAKE #1: No Contract

You must have a affiliate partner contract drawn up and ready to read on your Web site. No affiliate worth his salt will sign up for your program without knowing the rules, limitations, and compensation structure. And by the way, don't write your contract in legalese. Use every day language and make it easy to understand. Also, spell out in detail the terms of your agreement. When the affiliates get paid, how they get paid, and how they can be dropped from your program.

MISTAKE #2: No FAQs

Well-written contracts are good, but for a quick read on your program your company should provide a set of FAQs (frequently Asked Questions) about your affiliate program on your site. List everything that your affiliate partner needs to know in an easy to understand question and answer format. As your program grows, you'll receive questions from your affiliates. So, whenever you answer a new question, add it to the FAQ.

MISTAKE #3: No Affiliate Manager or Affiliate Support

Don't think that once a program is launched and Web sites are signed up, there's no further need of your program commitment. No so. Affiliate marketing programs are NOT self-administered. It's necessary to have a full-time affiliate manager—and even a staff—dedicated to the day-to-day operations of your company's affiliate marketing program. This person should be easily reached by your affiliate partners to answer their questions and solve their program problems. Without this kind of support, your program is doomed from the start.

MISTAKE #4: No Privacy Statement

State categorically that you will not share your database of affiliates with any other company for any reason. Affiliates don't want their names and e-mail addresses showing up on spam lists. Let your affiliates know that tier privacy is secure.

MISTAKE #5: No Marketing Help for Your Affiliates

Thinking that a sale will just happen on an affiliate partner's site is a big mistake. Affiliate partners must be trained and educated on how to sell your product or service and the objectives of your program. They need to know the best ways to promote your program and how they can increase their potential revenue. You should also change your banners, links and offers regularly offering fresh content to your affiliate's sites.

Post a Privacy Policy on Your Site

Make sure you have a posted privacy policy on your Web site. You can create a privacy policy by using the TRUSTe Wizard at www.etrust.com/wizard.

MISTAKE #6: No Reports

It critical that you provide your affiliates online statistical reporting. They need to know impressions per day, click-throughs, and sales and performance figures on a 24/7 basis. They are going to expect this feature so either design a reporting mechanism yourself or use one of the third-party affiliate solution providers such as BeFree at www.befree.com, Linkshare at www.linkshare.com, or Commission Junction at www.cj.com.

CHOOSING THE RIGHT AFFILIATES

A good, effective promotion strategy will net you thousands of affiliate sign-ups. But quality—not quantity—is what guarantees a successful affiliate program. Affiliates must be chosen carefully, just like any business partner. Look at the content of their site, their traffic, and especially the image they portray to visitors. As affiliate partners of your business, their image will be your image.

When you've received an application from a Web site, visit it. Look it over and see what it offers and what audience its directed at. Look at its content. Are the site owners trying to reach anyone and everyone who visits their site?

For example, is the potential affiliate offering visitors search engine placement AND credit card applications AND phone cards AND long distance service AND pre-paid legal services, and so on, and so on? This called the "flea market" approach. If the site sounds like this, then your products or service will be offered to anyone and everyone—and selling to everyone means selling to no one.

Think of yourself as a visitor to the site. Does the content satisfy the need of a person who has chosen to come there? Does the Web site's content synergize well with your offer? You must select affiliates that complement the products or services you are selling and would be of interest and relevance to their site visitors. This helps ensure that site visitors are pre-qualified, which will result in a higher conversion rate than would normally be the case. A site with targeted traffic provides a targeted customer prospect—and more sales for both you and your affiliate.

When you evaluate a potential affiliate site, keep these points in mind:

- See what type of visitors the site is trying to attract. Do they make an attempt to reach a targeted audience?
- Does the Web site's content synergize well with your offer?
- How is the site design? Is it professional? Would you want your offer to appear on their site?
- How about traffic? How much does it attract? Little traffic may bring few sales or referrals.
- Do you ship internationally? If not, don't accept international affiliate sites.

Finally, keep in mind the 80:20 Rule of affiliate marketing. 20% of your affiliates will generate 80% of your affiliate program revenue. So which is better? To have thousands of affiliates in your program, or to shoot for the hundreds that will generate the best results for your program?

All in all, if you have a product or service to sell on the Net, considering an affiliate program of your own should be at the top of your marketing to-do list.

CHAPTER 24

TEN WAYS TO DRIVE CUSTOMERS *AWAY* FROM YOUR SITE

In This Chapter

- Learn how to treat your shoppers with respect
- Find out what shoppers expect when they arrive at your Web store
- Discover what information to keep private and what you should reveal to your shoppers

Your Web site is here to serve your customers—not impress them. You job is to design a site and offer a shopping experience that gives consumers a quick, safe, and easy way to purchase something from your Web store.

So before you sit down with your Web consultant, and before your Web designer puts pointer to screen, be sure to avoid the 10 ways to drive customers *away* from your site.

- Confuse your customers
- Stay anonymous
- Offer at retail
- Frame your page
- Surprise them with shipping costs
- Make them work
- Make them wait

- Neglect to address privacy
- Keep security a secret
- SPAM your customers

CONFUSE YOUR CUSTOMERS

Rodney Dangerfield gets no respect. He told his psychiatrist that he had suicidal tendencies. His psychiatrist said that from now on Dangerfield had to pay in advance.

That might be funny to you, but treating your customer with no respect will drive him away from your site for sure. And one sure-fire way to drive him away is to confuse him.

Keep your navigation simple. You're there to sell. Customers are there to buy. Make it easy for them to find your products and buy them. If they can't find what they want and order it in three mouse clicks, you run the risk of losing them. So, organize your site material logically from the customer's point of view. Be sure to include clear directions for navigating the site from your home page. Remember that the home page of your Web store serves a variety of functions. It's a map of your store, a welcome mat, and a marketing message all in one.

People get lost easily, so include a "Return Home" link on every page of your site. Include a FAQ page and have links to the FAQ on every page where you think a customer might have a question about your store or service. Anticipate the needs of your users. If your site has a lot of product to sell, provide a search engine to easily find it.

Go light on the technical jargon and don't adopt a hipper-than-thou attitude in your writing. Shoppers want information—not a sales pitch. Let your shopper discover what they want at their own pace. Don't persuade. Inform.

Finally, look at your URL. See that WWW in front of it? It stands for the *World* Wide Web. So think globally. Users from other countries can easily access your site. If you want to make an international sale, respect cultures other than your own. Remember—they might not be familiar with American slang or expressions, so keep the wording simple.

STAY ANONYMOUS

Here's another cute trick that will drive customers from your site—stay anonymous. It never ceases to amaze me when the only means of contact on a shopping site is an e-mail address. Come on! We all have an address. Use it. Put your company mailing address, phone number, fax number, and customer service number on your site. And, while you're at it, don't forget to give your customers several ways to order from you—online, by phone, fax, and mail.

Why? People want some indication that your company is real. Supplying just an e-mail address or a P.O. box could seriously impact your sales. But if you're running a business out of your home, you may have little choice. You could make use of a Suite Box at one of the private mailbox companies like MailBoxes Etc., but many consumers these days are wise to the fact that a Suite Number can masquerade as a business address.

Also, consider putting a picture of you and your team on your Web store. Make your Web site seem more personal and you more approachable. Be sure that you have an "About Us" section on your Web store that tells the shopper who you are and what your store is about. Use this area of your site to drive home your Unique Selling Position and why the shopper should buy from you.

OFFER AT RETAIL

Shoppers believe that because an online merchant doesn't have a brick-and-mortar store, his overhead is low and he can pass these savings on to them in the form of lower prices. I know. I know. That server farm you have taking up the space of a small condo costs as much, if not more, to set up and maintain as a storefront in a strip mall. But shoppers don't believe it. So don't sell at retail. Sell at some kind of discount—at least 10% off suggested retail price or more.

If you can't offer a discount on the first sale, then offer some value-added service; perhaps a coupon good for a free item or a discount on a future purchase. You might consider partnering with another Web merchant selling products that are compatible with yours. If so, offer shoppers a bundled price of your product or service with your merchant partner's product or service.

FRAME YOUR PAGE

If you really want to drive customers away, then frame your pages.

Frames are a way to display several sections of several pages all at once. This is done by dividing the screen into several segments, or *frames*.

Frames are bad for two reasons. First they confuse the shopper and second, it makes it nearly impossible for a shopper to bookmark a framed page if he wants to return to it again later. When he does bookmark it and return, he only sees the framed page in his browser, losing any and all frames that surrounded the framed page originally.

Frames on your merchant site should be used for only one reason—to keep your navigation bar in front of your customers so they can find their way back to your site when you send them to another. For example, if you have set up reciprocal links or banner exchanges with other sites, a one-frame navigation bar directs customers back to your site from the site where you sent them.

SURPRISE THEM WITH SHIPPING COSTS

Shoppers don't like surprises. Before you put your customers through your order taking process, let them know what the actual shipped price of their order will be.

You can do this in one of two ways. First, present the customer with the full amount of his order *before* you ask for his credit card. If you can't offer that calculation, then have complete shipping and handling charges listed on your Web store—and make that list easy to find. This is even more critical for your international customers.

If you want to sell to international customers, then you have to let them know it. Give them the international shipping costs *before* they reach your order form.

MAKE THEM WORK

Speaking of order forms, here's a way to stop a customer's order dead in its tracks. The customer searched for, found, and is about to order your product. He reaches the order entry screen and it asks him to fill in the product name, code, description, and price of the product! Now the customer has to navigate back to the product page—or even multiple product pages—to retrieve and record the information. Their response? "Fuhgetaboutit! I'm outta here!"

So invest in a shopping cart software program that keeps track of what the customer is going to purchase and fills in the product information for him. These programs can be bought easily on the Web, and some are even free. If you're not technically adept at installing it on your Web store, hire a programmer for a few hours to do it. But do it!

Another big Don't is to ask shoppers to register with their name and contact information before they can shop in your online store. Would you fill out a form to enter a store in your neighborhood? Yeah, right!

MAKE THEM WAIT

The WWW stands for the World Wide Web—not the World Wide *Wait*. Shopping sites are a challenge to design. You want to keep page-download times low while at the same time customers want to see what they are getting. Don't use bells and whistles just because you can. People don't want to have to download anything to view your site. If you must use plug-ins, tell your customers where to get them. Be sure to include links to the software necessary for a full appreciation of your site. If you say your site uses RealAudio, then be sure it links to a download page for RealAudio.

As bandwidth increases, this issue will become less relevant. Until then, heavy use of graphics, video, and audio programs is time-consuming for the user.

Next, keep in mind that people want simplicity over cool graphics. Faster loading is better than eye candy. So keep your graphics small. Small is better where images are concerned. Try and keep them less than ten kilobytes each and your download time will speed up. If heavy graphics are necessary to display your offerings, at least be sensitive to customers with older systems. Offer a text-only option for viewing your site.

Finally, remember the three-click rule. It should take no more than three clicks to access the information they need. That means three clicks to a buy button.

NEGLECT TO ADDRESS PRIVACY

You want to keep your personal information private, right? So do your customers. Privacy concerns are a big thing these days and shoppers are worried about how their personal information will be used when they give it to a merchant. So create and state your privacy policy and have a link to it from your home page where shoppers can easily find it.

KEEP SECURITY A SECRET

Don't skimp on security. These days, there's no way to hide that your site doesn't sit on a secure server. Both Internet Explorer and Netscape Navigator tell the consumer when they are on a secure page of a site—and when they're not.

The words "secure server" can have a very calming effect on shoppers. Use a secure server for all your transactions—and tell your customers this when they use their credit card at your site. Put this information in your FAQs and even on a separate page on your Web site. Explain to them that their credit card transaction is secure.

SPAM YOUR CUSTOMERS

Finally, after you have a customer, you don't want to lose him. Keeping in touch with previous customers and prospects through e-mails and newsletters will keep your Web store in front of their mind. But you can overdo it.

Never spam your own customers. Offer your customers the option of receiving notifications of sales or new products, but be sure you have permission before sending anything. Unsolicited e-mail is more likely to generate more annoyance than sales.

As for frequency, try not to contact customers more than once a month, unless they have opted-in to a more frequent promotional program with you first.

There you are. Avoid these ten all-too-common pitfalls, and you have a good chance of making that sale and retaining your customers. After all, isn't that what you went online for?

G L O S S A R Y

ADSL (Asymmetrical Digital Subscriber Line) This strange-sounding name is the phone company's answer to cable modems. Unlike a cable modem where many subscribers are on the same line, an ADSL circuit connects two specific locations, is much faster than a regular phone connection, and could be faster than a cable modem.

Affiliate A Web site owner that earns a commission for referring clicks, leads, or sales to a merchant.

Affiliate Agreement Terms that govern the relationship between a merchant and an affiliate.

Affiliate Information Page A page or pages on your Web site that explains clearly and concisely what your affiliate program is all about.

Affiliate Link A piece of code residing in a graphic image or piece of text placed on an affiliate's Web page that notifies the merchant that an affiliate should be credited for the customer or visitor sent to their Web site.

Affiliate Manager The manager of an Affiliate Program who is responsible for

creating a newsletter, establishing incentive programs, forecasting and budgeting, overseeing front-end marketing of the program, and monitoring the industry for news and trends.

Affiliate Program (also an **Associate, Partner, Referral,** or **Revenue Sharing Program**) A merchant pays a commission to an affiliate for generating clicks, leads, or sales from a graphic or text link located on the affiliate's site.

Affiliate Program Directory Directory of affiliate programs, featuring information such as the commission rate, number of affiliates, and affiliate solution provider. Associate-It, AssociatePrograms.com, and Refer-it are among the largest Affiliate Program Directories.

Affiliate Solution Provider A company that provides the network, software, and services needed to create and track an affiliate program.

AltaVista One of the top 10 search engines. It indexes actual Web pages, not just Web sites (see *Yahoo!*). When you do a keyword search, it returns Web pages instead of Web sites.

Anonymous FTP Anonymous FTP enables users to access an FTP site for downloading without a password. With regular FTP, you must enter a user ID and a password to access the site.

Associate Synonym for affiliate.

Auto-Responder An e-mail feature that sends an e-mail message to anyone who sends it a blank message or a message with certain key words.

Backbone Networks This is the backbone of the Internet that consists of central networks with high-speed computers to which all the other networks of the Internet are connected. Once maintained by the National Science Foundation, backbone networks now have been privatized and are maintained by companies such as Sprint and MCI.

Bandwidth The transmission capacity, usually measured in bits per second (BPS) of a network connection. Video streaming and other multimedia applications require a high bandwidth.

Banner An electronic billboard or ad in the form of a graphic image that resides on a Web page, many of which are animated GIFs. The newer banners are interactive with the capability to take an order through the banner ad.

Baud The Baud rate refers to the speed of a modem. Common speed for modems today are 14.4, 28.8, 36.6, and 56K. Cable modems and ASDL approach the speeds of a T1 telephone line.

Bot Small pieces of software that search the Net looking for sites—or product pages if they are shopping bots.

BPS (Bits Per Second) A measurement of how fast data is moved from one place to another, usually in thousands of bits per second (Kbps) or million of bits per second (Mbps). A 28.8 modem can transport 28,800 bits per second.

Browser Software program such as Netscape or Internet Explorer that enables you to browse the World Wide Web and access the millions of pages that it contains.

C++ Superset of the C programming language that adds object-oriented concepts. Java, another programming language, is based on C++ but optimized for the Internet.

Cable Modem A modem connected to your local cable TV line. The bandwidth of a cable modem far exceeds the bandwidth of the 28.8Kbps and can be as fast at a T1 connection.

Cache An area of your computer memory or directory on your hard drive. This is the place where your browser stores viewed Web pages. When you return to a page, the browser gets this page from the cache, saving you download time.

CGI (Common Gateway Interface) An interface that allows scripts (programs) to run on a Web server. CGI-scripts are used for a variety of purposes, including Web page forms and shopping carts. The most popular languages for CGI scripts are Perl and C.

CGI-bin The name of the directory on a Web server where CGI-scripts are stored.

Chat You can talk in real-time with other people in a chat room, but the words are typed instead of spoken.

Click   Used in online advertising. A click is when someone clicks on a banner ad or link. The click rate is the number of clicks on an ad as a percentage of the number of times that the ad was downloaded with a Web page. A click rate of 1% means that 1% of the people who downloaded the page clicked on the ad.

Client/Server   The Internet is a client/server network. The client is the computer that requests a service or a piece of information from another computer system, or server, on the network. The PC you use to access the Internet is the client. The Web server you view pages on is the server.

Co-location   If you want to have your server on a high-speed connection, or want someone else to maintain it, you co-locate your server with other servers at a hosting service.

Cookie   A cookie is a small piece of information that a Web server sends to your computer hard disk via your browser. Cookies contain information such as login or registration information, online shopping cart information, and user preferences. This information can be retrieved by other Web pages on the site so that your site experience can be customized.

Cracker   A person who breaks the security of computer systems to steal or destroy information. A nonmalicious cracker is called a *hacker*.

Cross-Posting   Posting one message to several newsgroups at a time. This can be used by commercial enterprises to promote their business with unsolicited messages. Can also be considered spamming the newsgroups.

Cyberspace   First coined by author William Gibson in his novel *Neuromancer*, cyberspace is used to describe the Internet.

Data Encryption Key   String of characters used to encode a message. Someone can only read this encoded message with another related key.

Dedicated Line   A direct telephone line between two computers. Dedicated lines have permanent IP numbers whereas dial-up connections are assigned a new IP number every time you log on.

Dial-Up   Temporary connection over a telephone line to the computer server of your ISP to establish a connection to the Internet. You get a new IP number every time you log on.

DNS (Domain Name Server or **Domain Name System)**   A Domain Name Server maps IP numbers to your URL on the Web. When someone types www.mybusiness.com into their browser, the DNS searches for your Web site's IP address, such as 208.12.111.89, and displays your Web page.

Domain Name   A unique name that identifies an Internet site like mybusiness.com. A domain name always points to one specific server on the Internet where your Web site resides.

Download   The transfer of data from a server on the Internet to your PC. You can use your browser or an FTP program to download files to your computer. When retrieving your e-mail, you're downloading your e-mail to your computer.

E-cash (Electronic Cash) A currency that can be exchanged over the Internet. It requires the buyer to purchase the electronic currency from a special bank via check, credit card, or debit card. He then can use it to purchase goods from Internet vendors who accept e-cash.

E-mail (Electronic Mail) A message containing text or HTML sent over the Internet from one person to another or to a large number of e-mail addresses using a mailing list.

E-mail Address An electronic mailing address. E-mail addresses are in the form of *user@domain*, such as frank@aol.com.

E-mail Alias These are additional e-mail addresses that point to another e-mail address. All messages sent to an e-mail alias are automatically forwarded to the specified real e-mail address. This way you can have more than one e-mail address on an e-mail account.

Encryption Procedure that scrambles the contents of a file before sending it over the Internet. PGP (Pretty Good Privacy) is a commonly used encryption program. The recipient must have software to decrypt the file on her end.

FAQ (Frequently Asked Questions) A Web page that contains the most common questions and answers on a particular subject.

Firewall Internet security to protect a local area network (LAN) computer system against hackers. A combination of hardware and software acts as a firewall to separate the LAN into two parts. The data you want public is available outside the firewall, whereas sensitive data, such as credit card numbers, are kept inside the firewall.

Flame The e-mail equivalent of hate mail. Such hate messages are usually sent to the victim's e-mail box tens and even hundreds of times. Sophisticated Internet users use this technique against businesses that send them SPAM (unsolicited e-mail).

Frame Enables Web designers to break the browser window into several smaller windows, each of which can load different HTML pages. Using frames, Web designers can create navigation bars and advertisements that stay onscreen as you click through a site. If used incorrectly, frames can be a great annoyance to your visitors.

Freeware This is any kind of software that is distributed or downloaded free of charge for unlimited use.

FTP (File Transfer Protocol) FTP is used to download files from another computer as well as to upload files from your computer to a remote computer. Through (regular) FTP, you can log in to another Internet site, but you must have a user ID and a password. Anonymous FTP servers don't require usernames or passwords, but you can't upload files to anonymous FTP servers.

GIF (Graphics Interchange Format) Common graphics file format on the Internet. This format can display only 256 colors at the maximum of 8 bits—therefore a GIF is mostly used to show clip-art images.

Gigabyte (Gb) A gigabyte = 1 billion bytes.

GUI (Graphical User Interface)
Windows and Macintosh operating systems use a GUI where the operating system is displayed to you with icons on your computer screen. GUI is not like DOS and UNIX, which use command-line text commands.

Hacker An expert programmer who uses his skills to break into computer systems or networks just for the fun of it or to expose security risks. Unlike a cracker, a real hacker doesn't want to harm anybody or anything.

Hit A single request from a browser to a server. All text on a Web page is a hit, and each individual graphic on a page is also counted as a hit. If a Web page consists of text and three graphics images, then one Web page would serve up four hits.

Home Page The main page of a Web site. A Web site containing only one page is also called a home page.

Host A host is any computer that allows another computer to retrieve information or access its files. An example of a host is the server on which a Web site is stored.

HTML (Hypertext Markup Language)
The coding language used to create hypertext documents on the Web. HTML is a way to format text by placing marks or tags around the text. The tags `<i></i>` around a piece of text will make it appear italic.

HTTP (Hypertext Transfer Protocol)
The Web protocol for moving hypertext (HTML) files across the Internet. The `http://` in front of your URL tells a browser to transfer your Web site files (pages) to a computer for display. When it reads `https://`, that signals that you are on a secure Web page—for example, an order-entry page requesting a credit card number.

Hyperlink A highlighted word (hypertext) or graphic on a Web page. When you click a hyperlink, it could take you to another place within the same page, to another page on the site, or to a different Web site entirely.

Hypermedia Pictures, videos, and audio on a Web page that act as hyperlinks.

ICQ ("I Seek You") A communications network on the Internet. If you want to know whether your friends are surfing the Web right now, ICQ does the searching for you, alerting you in real time when your friends sign on. AOL Instant Messenger and Yahoo! Messenger are two other instant messaging services.

Impression Each request from a user for a Web page on a particular server. Counting the impressions is a good way to measure the popularity of a Web site. If a user views three Web pages on your site, that counts as three impressions.

Information Superhighway U.S. Vice President Al Gore's term for the Internet.

Internet A network of computer networks. The Internet evolved from the ArpaNET (a U.S. military network) to an academic research network, to the current global commercial network. Other names for the Internet are the Net, cyberspace, and the information superhighway.

Internet Explorer   The Web browser from Microsoft. Also known as IE.

InterNIC (Internet Network Information Center)   The InterNIC is the entity that keeps track of domain names. When you want to register a new domain name, you do it through InterNIC.

Intranet   A private company network of computers using the same protocols as the Internet, but only for internal use.

IP (Internet Protocol)   These are the common rules that provide the basic Internet functions. Internet Protocol enables computers to find each other.

IP Address   A unique 32-bit Internet address consisting of four numbers separated by dots, such as 208.56.111.89. Every server connected to the Internet has a unique IP number.

IRC (Internet Relay Chat)   A chat network where the words are not spoken but written. All words typed by any user are seen by everyone who is in that chat room or channel at that moment (see *chat*).

IRL   Stands for "In Real Life" or "meat-space."

ISDN (Integrated Services Digital Network)   Digital telephone system that can provide high-speed (up to 128 Kbps) transmission of voice and data.

ISP (Internet Service Provider)   An ISP provides Internet access to its members. Every time you log on, your ISP connects you to the Internet.

Java   A platform-independent programming language, invented by Sun Microsystems, that Web developers use to create applets, small software applications that are downloaded to your computer. Java-enabled Web pages can include animations, calculators, scrolling text, sound effects, and even games.

JavaScript   JavaScript has nothing to do with Java. JavaScript is a scripting language designed by Netscape. JavaScripts are embedded into HTML documents.

JPEG (Joint Photographic Experts Group)   An image compression standard optimized for full-color (millions of colors) digital images. Almost every full-color photograph you see on the Web is a JPG file, whereas GIFs are used to display clip-art images.

Kbps (Kilobits Per Second)   Measure of how much data can be sent per second. A 28.8Kbps modem transfers data at about 3.6KB (kilobytes) per second.

KB (Kilobyte)   Approximately a thousand bytes (1,024 bytes).

LAN (Local Area Network)   Computer network limited to one single location—usually an office or group of offices.

Link   A link can bring you to another Web page or another Web site (see *Hyperlink*).

Linux   A free UNIX-based operating system for personal computers. It competes with Windows.

Listserv   This is a mailing list. Similar to newsgroups but unlike newsgroups, listservs operate via e-mail. When you send an e-mail message to this group, your e-mail is copied and sent to all subscribers.

Location Internet address as displayed on your browser. When you type in the URL of a Web site into the location bar of your browser, your browser will take you to this page.

Log File File that contains detailed recorded events of a computer system, such as server access numbers, number of visitors, and error log files.

Mail Server Server that handles incoming and outgoing e-mail. This server is normally different from a Web server.

Mbps (Megabits Per Second) Measure of data throughput in millions of bits per second.

Meatspace Cyberspeak for the real world—anything outside of cyberspace.

Megabit About one million bits. Exactly 1,048,576 bits.

MB (Megabyte) About one million bytes. Exactly 1,048,576 bytes or 1,024KB.

Metatags Text tags added to a Web page that includes data such as title, author, content, or key words. These tags can be read by search engines.

Mirror or **Mirror Site** More or less an exact copy of another WWW or FTP site. Mirror sites are created when the traffic on the original site is too heavy. They are usually on servers that are located in different geographic areas.

Online Mall A collection of virtual stores on one Web site. Sometimes the online mall may host a Web store and at other times it only provides a link to their Web store.

Navigator A Web browser from Netscape and the browser that made the Web what it is today.

Net Short for the Internet.

Netiquette (Network Etiquette) Informal code of good manners on the Internet, such as typing in mixed case (typing in all uppercase is deemed as shouting). Spamming is not good netiquette.

Netizen A responsible citizen of the Internet.

Network Group of computers that are connected together so that they can share resources and exchange data.

Newsgroup Discussion group on Usenet among people who share a mutual interest. There are thousands and thousands of newsgroups covering almost every possible subject.

News Server Computer of your ISP that gathers Usenet newsgroups. From this server you can download the newsgroups you're interested in.

OC-1 to OC-48 OC stands for Optical Carrier, a standard for fiber optic transmission. They range from transmission speeds of 51.85 Mbps (OC-1) to 2,488 Mbps (OC-48).

Pay-Per-Sale Program where an affiliate receives a commission for each sale of a product or service that they refer to a merchant's Web site.

Pay-Per-Lead Program where an affiliate receives a commission for each sales lead that they generate for a merchant Web site. Examples would include completed surveys, contest or sweep-stakes entries, downloaded software demos, or free trials. Pay-per-lead gen-erally offers midrange commissions and midrange to high conversion ratios.

Pay-Per-Click   Program where an affiliate receives a commission for each click (visitor) they refer to a merchant's web site. Pay-per-click programs gener-ally offer some of the lowest commis-sions (from $0.01–$0.25 per click), and a very high conversion ratio since visitors need only click on a link to earn the affiliate a commission.

Perl (Practical Extraction and Report Language)   Perl is a computer lan-guage used for writing CGI scripts.

Permission Marketing   Gaining the permission of someone before market-ing to them. An op-in e-mail list is one form of permission marketing.

Plug-in   Small piece of software, usu-ally from a third-party developer, that adds new features to a Web browser.

POP (Post Office Protocol)   Internet protocol used by your ISP to handle e-mail for its subscribers. A POP account is another word for an e-mail account.

Portal   A Web site that attracts visitors by offering free information or free ser-vices on a daily basis. When you are on a portal site, you can use this site as a basis to explore the Web. The most famous portals are AltaVista, Excite, HotBot, Lycos, InfoSeek, and Yahoo.

Posting   A single message posted to a newsgroup, bulletin board, or mailing list.

Redundancy   This is a form of protec-tion against system failures. For exam-ple, if you want to be sure that you'll always have a power supply, you can set up two power supplies so that one takes over if the other one fails—or, you may have a mirror site for your Web site on another server.

Router   Computer that acts as an interface between two networks. A router sends data packets back and forth between networks.

Search Engine   An online database that enables Internet users to locate sites that have the information they need. Every search engine has its own strategy for collecting data, so one particular search usually produces different results on dif-ferent search engines. Yahoo! and AltaVista are two different types of search engines (see *AltaVista* and *Yahoo!*).

Server   A computer that has a perma-nent connection to the Internet. Web sites are stored on a Web server, and e-mail is stored and sent through an e-mail server.

Service Provider   A subscriber is con-nected to a service provider through a modem, and the service provider con-nects to the Internet through other net-works.

Shareware   This is software that is pur-chased on approval. The customer downloads it for a predetermined trial period and will have to pay the creator if he wants to use it beyond that period.

Shopping Cart   A Shopping Cart is a program that lets visitors make selec-tions from more than one product page before checking out of your Web store.

Shouting Typing in all capital letters in a chat room or on a discussion board or newsgroup. This is deemed bad netiquette.

Storefront Prefabricated HTML page for affiliates that displays new or specialized products with integrated affiliate links.

Sig (Signature File) A small ASCII text file of four or five lines that is automatically attached to the end of an e-mail message that includes additional information about the sender like your name, address, phone numbers, and Web address (URL).

SMTP (Simple Mail Transfer Protocol) Main protocol to send and receive e-mail between servers on the Internet.

Snail Mail Slang word for sending mail using the post office.

Spamming Posting an unsolicited commercial message to a newsgroup or sending unsolicited e-mail.

Spider Small piece of software, also know as a *bot*, used by some search engines to index Web sites. Spiders search the Web to find URLs that match the given search string.

SSL (Secure Sockets Layer) Protocol that enables you to send encrypted messages across the Internet. SSL uses public key encryption to pass data between your browser and a given server, such as when submitting credit card information. A URL that begins with https indicates that an SSL connection will be used.

Streaming Media (Streaming Audio/ Video) Technology that enables you to play audio or video while it is still downloading.

Surfing Browsing the World Wide Web.

T1 A telephone line that can transmit information at 1.544Mbps.

T3 A high-speed, high-bandwidth telephone line connection to the Internet. A T3 line can deliver information at 44.736Mbps—the equivalent of 28 T1 lines.

TCP/IP (Transmission Control Protocol/ Internet Protocol) A suite of communications protocols that defines the basic workings of the Internet. In fact, TCP/IP is *the* protocol of the Internet because it's the language with which all Internet computers talk to each other.

Telnet Internet protocol that enables you to connect your machine as a remote terminal to a host computer somewhere on the Internet. To Telnet into a remote machine, you have to enter a user ID and a password.

Timed Out When you request a Web page and the server that hosts the Web page doesn't respond in a certain amount of time, you may get the message "connection timed out."

UNIX Multiuser computer operating system. The Internet and the World Wide Web grew up on UNIX. UNIX is still the most common operating system for servers on the Internet.

Upload Sending files from your computer to another computer through the Internet. When making changes to your Web store, you must upload your new pages via FTP to your Web server from your computer.

URL (Uniform Resource Locator) Address of any resource on the World Wide Web, such as your Web store's home page: `http://www.mybusiness.com`.

Usenet Worldwide decentralized distribution system of newsgroups. There are at least 15,000 newsgroups available through the Internet.

User ID Unique identifier that you must enter every time you want to access a particular service on the Internet. The user ID is always accompanied by a password.

Viral Marketing The rapid adoption of a product or passing on of an offer to friends and family through word-of-mouth (or word-of-e-mail) networks. Any advertising that propagates itself the way viruses do.

VRML (Virtual Reality Modeling Language) A method for creating 3D environments on the Web. On a VRML page, it is possible to move around through a virtual room, see all sides of a product, and try on clothing. To see VRML pages, your need a VRML plug-in for your browser.

Web Page One single document on the Web. A Web page can consist of text, graphics, and pictures.

Web Site A collection of Web pages that form a complete site.

Webmaster A person in charge of maintaining a Web site.

Wetware Slang for the human brain.

World Wide Web An Internet client-server system to distribute information based upon the hypertext transfer protocol (HTTP). Also known as WWW, W3, or the Web. Created at CERN in Geneva, Switzerland, in 1991 by Dr. Tim Berners-Lee.

Yahoo! One of the Top Ten search engines. Yahoo! is one type of search engine: a directory of Web sites that searches by site category, not by Web pages (see *AltaVista*). It can be found at `yahoo.com`.

Zine or **eZine** This is short for online magazine. They're a good place to target-advertise your site.

APPENDIX A

IMPORTANT RESOURCES ON THE WEB

This appendix provides a list of Net-based resources that will broaden your understanding of e-commerce and provide valuable information that will help you succeed in your online business. These e-business resources will help your growing enterprise compete by giving information about sound business practices, establishing business and marketing relationships, building product and service quality programs, and entering international markets.

The resources listed here take a variety of formats. Many are standard Web addresses whereas others are mailing lists. To subscribe to the mailing lists, simply send an e-mail to the address listed, unless instructed otherwise.

E-MAIL DISCUSSION LISTS

TechTV.com

TechTV.com

TechTV.com contains just about anything related to technology products, software, and the Internet. The home page has links to the latest news, products, and topics discussed on TechTV. From the home page, five zones are easily accessed to get more in depth coverage.

1. **Tech News Zone**—To learn what is happening in the world of technology, click here. Topics include: e-business, education, gaming, electronics, computers, energy issues, viruses, hacking and security, business and money, computing, net culture, Internet, and politics and law.

2. **Products and Reviews Zone**—This zone has reviews and overviews on new products, Web sites, and issues. Hardware, software, consumer electronics, Web sites and services, soho, games, music tech and kid tech are also discussed. You can submit reviews of products to appear on the site. It's also a chance to get your first look at the newest products either on the market or soon to be released.

3. **Help and How-to Zone**—The zone for computer how-to. Featured topics include: getting started, technology experts, hardware, software, operating systems, and the Internet. There is a "Tips and Tricks" department for those lesser-known shortcuts. You can also get free stuff from the "Free file of the Day."

4. **Business and Money Zone**—If you need shopping tips, investment advice, or the latest news on personal finance, this zone is where to click. The market summaries help you decide where to put your money. The "Investment Challenge Game" will help you hone your skills so you can be successful at the real thing.

5. **Entertainment Zone**—For those into games, movies, music, and Internet culture, this is your zone. This area also includes message boards and chat so you can find others with similar interests.

All of the zones have links to news, chat rooms, and schedules of upcoming events on the site as well as on TechTV. Through "Interact" you can contact TechTV through the viewer mail (Vmail) department, answer the most recent viewer polls, and sign up for TechTV newsletters.

Another helpful feature is the "Superguides" section. These will help you get the most out of the more popular technologies, hardware, and software:

AOL—Stretch your America Online experience to the limit.

Broadband—Get ready to surf the Net at blistering speed.

Digital Cameras—Reviews of the latest cameras, scanners, camcorders, and related software, plus picture-taking tips.

Downloads—Our favorite tools and toys from around the Net. The best part: Most of it is free.

Linux—Tips, tricks, and latest developments for fans of the increasingly popular open-source OS.

Mac Station—Reviews of the latest Macintosh gear, plus tips and the latest on Apple's comeback.

Mobile Computing—For road warriors only: tips and reviews for PDA and laptop users.

MP3—One-stop site for the coolest music and the hottest players.

Virus—Find out how to keep the latest nasty viruses from trashing your computer.

Wireless—Tips and tricks for staying connected without all those pesky cords.

AdverTalk

`AdverTalk@fiestanet.com`

AdverTalk is an e-mail discussion group for small businesses to use to discuss issues and offer solutions related to small business marketing, including advertising, public relations, database marketing, and sales channels.

BizSupport

`join-bizsupport@marketserv.com`

BizSupport is the Business Opportunities Support Forum on `MarketServ.Com`. BizSupport is an unmoderated list on the topic of business opportunities and support of sales organizations.

E-Marketing

`www.webbers.com/emark/`

This list discusses electronic marketing techniques.

E-Tailer

`etd@gapent.com`

E-Tailer's Digest is a resource for retail on the Net and is published in a moderated digest form every Monday, Wednesday, and Friday. The *E-Tailer's Digest* topics include any, and all, subjects that pertain to retailing. To subscribe, send e-mail with a subject of `SUBSCRIBE_ETD`.

FrankelBiz

`www.robfrankel.com/frankelbiz/form.html`

FrankelBiz is the Web's only listserv devoted exclusively to doing business on the Web instead of talking about it. List members exchange reciprocal discounts, offer business leads, and do business with one another. Sponsors offer products and services at discounts to members.

GB Internet Marketing

subscribe@digitalnation.co.uk

The GB Internet Marketing Discussion List deals with all aspects of Internet Marketing relevant to the United Kingdom.

GINLIST

listserv@msu.edu

GINLIST has its own Web page. GINLIST (Global Interact Network mailing LIST) focuses on discussions of international business and marketing issues.

GLOBAL_PROMOTE

join-global_promote@gs4.revnet.com

This list is a forum for the discussion of issues relating to sales and marketing in the worldwide Internet marketplace.

GLOBMKT

listserv@lsv.uky.edu

Subscribers discuss global marketing issues in this forum.

HBBM-L

HBBM-L-Request@InternetWantads.com

The Home Based Business Marketing List, HBBM-L, is an open, unmoderated list geared toward marketing discussions and issues for home-based business owners. To subscribe, send the command SUBSCRIBE HBBM-L in the body of the mail.

HTMarCom

majordomo@listserv.rmi.net

HTMarCom has its own Web page. The list is dedicated to discussing the marketing of technology products.

I-Advertising

listserv@guava.ease.lsoft.com

This list offers a moderated discussion on all aspects relating to Internet advertising, including online media planning, media buying, campaign tracking, industry trends and forecasts, creative development, and cost estimates.

IESSlist

`majordomo@ix.entrepreneurs.net`

IESS (Internet Entrepreneurs Support Service) is a discussion group for entrepreneurs and businesses doing business on the Internet.

I-NET-PRODUCTIVITY

`listserver@netpartners-marketing.com`

The discussion group called I-NET-PRODUCTIVITY is a self-moderated list for discussing topics relating to using the Internet to improve any company's ability to market and sell on the Internet. To subscribe, type `subscribe I-NET-PRODUCTIVITY` in the body of the message.

Interad

`interad@iponline.com`

This name refers to Internet Advertising. The purpose of this list is to promote discussion and exchange ideas on the use of the Internet for advertising. To subscribe, e-mail the words `subscribe Interad` in the subject line or message body.

International-Business

`majordomo@globalbiz.com`

Discusses topics that concern business owners and marketing professionals as they relate to the Internet and the World Wide Web.

Internet Sales

`join-i-sales@gs2.revnet.com`

Internet Sales has its own home page. The goal of the Internet Sales Moderated Discussion List is to provide meaningful and helpful information to those engaged in the online sale of products and/or services.

I-Sales Help Desk

`www.audettemedia.com/i-help/`

This discussion list was spun off from the successful I-Sales list at the end of 1997. It too is targeted at those involved in online sales, but focuses more on helping people solve specific problems.

MKTRSRCH

`Listserv@listserv.dartmouth.edu`

MKTRSRCH is an open, unmoderated discussion list covering the topic of primary and secondary market research.

MKTSEG

`maiser@mail.telmar.com`

The purpose of this list is to allow and encourage an exchange of ideas and information relating to advertising and marketing to target segments.

NetMarket-L

`listserv@citadel.net`

The NetMarket-L list is unmoderated. It is for entrepreneurs, Webmasters, and pioneers— those of us who are testing out new ideas and marketing concepts on how to best promote our business, products, and services on the Internet.

NEWPROD

`majordomo@world.std.com`

NEWPROD is a mailing list devoted to the discussion of New Product Development in both product and service industries.

Online-Advertising

`www.tenagra.com/online-ads/`

The Online Advertising Discussion List focuses on professional discussion of online advertising strategies, results, studies, tools, and media coverage.

PRFORUM

`listserv@indycms.iupui.edu`

Corporate and PR communications is the theme of this list.

Product_Dev

`product_dev-request@msoe.edu`

The Product_Dev list is for discussing new product development.

Proposal-L

`majordomo@ari.net`

Proposal-L facilitates discussions regarding the development of business proposals, responding to Government RFPs, best practices, production, marketing, contracts, training, tools, and resources for planning, writing, producing, and delivering proposals.

Retailer-News

`majordomo@mailing-list.net`

The Retailer News Digest mailing list is a moderated discussion list for retail business owners, managers, and salespeople.

SMBIZ

```
smbiz-list-request@dandyweb.com
```

The Small Business Discussion List is for all small business owners, workers, marketers, and developers. To subscribe, send the message `subscribe`.

SYSOP-Group

```
listserv@property.com
```

The list is geared totally towards the business aspects of online services and marketing. Marketing, obtaining advertisers/sponsors, and new users is its only purpose.

Sales-Chat

```
sales-chat-request@listserv.direct.net
```

The Sales-Chat List was formed to provide a discussion forum for people involved in selling or interested in selling. Send e-mail with the one line message `subscribe sales-chat`.

SERVNET

```
listserv@asuvm.inre.asu.edu
```

This list is multidisciplinary and has been set up for discussions of service.

Webcontentstrategy

```
webcontentstrategy@lists.fourleaf.com
```

This webcontentstrategy list is for Web-based content business owners, executives, and advertisers to discuss strategy and funding issues. Subjects discussed are strategic or financial, rather than trading or operating in nature.

WTB

```
www.listhost.net:81/guest/RemoteListSummary/WTB
```

The We-Talk-Business list is set up as a discussion list for business topics.

E-BUSINESS PUBLICATIONS

American Demographics Magazine

```
www.marketingtools.com/
```

Online reproduction of the print version of *American Demographics Magazine*. The best demographic information online. A necessity for any good marketing plan.

Boardwatch Magazine

```
boardwatch.internet.com/
```

Guide to Internet access and the World Wide Web.

Business@Home

www.gohome.com/

Online version of print magazine devoted to those working at home. This is an online gathering spot and information resource for the working-from-home community.

CLICKZ

www.clickz.com

This column is published each business day and includes an eclectic mixture of online marketing news, opinions, and interviews.

CNET

www.cnet.com

As well as carrying all the latest technical news online, CNET publishes a weekly summary that provides links to all the major Internet stories from the previous week.

E-COMMERCE Alert

www.zdjournals.com/eca/

A biweekly newsletter, an interactive Web site, and an e-mail alert service.

Entrepreneur Magazine

www.EntrepreneurMag.com

A wide range of articles and suggestions for starting, managing, and maintaining a small business.

Fats Company

www.fastcompany.com

Contains plenty of articles about emerging businesses. The Web site is well organized, expansive, and covers up-to-date issues for today's entrepreneur.

INC. ONLINE

www.inc.com

The award-winning Web magazine for growing companies.

Interactive Week

www.interactive-week.com

Covers a variety of aspects about the Internet and interactive technology.

Internet World

www.iw.com

Weekly publication covering Internet news, marketing, infrastructure, and e-commerce development.

Net Magazine

www.netmag.co.uk/

Popular European Internet magazine.

Small Business Journal

www.tsbj.com/

The *Small Business Journal Magazine* has tons of small business articles and information.

Upside Magazine

www.upside.com/

Dedicated to providing its customers with high-quality, insightful media products that uniquely position the company as a leader in the information technology field.

Web Commerce Today

www.wilsonweb.com/wct

Monthly e-mailnewsletter on selling products directly over the Internet.

Web Developer

www.webdeveloper.com/

Covers HTML, Java, JavaScript, and Web site management.

Wired Magazine

www.wired.com/

Internet culture and business magazine.

Yahoo! Internet Life

www.zdnet.com/yil/

Covers entertainment, news, and useful Internet sites.

PROMOTIONS, SUBMISSIONS, AND SEARCH ENGINES

Add Me

www.addme.com

A free promotion, submission, announcement site that will submit your site to 34 various Web directories and search engines on the Internet.

Link Exchange

www.linkexchange.com/

A free cooperative service helping over 250,000 Web site owners get targeted exposure.

Netcreations

www.netcreations.com

Provides Internet promotional services, software development, and Web publishing.

Position Agent

www.positionagent.com/

Monitors Web site search engine rankings on top search engines.

Search Engine Watch

www.searchenginewatch.com

This site contains everything you ever wanted to know about search engines, including how they work and how to improve your site's ranking.

Submit It!

www.submit-it.com/

Announces your site to the top search engines and directories on the Web.

GENERAL RESOURCES

Builder.com

www.builder.com

If you're building a Web site yourself, CNET's Builder.com has an abundance of articles and advice to assist you.

Domain Name Availability

www.networksolutions.com/cgi-bin/whois/whois

Checks the availability of a domain name.

E-marketer

www.emarketer.com

This site aims to be the definitive online marketing resource. It includes news, statistics, and step-by-step guides to succeeding online. A weekly newsletter also is available.

Incorporation and Trademarks

www.corpcreations.com

Incorporation and Trademark services online (for all 50 states plus offshore).

NUA Internet Surveys

www.nua.ie/surveys/moreinfo.html

NUA publishes a weekly e-mail newsletter that summarizes all the latest Internet surveys and statistics. This newsletter is an invaluable resource if you want to know who's online and what they're buying.

Web Site Garage

www.websitegarage.com/

Has a large package of services including an HTML checker, site promotion tools, and a graphics optimizer.

Wilson Web

www.wilsonweb.com

This site contains a wealth of links to articles relating to every aspect of Web commerce. Much of the information is free, although some areas are accessible by paying subscribers only.

APPENDIX B

YOUR E-BUSINESS DO LIST

When running an e-business, it's easy to forget the day-to-day tasks that need to be done to keep your e-business on track. Let's face it. You've put a lot of work into building a foundation for your new enterprise. Keeping that foundation solid is an important task in making your e-business a success. So, here is a *Do List* of activities that you should perform on a daily, weekly, and monthly basis.

Daily To Do

- Check your customer service e-mail and respond the same day.
- Read new messages in the discussion groups that you participate in and respond to questions and calls for help that match your business offerings.
- If you run a bulletin board on your site, respond to all questions from shoppers.
- Read and respond to any e-mail discussion lists that you are on.
- Check the navigation on your Web storefront for broken links.
- If you are using an e-mail auto responder, send a message to it and make sure it's working.
- Promote a new product each day from your home page.

Weekly To Do

- Check your Web site's position in the search engines.
- Review your log files to see which pages are *not* getting hits and make changes accordingly.
- Review your advertising placements and see which ones are pulling traffic and which are not.
- Update your storefront with new information and products.
- Send out your weekly newsletter with product specials.

Monthly To Do

- Read your monthly industry and Internet publications.
- Create a seasonal promotion for your product or service.
- Look for new promotional activities for your Web store.
- Create a newsworthy event that can be used in a press release.
- Look for new directories and search engines to list your Web store.

PR DO'S AND DON'TS

Administrating a good publicity campaign takes a lot of work, so mind these Do's and Don'ts of news releases.

- DO make your press releases short and to the point.
- DO include all necessary contact information.
- DO spell-check your release. And do it twice just to make sure!
- DO keep typefaces large, legible, and readable for both e-mail and faxes.
- DO write a clear and meaningful subject line. The subject line should reflect the contents of your release.

- DON'T write unclear press releases. If it doesn't make sense to the reader, it will not be used.
- DON'T send a release to a publication without knowing the audience or what the publication is all about.
- DON'T send attached files. Don't send a word processing document or a zipped file that the contact needs to download, unzip, read into his word processor, determine the compatibility, print, review, and so on.

TOP SITES FOR POSTING YOUR PRESS RELEASE

PR Web (www.prweb.com/)   PR Web offers free posting.

PR Newswire (www.prnewswire.com)   PR Newswire requires an annual fee for posting.

Business Wire (www.businesswire.com)   Business Wire requires an annual fee as well.

URLwire (www.urlwire.com)   URLwire will post on demand and charges per posting, but does not have an annual fee.

Internet Wire (internetwire.com/release/index.htx)   Internet Wire will post on demand and charges per posting, but does not have an annual fee.

Internet News Bureau (www.newsbureau.com/services)   Internet News Bureau charges per posting but does not have an annual fee.

Xpress Press (www.xpresspress.com)   Xpress Press charges per posting but does not have an annual fee.

WebPromote (www.webpromote.com/products/prelease.asp)   WebPromote charges per posting but does not have an annual fee.

INDEX

G

H

I

INTERACTIVE WEEK

INDEX

MYSIMON

INDEX